# PDA by PDAers

*of related interest*

Can I tell you about Pathological Demand Avoidance syndrome?
A guide for friends, family and professionals
*Ruth Fidler and Phil Christie*
*Illustrated by Jonathon Powell*
*Foreword by Judith Gould*
ISBN 978 1 84905 513 0
eISBN 978 0 85700 929 6
*Can I tell you about...? series*

Pathological Demand Avoidance Syndrome
– My Daughter is Not Naughty
*Jane Alison Sherwin*
*Foreword by Phil Christie*
ISBN 978 1 84905 614 4
eISBN 978 1 78450 085 6

Understanding Pathological Demand Avoidance Syndrome in Children
A Guide for Parents, Teachers and Other Professionals
*Phil Christie, Margaret Duncan, Ruth Fidler and Zara Healy*
ISBN 978 1 84905 074 6
eISBN 978 0 85700 253 2
*JKP Essentials series*

# PDA by PDAers

## — From Anxiety to Avoidance and Masking to Meltdowns —

## Compiled by SALLY CAT

Jessica Kingsley *Publishers*
London and Philadelphia

First published in 2018
by Jessica Kingsley Publishers
73 Collier Street
London N1 9BE, UK
and
400 Market Street, Suite 400
Philadelphia, PA 19106, USA

*www.jkp.com*

**Library of Congress Cataloging in Publication Data**
Names: Cat, Sally, author.
Title: PDA by PDAers : tigers aren't just stripy / Sally Cat.
Description: London ; Philadelphia : Jessica Kingsley Publishers, 2018.
Identifiers: LCCN 2017059756 | ISBN 9781785925368
Subjects: LCSH: Pathological demand avoidance syndrome.
Classification: LCC RJ506.P28 C38 2018 | DDC 618.92/8581--dc23 LC record available at https://lccn.loc.gov/2017059756

**British Library Cataloguing in Publication Data**
A CIP catalogue record for this book is available from the British Library

ISBN 978 1 78592 536 8
eISBN 978 1 78450 934 7

Printed and bound in Great Britain

# Contents

# List of Graphs

# Introduction

The task of writing an introduction has triggered my Demand Avoidance, but I can appreciate the need and I am going to attempt to write something helpful and appropriate. I am a PDA adult. I learned this, after receiving an adult autism diagnosis and then – after hearing about PDA – joining the Adult PDA Support Network Facebook group to find out more. This group quickly proved to be my home from home.

PDA (Pathological Demand Avoidance) is an Autistic Spectrum Condition that is very real, but sorely ignored by a majority of health professionals and services. It comprises a pathological (hardwired) drive to avoid everyday 'demands' (commands, expectations, pressures, etc.) coupled with extreme anxiety and a host of other goodies such as being interested in people and enjoying wordplay.

At this time, this Adult PDA Support Network Facebook group is the only real dedicated resource for adult PDAers (thank you, Julia Daunt, for setting the group up) and, as the wider world has started to realise that adult PDA exists and merits recognition, this thriving Facebook community represents the best resource.

I felt inspired to communicate adult PDA to the now perhaps curious wider world via 20 PDA topics discussed (in a PDA-friendly way) in the adult PDA group, with 'quick poll' results at the end of each section, targeted Sally Cat graphic memes and Riko Ryuki's blog posts (Riko Ryuki is a member of the Adult PDA Support Network Facebook group and also blogs about PDA).

The recorded discussion was spontaneous. I haven't directed anyone's answers beyond my phrasing of starter questions and my in-topic comments (all of which are included in this transcript). My only direction has been in occasionally switching the order of responses (fair enough, I feel, as these adult PDA group contributors, who often live in different time zones, contribute when they come across a post, regardless of what others have already written, and also, once they are in the 'zone' to do so).

Perhaps I'm just autistically inflexible in my thinking to use this Facebook group template to communicate adult PDA, but this platform seems to me to be the arena in which we jell and flourish as a friendly, self-aware and dynamic community and our discussion, I feel, represents something significant: something key about our PDA personalities.

No single one of us is more PDA than any other. There is, in my opinion, no 'pure' form of PDA. We are PDA, adhering to a certain pattern, in our own unique ways. To me, this collective description provides a broader glimpse of the adult PDA whole than can be provided by a single PDA individual – although it should be noted that the contributors are PDAers who have heard of PDA; considered it; joined the Facebook group; felt motivated to interact there and joined the book post discussions. The majority of these are women. There may very well be a wide population of adult PDAers whose profile is markedly different. However, I feel this recorded discussion clearly demonstrates that PDA is not a hung-onto excuse for not bothering in life and illustrates both the diversity of distinct PDA traits (it's not just demand avoidance) and how we have lived with these differences all our lives, since long before ever having heard of PDA. To think of PDA as merely involving Demand Avoidance is to me akin to thinking of tigers as merely having stripes. Both Demand Avoidance and stripes are distinctive features, but both 'beasts' have much more to them than this: tigers have fur, tails, four legs, retractable claws, strong teeth, etc. PDAers also have high anxiety, intolerance of uncertainty, need for personal control and joy in wordplay, etc. And just as all stripy things are not tigers (zebras, corn snakes, railing shadows, etc.) all demand avoidant people are not PDA (people with Oppositional Defiance Disorder, autistic people sometimes, depressed people, etc.).

Many of us, myself included, within the group have freely enthused that the adult PDA group is our favourite group and safe space and I believe that there is a unique PDA chemistry that merits wider (consensual) broadcasting as a means of descriptively communicating our collective PDA personality. This is our melting pot arena. We often don't get on so well by phone or face to face. We flourish in the Facebook closed group world of text-based communication in which we can consider our replies and come to them as and when we feel sociable and able. We are in general sociable, but in our own times.

Another reason for my choice of discussion format for this book is that it's PDA-friendly in that it's kind of round table: there is no chief and we can all chip in as we feel inspired to do so, with no demands that we MUST.

As such, this book is compiled via a series of open questions I have posted in group with freely given responses from over 50 different adult PDA members, with the resulting discussions branching off in a happy, open and explorative PDA manner.

I believe that this book provides a unique window into adult PDA and, to boot, it makes a fascinating, sometimes very moving read.

# Original post in the Adult PDA Support Network Facebook group introducing the project to fellow members

Hello fellow PDA super people. I've got a book idea (probably an ebook to begin with). It will be *PDA by PDAers* (working title) and involve chapters/sections about different aspects of PDA, such as Demand Avoidance, anxiety, etc., which will involve one or more descriptive text/s written by us, targeted Sally Cat memes and descriptive comments by any of you guys who'd like to contribute (your identities can be disguised, if you prefer). So many of us have gained by joining this group in order to learn about PDA in adults and gauge whether or not we have it, and I think 'canning' this group's essence and putting it in a tin (book) would make a very useful resource for others out there. Who's interested?

# Prologue

Sally Cat Ugh! I've got Demand Avoidance against finishing the *PDA by PDAers* book! Riko helped me earlier by (on my request) telling me not to finish it, and this has helped in as far as I'm now able to be curious about whether or not I've included one of my new graphic memes, but the thought of opening the Google Doc to actually check is abhorrent to me. Ditto re checking the folder I've saved the book-converted memes in. Even thinking about working on the book is still pretty abhorrent to me (but less than it was – thanks, Riko – because I'm able to think about it this much and make this post). I'm wondering whether a useful strategy for myself would be to find some aspect about working on it that's exciting for me... Bloody Demand Avoidance!

Pickle I feel your pain. My life seems to be one long exercise in procrastination.

Sally Cat I'm great at procrastinating (witness me here on FB whilst cooking!). As a plus, I did succeed in working on my avoided website rebuild for a couple of days, but this allowed working on the book to become a demand...and then they both became a demand yesterday and I spent the day procrastinating instead. Perhaps I am needing recharge time and it's all OK?

Becca B I forbid you from even thinking about looking at it, Sally!! It's totally off limits to you!

Becca B Worth a go!

Sally Cat I just opened the Google Doc!!!! Motivation = to copy my opening post here into it as a descriptive prologue!

Becca B  Stop!!!!!

Silva  No Sally; don't do it!!!

Sally Cat  From experience, describing my demand avoidance helps it to 'burst'.

Mud Wildcat  Just hand it over to someone else to finish and edit. They will probably finish it quicker than you.

Sally Cat  Oh, that's a good one!!

Mud Wildcat  I'm The Master.
        They will though. Faster and better.

Sally Cat  NEVER!!!!!!

Mud Wildcat  Yes, they will. You are in total denial. Not only will you never finish it, it's because you CAN'T finish it. Just chill instead and go back to the smelling salts. Don't even try, you're depressing me.

Mud Wildcat  I am not finishing my book, even though it is all that I live for beyond my kiddliewinks. Beat that.

Silva  I think you know you've bitten off more than you can chew on this one, Sally. Just too ambitious. Shelve it – you know you'll never finish it xxx

Silva  And hugs, by the way!

Mud Wildcat  We could do it for her in return for a credit, Silva.

Silva  Mud Wildcat, of course we could! Brilliant idea! We'd be saving her from herself really... She'll never do it!

Sally Cat  I've just checked whether or not I'd included that graphic meme (I had): go me! I'm now feeling quite sick contemplating the task of finding out which section summary I finished last (demand #1), finding the start of the next section on from it (demand #2) and summarising this (demand #3). I think I'm going to go and procrastinate for a bit while I summon up the resolve...

Alice  Sally, I seriously think you should put it in a cupboard and ignore it for a month. You've done far too much already x

Silva  Seconded xxx

Sally Cat  Yay, I've just written the summaries for Routine and School (which is a huge section!). Head now hurts and going to read Game of Thrones for a bit.

Alice  What!!!!! You are not taking our advice here, Sally. It's very worrying.

Sally Cat  I. Am. So. Sorry.

Mud Wildcat  Wilful insubordination. Not really on.

Sally Cat  I am just so rubbish, appallingly rubbish at compliance!

Mud Wildcat  Disgraceful behaviour. You are letting the side down.

Silva  She just can't help herself...

Sally Cat  Lovely people, do any of you object to my transcribing this thread (with your chosen pseudonyms, if you have them) into the prologue of the book. Liking this comment equals a 'yes'. Anyone who doesn't 'like' I'll leave out xxx

Sam  If I told you someone else is about to send out a PDA adult book does that help? Depends if you are a little competitive?

Sally Cat  Who is??????

Sam  No, there isn't but I know for myself it would stir up enough panic to finish it this morning. Sorry Sally. Did it work? X Was genuinely trying to help. I can't wait to read it. Clever and brilliant you can do it x

Sally Cat  I have re-motivated myself thanks to you guys helping me. I'm much more motivated if I have new stuff to add, like this intro (may I quote your comments also, please – same pseudonym as in the book text)? I think I can get it together to do more of the 'donkey work' part of finishing it off, but I'm feeling a bit sick and headachey thinking about it! I shall NOT be defeated by Demand Avoidance though!!

# — 1 —

# DEMAND AVOIDANCE

» What the Demand Avoidance aspect of PDA is
» What it feels like (tightening in head and jaw; anxiety;
  Fight/Flight reaction triggered; an electric storm...)
» Whether it can be controlled
» The need for downtime either side of facing demands
» Whether it is always obvious
» 'Invisible' Demand Avoidance (that has operated
  without conscious awareness)
» What makes it pathological

---

What is the Demand Avoidance aspect of PDA? What does it feel like?
Is it always obvious? Can it be controlled? What makes it pathological?

---

Stephen Wright  A demand is anything not generated by the person
   with control issues. The level of demand perceived is based on
   the amount of control the person with PDA has over their life.
   Not everything is a control issue and not everything is a demand.
   This question can't be fully answered except for 'it depends'.
      I don't have to go to work...I found a job I love. Other people
   not trusting me has made it so I couldn't show up to work with
   a smile and actually have my first true day of work.

Dee Dee  I can't take being told what to do, I need choices.

17

Pickle  Even the demand of thinking about this question has caused the inside of the front of my head to tighten, my mouth to salivate and my jaw to feel tight and also my brain to fog up a little bit. I thought I wouldn't be able to answer that question but I guess I just did. Add to that anxiety if it is a bigger demand or one that is further ahead in the future.

Little Black Duck  It feels like this post with 5 questions and my brain just frazzles itself immediately, not able to find a starting point to even begin. It loops. And loops. And loops some more.

It's like my body is on freeze frame and my mind is on fast-forward. Within this one person and entity, my response is polarised. Always polarised. Never certain. Never confident. Always fearful. And a lifetime of that response, then creating a secondary 'fearful of fear' response.

Alice  What you say resonates with me (as it often does, wise one) about my reaction to the initial question in this post, and others. When I read Sally's questions, my mind frazzled and I almost had a sensation of word blindness and this is something I often experience when faced with a lot of text and the need/desire to respond. I think that this might be Demand Avoidance too.

Julia Daunt  It can't be controlled. It can be juggled in the sense of if I have something important that needs my time and energy then something else will need to be removed for the time being. I can only handle so much anxiety and demands at any one time. It's a constant juggling/balancing act.

The anxiety that stops me completing things is what I need to reduce/keep low. So if I've got an appointment that I must keep then I need to lower my anxiety enough beforehand for me to go to it. This means shrinking back on the demands on me. Everything from washing and dressing to socialising is reduced, sometimes to zero if it's a big event or something that will require a lot of energy from me, and then I'm able to keep the appointment. If demands are low the anxiety is low and the more 'able' I am mentally/cognitively and therefore the more able I am to mask. That's an added bonus.

When I'm pushed over my limit then I need recovery time. This can be hours, days, weeks or even months. It's a process that can't be skipped or hurried. I have to carefully plan out my diary so that there is enough time between events for that recovery and prep time.

**Sweet F All**

If I'm doing sweet F all

Please know this is super cool

I've done so much you didn't see

To you it's small, but great to me

Washing, brushing, getting dressed

Please cut me slack, I need to rest

**Sally Cat** I do this, I kind of super-charge my robustness ahead of appointments, etc., so I can cope with them and then I need quiet space recovery time afterwards. And, yes, too many events lumped together overload me, it's extremely stressful, my anxiety soars and I can be completely knocked out so I am bedridden.

**Julia Daunt** I cannot prep for the next thing whilst still recovering from the last. Events are anything – telephone calls, outings, doing lots around the house, admin of groups, emails, talking to friends on Facebook, public speaking – it's all an event and must be handled carefully. I can feel when I'm close to my limit so I simply withdraw and recover.

**Sally Cat** I even need recovery time after hoovering the living room, LOL.

**Julia Daunt**  Simple things take only a few hours to recover from and it's normally a nap. A shopping trip to Tesco, for example, but the big things like a weekend away will need days of prep (doing zero and zero demands) and then about a week's worth of recovery after. If the event was traumatic, like my train journey to Dover last year, then it can take months of recovery time.

**Lauren**  When talking about PDA with my fiancé, he said, 'But doesn't everyone want to avoid demands?' I said, 'To an extent, that's probably true. But how many people have had an experience where they had to shower and do homework in the same night, had an internal struggle to accept and accomplish those two daily demands that was so taxing mentally that they didn't do either one and couldn't go to school the next day? Not once, but they had this same struggle almost every day.' I'm 30, and sometimes I really feel like I'm just being a stubborn child. But then I have to remind myself that it really is a medical condition that's out of my control (mostly) and I can't be too hard on myself.

It was much more challenging for me to deal with when I was in high school versus now as an adult. I think it was a combination of things: not being as in control of my life as I am now, because I was a child and many decisions were just made for me. Also, not knowing myself as well as I do now. I can compensate better now as an adult because I can make compromises with myself. For example, I'll have a discussion with myself in my head like, 'Okay, I don't want to shower tonight before bed. But if I don't shower tonight, that means I have to wake up earlier in the morning to shower (which, to be honest, probably means I'll be late to work). So which one is it?' Having options always helps me cope with demands.

## OBSTACLES
This is what I plan to do:

But Obstacles get in my way:

Rules, conventions, calls, expectations, even my own body's signals:

All of these are Demands

And I want to Avoid them so I can keep heading straight towards my goal.

**Tracy** The internal feeling of demand avoidance, for me, is anxious and tense and overwhelming and LOUD and gets worse as long as I keep trying to push through it to meet the demand...

I tried to describe it to my therapist as saying, 'Maybe it's like listening to someone scraping their fingernails on a chalkboard, a sound you absolutely can't stand, but it just keeps going ON and you have to pretend it's normal and do stuff like it doesn't bother you (and maybe even you're the one causing it but you have to!).'

Or it's a feeling like if someone gave you a cup of worms and you knew you had to eat them and act like you don't hate it, but you really do think it's just gross and awful, but everybody else just thinks it's not a big deal.

Or it's like as if you have a really gross scary bug on your skin and you can't squish it or flick it off, you just have to let it crawl on you while you keep working and pretending you don't absolutely hate it.

You just have to tolerate that awful feeling, in fact you have to embrace it and do the things that make you feel that way even though they do, and usually also pretend you DON'T feel that way so that you can pass in 'normal' society. It's a really awful terrible feeling but hard to explain or describe to someone who doesn't seem to get it.

When I feel that way, I get very uncomfortable and amped up and my mind will try to get me to do almost anything to avoid doing the things I still know I have to do, while I am also simultaneously strategizing to try to get myself to get the tasks DONE and OVER WITH (this is at work where I feel I have to get things done OR ELSE).

And I feel very bad about myself because I want to be a person who acts out my values and meets my commitments and yet I never seem to be able to do all that I say I will do, or think I SHOULD do. So I'm not the person I want to be, and that sucks.

And of course she wants to know what is happening when I feel the feeling. So I can give her examples...

I told her that although I love my coworkers and my boss and am passionate about what we're accomplishing, I am looking for another job. And WHY I am looking for another job is: I have to resort to more and more extreme measures in order to get myself to do the regular, ordinary tasks of my current position, and I want to move on before it gets so bad that I lose my coworkers' and boss's respect. I am always excited about a new job for about 3–6 months, and can do it pretty well while I am learning, but then my performance falls off as it becomes routine – because the ordinary tasks become demands. I've been at this job for two years and I'm starting to hate myself, and this happens EVERY TIME I have been in a job for this long, no matter what I'm doing or how much I love it.

Or, for an even simpler example, I could tell her what happened last night – that even though I love my husband, when he comes home I get that awful feeling inside when I am thinking I have to go say 'hello' to him. It feels like a demand... But when she inevitably asks, 'Then, do you not like him?', I have to say, 'NO! I like him, but I don't like feeling like I HAVE to say Hi.' And that doesn't make sense, and of course it seems like no big deal to her, so she struggles to figure out why it's hard for me. And everything she comes up with isn't quite right. So in the end, we don't relate and I still feel like an alien.

Lucy Clapham If someone tells me I have to do something: 'go hang up your coat', for example, I can feel the fight or flight response taking over my body. My stomach feels like it is in knots and I begin to shake. The only way I can calm down is to regain control of the situation. Often this isn't possible and can lead to what others will call 'challenging behaviour' but in reality I am terrified like a small bunny who has seen a hawk! Sometimes, to make matters worse, even demands I set upon myself can trigger this same reaction and this can lead to me living in squalor or not looking after myself. It's ever so frustrating!

> **Self-observation whilst tackling a long-avoided task**
>
> I might try and do the f**king thing
>
> … I'm trying to get it together to do it: my forehead feels tight, I've got butterflies in my stomach, I feel a bit sick.
>
> … Yup, I still feel sick. I'm panicking about individual Demands involved. I find it difficult to fully think about them because I don't want to give them thought space.
>
> … I've achieved the first part of the task!!!
>
> … I realise I should maybe spend more time & do it better.
>
> … I've achieved even more of it: feeling less head explodey and sick.
>
> … I've done it!!! My head still hurts. My ears feel hot now for some reason, but I feel less sick

**Sally Cat** For me, demands are things out of my conscious control (including body signals) and feel like an encumbrance upon me to 'have to' deal with them and I automatically resist.

I severely struggle if people give me advice or guidance, even if logically I know it would benefit me. Accepting what they say and following their directions feels like demands and I just automatically want to refuse. I can make myself listen, but every moment is excruciating. Although I love learning, formal education has been quite challenging for me because of this.

**Tracy** I had demand avoidance even as a pre-verbal infant. It was very clear to me that family members wanted me to practise and learn walking and talking, and I perceived this as their demands and expectations. I refused to practise walking or talking unless I was left alone in a room to do it by myself. I wanted to learn, but I just couldn't do it when everyone was trying to get me to! When my folks left the room I would start to pull up on objects and walk around them – by myself. If someone came into the room when I was practising, I would just let myself fall and pretend I wasn't doing anything, and if they tried to 'help' me I would go limp.

I only said one nonsense word and nothing else for about a year, even though I understood everything people were saying and responded non-verbally and made my needs known. Demands don't have to be spoken to cause demand avoidance!

---

### Invisible Demand Avoidance

Demand Avoidance is not a loud response inside me.

It's feather-light and hard to feel.

It's only really noticeable when thwarted.

Just as you only feel air when pressure forms winds, my Demand Avoidance is not obvious unless demands are forced.

Forcing triggers anxiety and my adrenaline Fight / Flight / Freeze response.

---

What it feels like: out of control. I start feeling uncomfortable (but I don't notice it at first, I just react). I can't do what's expected of me, what I expect of myself, and there's a conflict – a disconnect – which I can't resolve. Then that feeling starts to build until it's all I can think about. It feels like I'm being forced into a corner – no options. Fight-or-flight kicks in, and my rational brain, and my ability to communicate and empathize, shuts down. In addition, I become frustrated and disappointed in myself because at that point I will pick fights, shut down completely, become irritable or sad or angry or ANYTHING to get out of the situation. I say things I don't mean. I get totally overwhelmed. I am no longer ME. I am no longer a person. I am just trying to escape. And then I come back and I have to deal with the aftermath.

And no one understands what has happened. It seems like they have all kinds of explanations for why I behave the way I do, but none of them is right. None matches what I feel. So they act like I don't like them, or that I am lazy, or that I don't care or that I am a bad person. And I feel terrible about myself because, despite my plans, despite my best intentions, I am back in this place again. And I have no explanation for them. I can't fix it. I can't stop it from happening.

Macushla  A laid-back, non-aggressive form of PDA is procrastination, which most people do from time to time, but not to the same crippling extent. Even if it is something I want to do or somewhere I want to go, I find the motivation difficult and find myself doing all sorts of odd jobs, a number of which I have previously avoided.

Sheila Murphy  I am avoiding something very important at the moment. So to avoid doing it I have started painting my hall and now am bored of it, so it's unfinished yet it annoys me. I can't seem to blank it out.

Macushla  So frustrating. If only we could switch our brains over to 'autopilot' life would be so much less stressful.

Sheila Murphy  I am permanently having a debate with myself.

Dee Dee  Relate to that, it's late I should be going to bed but end up doing the housework before bed. I've had all night and done nothing.

Tony Enos  I describe the experience of being under a demand as similar to claustrophobia. The anxiety keeps rising steadily until it becomes a non-negotiable, panic-driven need to flee from the source of the demand. My level of anxiety going into the situation essentially dictates how quickly I will get to this point. Initially I can focus on the novelty of the situation or for a short while the idea of doing something (very) temporarily for a greater purpose can get me by. But in those instances I am borrowing heavily from tomorrow's spoons, so to speak, and a meltdown or shutdown in the near future can be imminent.

A demand can come in many shapes and forms. The worst for me is when I feel I am being coerced or bent against my will to do a task – having to do something because a reward is being dangled over my head contingent on my completing the task. If someone requests I do something for them, then I can choose to do the activity out of my own free will, sometimes without a problem. But if a reward is withheld contingent on my completing the task, 10/10 times I will forgo the reward and choose free will over coercion.

If I put too much pressure on myself as far as it being one of the 'I should be doing this but I'm not' tasks, it is as if I can feel anxiety radiating from the task and approaching the task feels like trying to slowly reach out and touch a lit burner on the stove. Things like: having to go to work because without it you don't get money and without money you become homeless so you have zero choice, you must go to work, feels like people grabbing my hand and forcing it into the lit burner – the means I will use or actions I will take to stop this scenario will intensify at a steadily increasing rate and can spread well into the realm of self-harm – just as a wild dog may chew its own leg off to escape a snare.

Clusters of smaller demands: call the part shop because they forgot to put a part in my order + make an appearance at my sister in law's baby shower then babysit my dog across the street while everyone else interacts with one another + help a friend move a piece of furniture from one room to another, all compile to deplete my available spoons for handling demands. Any one of those things isn't so awful and doing them individually from a well-rested state can even make the tasks seem nominal... But life doesn't meter things out like that, sometimes they come all on the same day, on top of other stressors, after not enough sleep. As the day progresses, each individual demand becomes more and more unbearable and if pushed, or if I push myself too hard, a meltdown or shutdown becomes imminent.

This is pathological in that there is no choice. You can explain to a pathological liar why lying is bad and how much it can hurt people all you want and the person may be cognitively capable of understanding what you are telling them, but will then turn around and tell you that they rode a bicycle from Hawaii to Spain or something. I am cognitively capable of understanding that I am doing a task for a fair reward, even for an unfair reward in my favor, but if pressured too hard or too long by myself or another,

I will flee the task no matter how detrimental the outcome may be to myself. This is pervasive and affects every aspect of life, often destroying any possibilities of a normal and independent life. Long before I knew what PDA was, I was self-aware enough to know that I would die of thirst in the desert if someone tried too hard to sell me a bottle of water, even if I had gobs of money.

Alice  Demand avoidance in my view is pathological as defined by the dictionary, therefore 'being such to a degree that is extreme, excessive, or markedly abnormal'.

Dee Dee  To me it feels like I've been stabbed in the heart then flight. If I can't get away sobbing uncontrollably.

  If I can get away I rant, verbally unpleasant...never violent until I can be calm again. Think that's the pathological bit.

  Demands on me, I have to have a good think. I can't stand being put on the spot and feel incredibly irritable. I always do things in my own time after I've thought about it a lot first.

Joan Watson  One time I was running to hand a paper into uni on time (they locked the doors on the hour and anyone who wasn't inside by then basically failed the course). I had an asthma attack as I ran and it felt like I was trying to run through a thickening wall of treacle. It feels a bit like that to me.

Sally Cat  Demand Avoidance feels like this to you, Joan?

Joan Watson  Yeah, like a wall of treacle you can work to push through if you have the energy, or just avoid which feels wonderful and freeing.

Sally Cat  Yup, I get that – sometimes for me it feels like trying to push same-pole magnets together: no matter how hard I force them, they won't meet.

Sheila Murphy  PDA for me can feel like a rush of fiery anger or being frozen, stunned, stuck unable to do anything.

Gillian Mead (mother of adult PDA daughter)  When given any kind of demand it triggers anxiety and meltdowns in my daughter!

For me, battling Demand Avoidance can feel like trying to force two same pole magnets together...

No matter how hard I push, I'm just not going to overcome the resistance

Miguel (9-year-old transcribed by his mum) Demand Avoidance is like a dark cloud that builds like a violent storm with thunder, lightening and wind.

As it builds I feel cold, shaky, scared and like I want to jump out of my skin. The feeling of anxiety is so unbearable that it takes over.

It makes me feel down and horrible like I want to jump out of my skin.

Jenny Penny My frontal lobes feel like an electric storm; this is why I've always wished boyfriend or husband would stroke my head to reassure me. Earliest memory is of being desperate newborn finding comfort with my tiny head wedged in the little gap between the hard plastic mattress and headboard of cot. Pressure on head helps, you see. Now I realise this I can do it to myself if necessary – lie down, close eyes and hold my own head!

Sally Cat I often feel anxious about demands, but sometimes – possibly more frequently – feel irritated and angry about them being imposed on me (even by myself). I think it's maybe because my Fight/Flight/Freeze response gets triggered by demands.

It feels like I'm hypersensitive to a Sense of Demand (that most people probably don't even realise they have).

A Sense Of Demand?

My Pathological Demand Avoidance feels like Hypersensitivity to a Sense of Demand

I wonder whether Sense of Demand is something everyone has, but is unaware of?

It might work invisibly for most people (non-PDAers), who'd just feel uncomfortable if people were very rude or pushy

But with PDA hypersensitivity, our triggered Sense of Demand screams in our heads

This is how my Demand Avoidance feels...

Tracy Yeah, me too, I get irritable. I've tried to tell my husband, basically, that when he wants something from me I can't hear myself think. As soon as I know he wants something from me, I don't know what I want anymore, and of course that makes me feel very irritated! Despite the fact that I do want him to be open about what he wants, as that's appropriate communication, it can be hard for me, too.

Sally Cat It's kind of like there's ethical me that likes justice and fairness and then there's Demand Avoidant me that hasn't got patience for anyone else and wants them all to enable me to do as I please and be exempt from their needs and wants.

Alice I think I get irritated too, but I have only just realised why! Over the years I've put myself down as lazy, but it could be PDA.

Alice I have recently learned that demands are not always obvious to me, and I now can't rule anything out as a demand which I find really challenging and sad. A demand feels like a fear, my heart may race and I can think of nothing else until, one way or another, it is resolved. If I manage to complete the demand, I feel proud, but more often than not, I fail and avoid it by either postponing an event or activity or cancelling it completely which initially causes huge relief, thereafter guilt and frustration. There is also a more complex and subtle process that I have noticed recently which is a self-sabotage element where I can actually do the opposite of what is required/requested which makes me feel angry and even more frustrated with myself.

Sally Cat  Having gained awareness of my PDA, I sometimes spot Demand Avoidance operating in myself that I wouldn't previously have been aware of. For example, I was recently seeing a counsellor, and I noticed myself just kind of mentally disengaging whenever she invited me to reflect on something. I realised that her well-meant invitations had triggered me. She was a bit upset about this when I told her, I think, until I explained that Demand Avoidance reactions aren't to do with how polite someone's been (although rudeness makes it worse). I'll even resist my own body's signals (like feeling too hot).

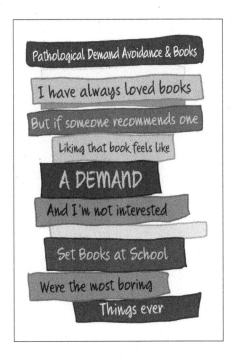

Pathological Demand Avoidance & Books

I have always loved books

But if someone recommends one

Liking that book feels like

A DEMAND

And I'm not interested

Set Books at School

Were the most boring

Things ever

**Tracy** Absolutely! I struggle so much to drink water when I am thirsty! I am thirsty and I want the water and I HAVE the water in my HAND and I just can't bring myself to drink it! So hard to explain without people getting upset or confused... Thanks!

**Sheila Murphy** I do this too!

**Kamala McDaid** adding 'please' in 'most' cases makes a demand a request if said in a calm voice, which makes it a little easier to comply with if not already 'heightened'/stressed.

**Sally Cat** Demand Avoidance can make things I might well otherwise have enjoyed totally unappealing. For example, if someone suggests I'll like a particular author, liking them feels like a demand and I actively resist reading their work.

**Alice** That definitely applied to me at school! I have read voraciously all my life, yet set books at school were a real trial!

**Sally Cat** Euch! Set books: the most boring things on Earth!

**Laura Mullen** This! I'm told I should read the classics, I'll love them... bite me! Boring, horrible, and just plain eww...lol. Now if I read them because I'm interested in them, it's great!

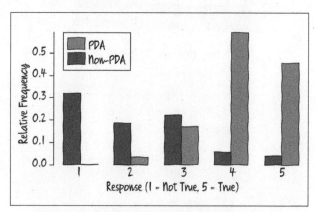

Graph 1: My Demand Avoidance impacts my life
*From a 'Quick PDA Poll' with 240 PDA and 145 neurotypical respondents*

# D IS FOR DEMAND

## From Riko Ryuki's blog

You might have noticed the word 'demand' used a lot in this blog. But what exactly is a demand?

For most people a demand is something they have to do, something that takes time and energy to complete that might be better spent elsewhere. For these people a demand can be anything from having to get up early in the morning and having to go to work to having to make dinner for their family and having to complete extra work for their boss.

In most people's lives the demands of family and work and sometimes even friends can be seen as added work, extra stress or simply something they just have to get on with.

Not everyone perceives the same things as demands though. For some, making dinner for a large family can be a fun activity if they like cooking. For others they may love their job and find the concept of extra work exciting. Still others may find enjoyment in everything to do with their families' lives, including the constant nappy changes.

What might be seen as a demand to one may be seen as something enjoyable to another. So what constitutes a demand for PDA people?

Due to the added anxiety that comes with PDA, PDA people will feel that nearly everything is a demand. Work, family, friends, school, housework, etc. may be at the top of the demand pile for these people, with other things coming in as lesser demands underneath. When you hear a PDA person or their family saying that everything is a demand, they are not far wrong.

Throughout my life I've found that we have a much, much larger number of things which are perceived as demands. Everything from having to say 'hello' and 'goodbye' to being in the same room as strangers. From having to eat a meal to going to the toilet. Even breathing can be seen as a demand. Things that come naturally to most people, that they often do without even thinking about them, are a constant struggle to PDA people.

One of the main differences is that for most people a demand is something annoying that they have to do, but for PDA people they are something unpleasant that they have to avoid doing at all costs.

You might hear some parents of PDA people saying, 'If they put as much energy and time into doing the activity instead of avoiding it then they'd get so much more done.' Yes, this is true. The same could be said for people with a phobia of flying. If they just got on a plane and enjoyed the journey instead of planning to travel by car, then boat, then car, taking more than double the time and cost, then they'd get there much faster and with less hassle and cost. But it doesn't work like that. If it did then there'd be no such thing as a phobia or anxiety. The PDA person would be just like other Autistic people (maybe) and they wouldn't put up such a fight over something as simple as eating a sandwich (because their parent has told them to as opposed to any sensory reasons).

I know it sounds silly. It does to me. When you're trying not to breathe because it's turned into a demand. When you start to have a panic attack because you can't stop breathing, there's no way to avoid it. When you start to hyperventilate because you can't control your breathing but that also makes you lose control and the whole thing snowballs and inside you're screaming with frustration at yourself that the whole thing is stupid and 'why can't I just breathe like a normal person?' When you want to go out and enjoy the lovely sunny day but the thought of having to stand up and put shoes on and go out that door makes you feel so ill that you just can't do it. So you stay inside hating yourself because even the things you want to do are too much of a demand. Where it's easier to wait until you're ready to clean the bathroom and then you do it without many issues as opposed to trying to force yourself to clean it immediately and end up avoiding even going into the room for weeks on end because you feel too ill to even walk through that door, never mind clean anything.

For most people, certain things are demands. Those things are the things that are hard work for them and are often things they don't want to do.

For PDA people, anything and everything can be a demand, regardless of whether it's hard work or easy, unpleasant or fun, whether they want to do it or not, whether they've been asked/told to do it or have decided themselves that it would be a good idea to do. It doesn't matter what it is, chances are it's going to be seen as a demand, whether we want it to be or not.

# WHAT SORT OF THINGS ARE WE DRIVEN TO AVOID?

» Demand Avoidance levels fluctuate
» A range of things avoided, some pleasurable, including:
  – Drinking water
  – Hanging coats
  – Bills
  – Housework
  – Correspondence
  – Things, like artwork, to which others have assigned meaning
  – Ironing
  – Family time
  – Picking up dropped items
  – Being healthy
  – Clearing the fridge
  – Cross stitch
  – Holidays
  – Time with friends
  – Playing the piano
  – Breathing
  – Red tape
» The strategy of immediacy

Is your Demand Avoidance always towards things you don't want to do?
Or do you also avoid doing things you enjoy – or even silly things?

**Idleness Is A Demand**

I can't just potter around or sit in the sun

Idleness is a Demand

It's intolerable

I have to be doing SOMETHING

Even if this something is very little!

Sarah Rebecca Arbery–Hinkle  I avoid things I enjoy as well as things that are demanding or perceived as threatening.

Julia Daunt  I avoid everything. Things I don't like, things I enjoy and things I want to do. That is what can be the most frustrating bit about PDA for me. I want to but can't. I need to but can't. I wish it was just a case of 'don't like that so won't'. Demand avoidance is SO much more than just 'don't like'. Much much more in fact. I think people often overlook that or just don't understand but say they do.

Tracy  Exactly. This is what I was struggling so hard to explain to my psychologist (and also trying to get across to my partner). It happens even with things I WANT to do...

Alice  Yes!

Silva For me it seems to fluctuate. At times I can face things. Other days I'll avoid like the plague – and it's all kinds of things, not just things I don't like though they are more frequent. I've even avoided visiting people I love or meals out with friends...and anything that is a regular event drives me mad and I give it up. Even when I enjoy it.

Tracy I avoid things I am told to do, things I want to do, things I don't want to do, silly things – all of the above. It's worse when I'm tired, hungry, sleepy, stressed, overextended or scared. Example: drinking water. I like doing it, I want to do it, everyone says I SHOULD do it, I take all the steps up to actually doing it, and a lot of the time I still can't bring myself to actually DO it. Frustrating!

Little Black Duck Anything your mind can conjure up could be included. From the ridiculous to the sublime. And it gets better because you can even try to distort reality. You can convince yourself that important things aren't so important and inconsequential things are life-changingly huge.

It fluctuates a lot. From world-conquering superhero, to can't get out of bed. Mood plays a big role, for me.

Riko Ryuki  Anything and everything.

Riko Ryuki  Someone knocked the coats off the bottom of the banister where they live. It's been two days so far of people walking past them all the time and yet no one has picked them up. Would take two seconds but it seems no one has the spare spoons lol.

Sally Cat  Maybe they're all PDA? Is this where you live, perchance?

Riko Ryuki  Lol yep. I know eldest two boys are just not sure about youngest, he's def autistic so maybe.

Sally Cat  I'd reached the stage in life of being able to maintain a relatively tidy home – wow!

But now I have PDA 6-year-old DD and she is extremely skilled and dedicated at moving things around into piles and clusters and strewing other things around. It's too much for me to keep on top of!

Riko Ryuki  I'd say mine mess the place up after I've just tidied it but I don't even get that far. As I'm putting toys away in a box they are being emptied back out at the same time. I tidy sometimes after they've gone to bed but it's rather pointless as they literally empty it all out again once they wake.

Sally Cat  And you likely need that time to recharge anyway?

Riko Ryuki  Yep. Though that time is spent watching programs with eldest, it's the only time he gets me to himself.

Sarah Johnson  I avoid...bills, phone calls, paperwork, washing, ironing, going anywhere there are strangers, cleaning, cooking, washing myself, school correspondence, nits and lice, illness, feeding my family, putting the shopping away, answering texts and messages on Messenger, loud talking and TV, the cinema, putting fuel in the car, talking to my parents, doing my parents' computer work, replying to my friends, getting photos done and sending them, requesting anything, shopping.

Things I do...go out for a casual drink (no pressure), go to work (new), talk to the dogs for a little bit (they're happy), Facebook (I can pick and choose), eat (I'm hungry), drink (self-medication), argue and debate (novelty), counsel friends (I can make a difference), argue (it's right!!) and then give up...learn – the best bit as it's new and adds to my persona.

Andrew I would have to say I'm not limited to avoiding just the things I don't want to do. Generally though my avoidance for things I like doing kicks in when other people have started to assign meaning to it, or influence it in any way. For example people sometimes get overexcited about my artwork and a few times friends have said I should sell my artwork online; suddenly I get this awful dread about art and don't want to draw or paint anymore.

Tracy YES. So crippling, unfortunately. I end up not wanting anyone to be aware of anything I do which I want to do, in case they assign meaning to it (which they will, one way or another), which is hard since I share even my home and don't have any space to myself. I end up feeling like I can't do anything at all for fear it will be taken from me.

Dee Dee I avoided housework and ironing clothes for 3 years with the ex...not so much in my own house with housework but I still haven't ironed a thing.

Dee Dee The thought of ironing just makes me tired. Mundane stuff makes me tired.

Pink I only iron stuff if it needs it when I get it out of the wardrobe. Most of my clothing is jersey and I dry things on the airer or the line, making sure they are super flat, and fold them neatly, so I don't have to iron. Oooh and socks need to be paired up as I peg them out otherwise they don't get matched.

Sally Cat Socks must always be paired!

Sally Cat And I'm not good at neat folding (too demandy) but I buy clothes that don't crease easily.

Sally Cat There's things on the floor I just can't pick up, sometimes for months.

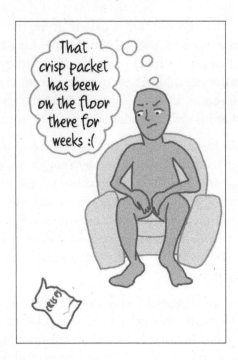

Sally Cat  It's like they have a repulsive force field around them.

C. Keech  Hahaha I always do that. Acknowledge its presence, acknowledge it's an eyesore, acknowledge I'm uncomfortable with that, walk on by.

C. Keech  Nothing is totally exempt, though if I've built 'trust' with a certain activity or pastime, in that it has been a reliably positive experience, I am much more likely to go into it with less debilitating analysis/be able to talk myself round if the initial instinct is to avoid it. I must spend minimum 70% of my daily brain activity quota just...arguing with myself.

Sally Cat  Did part of you want to add, 'No, I don't'?

C. Keech  Trying, in vain, to conceal the true extent of my madness xx

Sarah S  Cooking. I'm a grazer in general, so when my kids need feeding I feel almost resentful – awful, I know.

Sally Cat  I actually like cooking, always have done, but not when it feels like a demand. I can see this in my mum too (who I strongly suspect to be PDA). She used to provide home-cooked meals every evening when I was a child. She discovered making stir fries when I was about 12 and used to carefully cut carrots into matchsticks. We all liked her stir fries. Then, just recently, her stir fries came up in conversation for some reason and she grimaced and complained kind of accusingly, 'I had to cut the carrots into perfect matchsticks! It took ages. Really fiddly!' I felt a blow to my heart and disappointed that yet another happy memory had been tarnished by my mum unexpectedly complaining about it (she has done this sort of thing a lot). Since learning about PDA, I can see that her attitude was driven by Demand Avoidance (coupled with an unhealthy coping strategy of blaming her problems on myself and others).

Pink I used to batch cook some breakfast pockets, for those days when I was refusing to be healthy and eat well, that I could just bung in the microwave to defrost and cook and 90 seconds later I had a balanced meal. In order to make these, I had to have all the ingredients in the house and completely run out of them in the freezer. I would force myself to cook them in a passive aggressive kind of a way, by starting off the dough in the bread maker and then kind of going well, sod you, brain, you can't cope with wasted food so you're going to have to get on with the rest now.

These things were an absolute life saver and still I had to find a way to make my brain do them!

Sally Cat There's an out-of-date Dairylea cheese triangle in our fridge. I bought the pack back in about February and enjoyed eating the first 4 triangles as snacks. Retrieving the fifth as a snack became an avoidance issue, but I eventually managed to get it from the fridge, unwrap it and scoff it. It was tasty. I enjoyed it. One triangle remained. I was aware of the use by date of mid May, but could not overcome Demand Avoidance to eat the bloody thing. We'd even got a new fridge and transferred the lone cheese triangle into it, but could I bring myself to eat it? No. And the carton with it in is still lurking in there three weeks after its use by date (throwing it away is a demand as well! Hell, bloody use by dates are demands).

**Pink** The only way I can clear out stuff from the fridge that's past its sell by date but still looks OK and yet I'm refusing to eat it is to dig it out and leave it on the side until it's definitely gone off, then I can throw it away!

**Dee Dee** I love doing my cross stitch but it can be months and months before I pick it up...when I'm focused I can spend all day doing it until the early hours.

My biggest avoidance is seeing the family sometimes only twice a month. I haven't seen my boy for a while.

Mum and Dad are going away for 2 weeks; this may sound nasty but it's a relief coz I can forget about them for 2 weeks.

**Alice** I think the saddest things that I avoid are time with friends, going to the theatre, holidays and family visits (although the family visits can have additional problems for me).

**Emily Cool** I totally avoid doing things I love doing. I play the piano, except I rarely do these days. I used to not play for ages but then as soon as I did it was hard to stop. I also wouldn't be able to practise as a child if my mum had told me to do my practice! I'd have intentions to do it but would have to do it when it felt right. As soon as someone said I had to, I just couldn't! I would go in the music room and go through the motions but it was so stressful I got knots in my stomach and had to keep stopping. My fingers were literally going through the motions but my brain was just going through all these other thoughts. I felt so cross as I really wanted to do it but couldn't because I needed to do it in my own time. These days I don't have the time or brain space to put what I want into playing so I avoid it altogether. Reading is another thing that I love but can hardly ever bring myself to do!

Sally Cat It's maybe similar to my avoidance of listening to music. I tend to get into particular songs so intensely that it overwhelms me so that I want to listen to them repeatedly and I find it easier to just not listen to anything at all.

Emily Cool I'm the same with listening to music. It's odd, as I'm a musician, that I don't listen to music at all. I used to in the car, and it would be the same CD over and over, often repeating one track until it suddenly became too much.

Sally Cat Yes, I'm like that. We've got a few CDs in the car and I resist having them played, then if DD really wants to hear something, I hope it's the one with my favourite song on. If it is, I'm happy, but impatient through all the other tracks and gutted when my favourite song finishes. If she wants a different CD, I'm kind of gutted. I prefer silence!

Emily Cool I do sing sometimes. I have phases of either singing loads or not singing at all with no in between. I think it depends on what I'm doing. When I was working with singing students I would get songs, or just a line or two from a song, stuck in my head. I would sing it over and over, mainly when I'm driving. I watched Britain's Got Talent last week so I've still got music from that going round and round. I like music in my head so sometimes outside music interrupts that! My children don't listen to music either. I used to try to encourage it when they were younger, but often they didn't like what I put on, and my eldest can't really cope with it. He used to like Calvin Harris and I hated it at first. After I listen several times to something I don't like it kind of grows on me!

**Sally Cat** I get lines of songs stuck in my head too. They kind of strike a deep chord with me. Just lately, it's been the notes and words of Dido's 'Thank You', where she sings 'get out of bed at all'. I get transfixed and tend to start singing the song. I make up songs as well and sing them to DD. She's PDA too and loves wordplay. We make up ridiculous names for each other and ourselves.

**Lauren Larson** I do aerial circus classes. And I LOVE them. But when I know I have to do it every Wednesday (or whatever day I sign up for) it becomes a chore and I dread it. Afterward, I'm so happy I went and feel great. But the idea of it being something I 'have' to do because I paid for it ahead of time makes me never want to do it. And that's just one example. I pretty much avoid everything I can for as long as I can, even if it's something I want to do. So because of that, I'm actually better off sometimes the more I HAVE to do...because then I'm productive in other ways by doing things to avoid the things I really need to do. (Like in college my hair was always done perfectly because I was doing that to avoid doing my homework.)

**Sally Cat** And writing my dissertation was the only thing that's ever made me keen to mop the kitchen floor!

Astrid van Woerkom  I avoid things I don't like more than things I enjoy, but I do avoid both to a degree. For example, I am a blogger, which I love, but I avoid writing posts many times. Basically, any time it feels like a chore, I avoid it.

Sally Cat  I get this; once the novelty wears off and a task becomes a routine I should follow, it feels like a demand and I just don't want to do it.

Tracy  Sally Cat, Yup!

Vanessa Haszard  Most days I resent having to breathe! I can get really enthusiastic about something new occasionally, but mostly I do very little. Driving my kid to and from school is my biggest achievement, and demand, at the moment. It is wonderful, but I know I need to return to reality at some stage.

Stef  I would say my biggest struggle is anything I call 'red tape'... if it requires me to fill things out and mail them, etc., it brings on major avoidance techniques. All sorts. Losing the papers, forgetting to send, directing them elsewhere, telling the person I can't (and after my husband died I did this whenever I could, simply refusing)...the more mundane but multiple steps, etc., the harder it is for me. Usually it's stupidly easy (my family wants me to apply for Canadian citizenship for my son. I've paid the fees years ago, filled out the computer form but need to find official docs needed and just assemble and mail. It's been 4 years of not finishing it!). I also don't manage well when backed into a corner with questions...whoa. I'll use any tactic known to get the heat off myself. It's not pretty. Finishing things is a bad demand too, especially once I've gotten sidetracked midstream. I would prefer to finish things at once because of that thing...

Sally Cat  I tend to do things immediately, perhaps for similar reasons. If I postpone actioning something it becomes a demand. I am self-conscious over how keen I may come across immediately replying to emails, but if I don't, it's opening the door for Demand Avoidance to creep in.

Stef  I am fairly prompt on answering people too...and if I don't send a response right away I often avoid responding at all.

Alice  Stef, me too! And I agree with Sally about not wanting to look too keen in replying, but have to for the same reasons. My children's school secretary once said to me that she thought I was extremely efficient!

Sally Cat  Time spent doing things is a demand for me, so I tend to do things super fast. I like to be as efficient as possible and have a tendency to cut corners so I can finish things more quickly. This depresses my inner perfectionist.

Sally Cat  If I drop something when I'm walking through the house, I resist the demand of immediately physically reacting and pick the thing up when I pass back through (it's more efficient this way!).

EFFICIENCY
I have always prided myself on doing things <u>efficiently</u>

Like I'm running a race

I've recently realised
This has been <u>Demand Avoidance</u> in action:
The more easily and quickly I can do a task,
the <u>less Demand</u> it involves.

Emily Cool  Yes! Torn between getting something out of the way as quickly as possible or doing it to perfection. I always thought of this as my ADHD versus my ASD.

Sally Cat  It's all very jumbled, IMO. ADD/ADHD are now apparently considered part of the Autistic Spectrum (this is what the paediatrician who amended DD's ASC diagnosis to include PDA told me). I definitely relate to having ADD as well.

Sally Cat  Too many TLAs (three letter acronyms)!

Tracy  For real? I have been diagnosed with ADHD as an adult, but everyone always pooh-poohs any suggestion there might be any element of ASD. I don't fit what they think of as the profile.

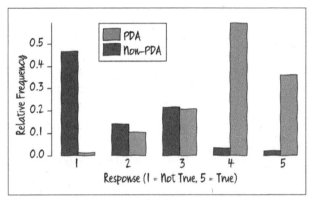

Graph 2: Demand Avoidance stops me doing things I enjoy
*From a 'Quick PDA Poll' with 240 PDA and 145 neurotypical respondents*

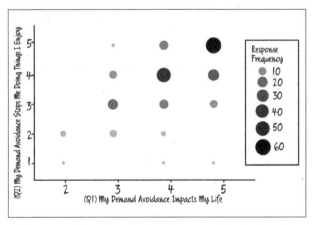

Scattergraph 1: Correlation between Graphs 1 and 2
*There is a moderate positive correlation between 'Demand Avoidance impacts my life' and 'Demand Avoidance stops me doing things I enjoy'*

# A IS FOR AVOIDANCE

## From Riko Ryuki's blog

Avoidance is the act of keeping away from something, a fitting action then to the fear that demand evokes. When a person avoids something they go out of their way to make sure they don't go near the thing, to not think about the thing, to not feel the thing or the emotions it represents.

It makes sense that people who have phobias will avoid the trigger as much as they can, the same as for people who have PTSD. If you know someone you don't like you'll try to avoid them, if there's a shop you had an embarrassing incident in you'll avoid entering that shop, if you ate some food which made you sick then you'd avoid eating that food again, it's instinctive, it's human, it's necessary for survival.

Except our brains aren't always able to tell the difference between a danger and something that's safe. It's why some children refuse to try new foods. It's why we feel anxious when going to new places. It's why people get scared of things that don't make any sense, like a fear of flowers or a fear of buttons.

PDA people experience anxiety or fear about a wide variety of things, and so they try to avoid them. School is scary, let's not go. That party I really want to go to is unpredictable and I don't know who will be there, let's avoid it. That sandwich doesn't look like it normally does, I can't eat it. When we get scared, we avoid. Makes sense.

So what form does avoidance take? Because for PDA people, it isn't just about not going near whatever makes them anxious. Avoidance takes many forms, especially in children where it's harder to just walk away. There's ignoring, refusal to acknowledge, drowning out, changing the subject, distraction, switching off, creating a fantasy world, taking control, destroying/damaging, distancing oneself, lashing out, turning others against themselves, running away/bolting, shutting down, etc. All of these avoidance tactics serve to avoid whatever is creating the negative feelings, it's a defence mechanism against the world. Most PDA people will start with the natural ones, ignoring, refusal, avoiding, walking away. If those aren't effective then they move on to the next lot of avoidance tactics by pushing others away, withdrawing into fantasy. If those don't work either then the person may become difficult, using defence tactics to create distance between them and others: 'if people don't like me they won't ask me to do things'; 'they'll leave me alone'. If even those don't work then they may become aggressive, lashing out verbally and physically, also known as a panic attack.

Avoidance. It's annoying and disruptive, especially for the PDA person. They want to do the same things as everybody else. No one wants to live in fear of brushing their teeth or saying 'hi' to a friend. But they do, we do. It's difficult for people to understand when they haven't gone through it themselves. Everything can be scary to a PDA person; we feel like we have to avoid everything. How can you avoid going to the toilet? How can you avoid eating? How can you avoid breathing? How can you avoid swallowing? Ask a PDA person, no doubt they'll have tried at least once in their life.

A is for Avoidance.

# – 3 –

# ANXIETY AND PDA

- » Quantity of anxiety (massive or minimal)
- » Delayed self-awareness of long-term anxiety
- » Alexithymia (being unaware of own emotions)
- » Denial of anxiety
- » The pluses of self-awareness
- » Anxiety as like an electric storm and lava
- » Anxiety from avoided demands
- » Anxiety expressed as anger
- » Distinguishing PDA anxiety from PTSD

---

Do you feel a lot of anxiety in life – or perhaps very little? How about social anxiety? Do you consider anxiety to be a hardwired part of PDA? Is it possible to feel Demand Avoidant and not anxious?

---

Martin Nightingale  A lot.

Vanessa Haszard  Enormous anxiety, only the level varies. I am aware of it the moment I awaken. It is only since discovering PDA that I have begun to tease it apart, and identify that some of it is sensory in basis rather than internal psychology if that makes any sense?

Very high anxiety is hardwired with my PDA

I try to hide it behind a bland mask

Riko Ryuki I don't feel a lot of anxiety, certainly not as much as I should. I do get socially anxious, especially when speaking in front of people, I get stage fright a lot. I feel anxiety often comes from demand avoidance and being pushed to comply. To me anxiety is a symptom of PDA though one that many PDAers feel greatly. I tried taking anti-anxiety meds once but while it did reduce my anxiety, especially socially, it actually made my demand avoidance worse because I cared less about not performing certain demands. For me, while anxiety works to make it harder to perform demands it also makes me want to.

Alice I've been unsure about this. When I had some sessions with a psychologist for depression some years ago, I was adamant that I felt fearful rather than anxious. My excellent GP enabled me to see that perhaps they are on the same continuum, which helped. I am now much more able to use the term 'anxious' at times when DA is in full flow (I still feel frightened too!). The anxiety makes me want to 'fight or fly', usually the latter. Initially, the relief felt when avoiding a demand is almost palpable. Yet if it is a demand that needs facing, guilt and frustration soon kick in.

Julia Daunt I don't know how to answer this. You see up until a few years ago I wasn't even aware I was anxious all the time, but I am. I think I was unaware of just how anxious I am because I lacked self-awareness but also because I was effectively born anxious. How can someone who doesn't know any different know what a normal or an excessive amount of anxiety feels like? Anxiety is my normal. By normal I don't mean nil. I don't have a nil. My normal anxiety is probably about a medium/high on a neurotypical level if that makes sense. Unless I'm not coping and my anxiety goes through the roof I don't normally even notice I'm anxious unless I make a conscious effort to think about it. If I'm out and about I do suffer with the added extra of social anxiety. Anxiety is definitely a hardwired part of PDA for me. If I'm demand avoidant then I'm naturally less anxious. Reducing demands is the key to finding that balance.

Sally Cat This is my experience too.

Alice Absolutely. It took me ages to agree that I might be anxious – without realising it is the norm for me! You describe it really well, Julia x

Sarah Johnson I never knew I had anxiety until I realised I had PDA. My anxiety manifested itself as anger, argument and control. Being there at the right time, doing it right, getting it right, the right clothes, the right kit, the right location. All examples of anxiety rearing its ugly head as me being in control – and why? To alleviate the anxiety. Once I realised I was always anxious, although I thought I was never anxious, things got easier. Acceptance and tolerance of one's own limitations and habits made me realise it doesn't matter – it's just me. And it's okay. It's just anxiety. No pre-ordained need to be sorted or better. Go with the flow. Who cares? Anyone died? No? So f***ing chill, baby...

Silva Sarah, reading this made me smile with moist eyes if that makes sense? I can so relate and you've really helped me to crystallise a few things in my own mind. Bless you! x

Sally Cat I have become much more aware of my anxiety lately. I have always felt it very strongly, but had become accustomed to it. For example, I went to see a GP about flu about five years ago and he spotted me having a full-on panic attack. He gave me a paper bag to breathe into (which made me panic more, LOL). I'd had had absolutely no idea I'd even been anxious before he pointed out my physical symptoms.

### Anxiety-Blindness

I've lately realised I'd had so much constant anxiety in life that it had become normal; I didn't notice it.

I was once very surprised when a GP pointed out I was having a full blown panic attack.

I've now learned to focus on my feelings And can spot these hidden panic attacks.

Little Black Duck Massive amounts of anxiety. But as others have said, took me decades to recognise it for what it was. It was just always there and pushed down. When it was suggested that I might be anxious by a clinician in my early forties, I scoffed in disdain. Me? Anxious? Laughable!

Oh, but hang on. Wait a goddam minute. Is *that* what that thing is coursing through my body every waking moment. And the answer was an indisputable YES!!!! It's an integral part of who I am. So integral, I hadn't recognised it for what it was.

Sally Cat That's how it's been for me too, I think: a major, major factor throughout my entire life, but something I'd become so used to I didn't notice it.

Little Black Duck  Yep. I only recognised it as 'anxiety' when it was at 'full panic stations' mode. And I just thought that was normal. How everybody was. What I didn't recognise was the ever-present swirling undercurrent that the occasional tsunami built from.

Sally Cat  When we've never known anything else it's not easy IMO to pinpoint individual currents within us and apply labels to them, like 'anxiety'.

Little Black Duck  Right. It's just *Me*. Strongly suspect that alexithymia is involved in that too. I recognise irritability and anger because they appear and make themselves known but the anxiety just has a permanent home, within me...so far more difficult to pinpoint.

The Toll of Self-Alienation

Severe self-alienation
Self-doubt &
Low self-esteem

When under pressure from others has led me to repeatedly force myself to do things despite Demand Avoidance

— but with a terrible cost of anxiety as a result.

I think this is what I was like as a child and younger adult.

Sally Cat  I scored significantly enough in an alexithymia self-test to be prompted to join the community. Counsellors – and I've seen many – used to get very frustrated with me for being wonderful at analysing my relationships, but completely failing to describe how I felt. I've managed since to learn to name my emotions more and become more in tune with them, I think, in the process. Perhaps the sheer bombardment of roller-coasting emotions we PDAers are neurologically subjected to from birth kind of numbs us?

Little Black Duck I think it was also the associations my brain had made. I saw anxiety as weakness. I wasn't weak. I was tough, stubborn, strong-willed, a fighter. Admitting I was 'anxious' felt incongruent to all of that. My brain spat out 'Error! Error!' It was a real relief to let all that go and just accept it, based on new neural associations.

Sally Cat I can relate to having a fundamental denial of vulnerability. I can also see it in my mum (who I strongly suspect is PDA) and young daughter (who is now diagnosed). My mum will NOT admit to feeling anxious. She did her 'weird thing' during her last visit and disturbed me by coming across as uncomfortable and not going along with things I suggested, but not saying she had any issues. In retrospect, I realise she'd had a concealed panic attack.

DD, since she learned to talk, has persistently denied being distressed to the point that she'd declare, 'I'm OK! I'm OK!' After a nasty bash and with tears streaming down her face (very hard to respond to as a parent!). I interpret this primary denial of vulnerability as rudimentary masking.

Little Black Duck I see it as the point where the anxiety meets the autism. I wasn't trying to hide it behind a mask...I just couldn't see it/believe it. I was masking for 40+ years too...but with little awareness of that, either. I just called it 'life'.

Sally Cat Yup, I relate to having had a similar existence.

Little Black Duck Knowing helps... A LOT!!

Sally Cat Definitely! For me, self-awareness = empowerment. And I like to have as much control as possible over my life.

Little Black Duck Strange, that! Lol!

Tracy I feel an incredible amount of anxiety, most of the time, but have only recently begun to realize that. Before therapy, I didn't know because it was just my usual state, the sea I swam in every day. Like a fish doesn't know what water is, I didn't know I could have felt any differently. In fact, most of the time I would numb it so I didn't have to feel much of anything. Perhaps my high anxiety comes from my not having accepted myself yet as I am; I always feel like I must accomplish far more than I am capable of, and every time I add capability, that enormous list of things I ought to do grows larger, not smaller. I think somewhere in me, I am always hoping that someday I will be able to be 'a real girl' and handle 'normal adult responsibilities', so when I see any hope of that, when I'm doing pretty well, I sort of expect even more, and then I fall even farther behind again because of the overwhelm. I was extremely anxious and fearful as a child, but did not share most of it with my parents or anyone else, other than trying to get to see a therapist when I was in high school (that did not go well; he had not a whit of empathy). I have a lot of social anxiety whenever I feel I may not meet expectations or am doing something I'm not 100% confident I can do, or something creative that requires investment and vulnerability, but I am quite good at hiding it, so people usually don't believe me when I tell them.

> **SOCIAL ANXIETY**
>
> Oh!!! I worry so much that I've said the wrong thing!
>
> My social anxiety is a killer!
>
> Sometimes I just want to curl up into a ball & hide
>
> It takes so much sometimes to overcome this horror of failure
>
> And self-loathing
>
> BUT
>
> I have learned to mostly keep it at bay
>
> To put it on the back burner
>
> These negative voices never disappear
>
> But I have learned to stop them ruling me
>
> It's so liberating!

Miguel (9-year-old transcribed by his mum) Anxiety is part of life. 99% of the time anxiety kicks in with DA.

The other 1% is the time I feel OK about just saying no to the demand and feeling OK about it.

I hide my social anxiety behind a mask, because I then have the demand of hiding it on myself.

This mask actually makes it worse.

I think this is why I get so exhausted at school.

My tolerance gets lower and lower and lower as the week goes on.

Lucy Clapham My primary emotion is anxiety. I have suffered from it for as long as I can remember, possibly earlier. I had my first of many panic attacks when I was 6. When puberty hit, my anxiety started to display itself as anger, whereas before I was more controlling and cried when I felt scared. I also suffer from an over-reactive fight or flight response, so a situation that would either annoy or upset anyone else will trigger me into fighting or fleeing. All of my problems are caused by anxiety in one way or another.

Sarah Johnson When I told my beloved friends my anger and need for control was anxiety because I have PDA they said, 'Of course it is, darling.' How annoying is that? They knew, I didn't. They couldn't tell me as I have PDA and I'm always right. They love me anyway and unconditionally. We laughed. I said thank you. They're my friends.

I think if I were to accept myself and learn to communicate well and be proud rather than ashamed of myself and of my experiences, my emotions, and my capabilities, I might not struggle with anxiety as I do. Therefore I would not say anxiety must be an essential feature of PDA, only that many of us probably do have it, at least at some points along the way. It can certainly be difficult to face expectations you have no way of meeting, and until you value yourself for what you are, the contrast between what you are and what it seems you ought to be is often a source of shame and anxiety.

Dee Dee My ex said I was a ticking bomb.

Laura Mullen My therapist says I have magical thinking; that is, if I worry enough it will all be okay. So that means anxiety is a constant for me. I can't stop, and then when someone asks me to do something the constant run in my head is 'Oh my gosh, I really don't want to do this, but I have to force myself to do this, not because they asked me but because my instant reaction is I'm making a demand on myself!' My anxiety keeps me from many things; my social anxiety is a lot worse now after a terrible battle with psychosis and PMDD. The demand to socialize is enough to make me a hermit for the rest of my life. I have a constant dialogue in my head about anxiety, tell myself to stop, struggling, etc., course my PDA is to the point where telling myself not to do something is going to make me do it all the more, even unconsciously, and because it's not recognized I haven't found anyone to help me with it. When I told my husband I'm a control freak because it means that I am in control and it lessens the

demands on me that way, he just said I wasn't a control freak.
Well, if only he knew what was happening in my head...

Sally Cat  For me, the control part of my PDA isn't about controlling others, but about controlling my world.

Gillian Mead (mother of adult PDA daughter)  Anxiety is the lava in my daughter's volatile volcano X

Tony Enos  I like how you put that.

Cara  I was close to 40 before I realized 'this' was anxiety and 5 years later I'm only now coming to understand that my body is displaying all the signs of anxiety and is in a constant state of fight/flight mode but I only really register it when it goes sky high and my eye starts twitching. It's usually off the scale when I'm out socially or have to phone people but like most others I mask – 40+ years of practice so pretty good at it now. Absolutely knackers me though. Still trying to get my head around the demand avoidance though so no clear thoughts there just yet. Only recently diagnosed!

Cara  On reflection, there is always anxiety with demand avoidance – if I'm avoiding doing something, I cannot stop thinking about the task I'm avoiding and it plays continually on my mind. If there is a very long list of things I'm avoiding I'll eventually get overwhelmed, my head will spin and I usually freeze/shut down completely.

Sally Cat  I'm like this: avoided tasks create a cacophony of alarm bells in my brain that don't cease until I – horror of horrors – face the demands.

Cara  Or my husband does them for me.

C. Keech  I think I have ever-present anxiety but it's so constant it's become run of the mill. I only notice it when I have too many things on. Then I go from semi-functional to a neurotic, crying mess and the inspiration for either reaction need only be a hair's breadth under or over 'the line'. I don't know where the line is and spread myself too thin so I start getting labels. 'Depressed, agoraphobic, body dysmorphic, disordered eating habits, anxious, insecure, over thinker, negative, etc. etc., then if someone/something comes along that lifts one tiny part of what I'm carrying off the pile, all those 'illnesses' instantly melt away. It's quite profound.

Shame no c**t'll help, really.

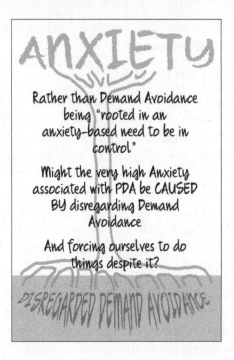

Sarah Johnson I thought I wasn't anxious at all. Until I discovered PDA and realised my anger is actually anxiety and the frustration to control my environment. Based on that premise I'm anxious all the time!

Francesca I've been thinking about this a lot lately with everything that's going on in my anxious little family. Out of the 4 of us, I'd say that half of us are likely PDA and we're all chronically anxious. With me and my son it's sort of reactive anxiety. We've got used to worrying about things, feeling uncertain, having high expectations of ourselves but low self-confidence. We are prone to staying awake till the wee small hours because our minds won't leave us alone and we both get migraines. Of myself, I would say I'm more conflict avoidant rather than demand avoidant and this has developed as a result of some heavy duty triangulation by my parents as a child. The worst feeling for me is to feel stupid or that people are judging me negatively. I feel like I freeze and agree to anything and everything as a means of escape. In fact this is partly what appealed to me about my husband when we met – he's certainly not afraid of saying 'no' like I am. He doesn't really seem to care much for social convention at all, but, oh my God, is he anxious! It just comes across as 'fuck you' instead of 'sorry'!

So he and my darling girl are the same in this respect. It's to my mind a subverted kind of anxiety that is part of who they are instead of a reaction to the slings and arrows life hurls in their direction. Those slings and arrows can certainly make things worse, but it's always there to a greater or lesser extent. And the primary expression of it is 'don't you dare tell me what to do, I am the boss of me and you can all go to hell'.

I don't know if this resonates with anyone else on here or if I'm completely off.

Tony Enos I experience an enormous amount of anxiety, but separating what anxiety is caused by PTSD and what anxiety is caused by PDA can get a bit hairy.

Some things are obvious. The fact that when my landlady slams her front door or car door and I get a knot in my stomach because I 'know' she is clearly doing it because she is mad at me is easy to decipher, that is because of my childhood. That I tiptoe around everywhere, try to make as little noise as possible, and sometimes even crawl by the windows so it doesn't look like I am home is also because of my childhood – when you have been taught that every ounce of your being and existence is offensive and bad, you try as hard as you can to make it seem as though you don't exist at all, and that becomes habit by the time you are an adult. But underlying all that is the knowledge that while you are not worthless, you are certainly worth less than everyone else. This in itself is not a result of PDA, but it is a result of treating PDA symptoms with violence. The memes that say 'Back in my day we didn't have behavior disorders, we had a belt' infuriate me. Those people may have received a spanking now and again which is one thing, but it is that mentality that convinced my mother to beat me badly enough to break teeth. My level of anxiety and PTSD is what happens when you try to 'beat the autism out' of your child, or you sadistically induce meltdowns in your child and then beat them for having a meltdown all under some sick delusion that you are somehow 'helping' the child. The PDA Society does a great job of explaining ways to help a child with PDA as is appropriate on the website, but if you want an example of what happens when you do the opposite, I suppose I am a good example of what can happen.

Some of my anxiety is obviously my PDA. There is a material used in some high-end motorcycle armor (D3O) that functions as impact protection. The molecules are generally free flowing so you have a semi-pliable piece of padding. During an impact, when energy is applied to the material, the molecules lock together causing the pad to become progressively more rigid, so the point of impact becomes rock-solid and spreads the force of the impact out. This is a great property in impact protection armor, but not so much when it comes to one's mindset. The harder I feel pressured (by myself or someone else) to do something, the more rigid I become in my mindset of avoiding that task. The harder I am pushed, the greater the amount of anxiety I can feel radiating from that task like heat from a flame. Pushed hard enough or long enough and the anxiety becomes so overwhelming that the autonomic nervous system takes over and decisions start being made out of an animalistic fight/flight/survival mentality – calm, collected logic ceases to be an option. That is clearly the PDA. When I have a task I enjoy doing, and someone requires that I do that task or a reward will be withheld, it not only takes all personal reward out of the task, but it makes the task, the withheld reward, and the person withholding that reward, detestable; all become the subject of burning resentment. The anxiety in that situation that builds to a fight/flight response is PDA.

But what is the cause of my social anxiety? It varies from situation to situation. Did I expect to talk to them? Will I ever see them again? Is it a single person or a group of 3 or more people? Does my girlfriend know them? Will their opinion of me affect her life? Is the subject matter something I know a lot about? Is the subject of conversation something specific or is it just small talk – the latter causes far more anxiety. Do I know what the other people's impressions of me are? Do I know what their expectations are and whether I live up to those expectations? Will there be anything we have in common? Clearly that is all anxiety.

It is all possibly caused by a generalized anxiety disorder, but is it rooted in my PDA or in my PTSD? Probably the PDA as it is an anxiety-driven ASD, but it is harder to pinpoint the cause of that.

It is possible to use this level of anxiety to get things done. If I am avoiding something because of my PDA, I can often accomplish other things on my to-do list to continue giving myself an excuse to avoid doing the one particular item. Sometimes, if I am not avoiding a certain task, I can feel like I don't know what to do with myself because I use avoiding doing one thing as a motivator to do something else so frequently. Sometimes having anxiety levels that high puts you very close to the tipping point for anger and that can also be a motivator. I can deliberately push myself over the edge into anger if I need motivation to exercise, for instance. Or sometimes I will accomplish a task just to spite a person who said I couldn't and letting the anxiety make me angry can help in accomplishing that task. But in those cases, I personally have to be the one making myself angry. If someone else tries to get me angry to make me do something, it will guaranteed backfire and I become angry at them and it will only motivate me to do something to make them as equally angry or unhappy. But again, PDA, PTSD? It is all entwined so it is hard to say what the source is; the battle becomes how to manage it or turn the anxiety to your advantage when you can.

Vanessa Haszard   Thank you for so clearly framing this, Tony Enos, it is something I have been thinking of myself. In my case PTSD has been repeatedly brought up, but never diagnosed, partly because BPD is often considered to be trauma induced, or in fact a form of PTSD.

Those considerations re how behaviour or presentation will reflect on a partner are very familiar to me. I really don't care what anyone thinks on my own behalf, but worry how I reflect on my partner in others' eyes.

Tony Enos   It is interesting. When I first sought help at 35, I was told that at my age it would be too difficult to distinguish my autism symptoms from my PTSD symptoms so I was initially given the diagnosis of Schizotypal Personality Disorder (SPD). I can understand why they would have considered that because childhood abuse is one of the fundamental causes of SPD, but there is a certain detachment from reality involved with Schizotypal disorders that I clearly do not exhibit. There is also a lot more magical thinking tied with SPD, and while I can exhibit some, it is more on the level of superstition where I can understand that there is no real connection between unrelated thoughts and events. I was very aggravated at the time because I wanted a diagnosis that was accurate, not one that was lazy and the first one to fit some of my symptoms – many personality disorders show some PTSD overlap. It took me a lot of reading and learning a new psychiatry-based vocabulary in order to distinguish what symptoms I had that supported one diagnosis or ruled out another. Putting all my hopes in the ability of the person sitting across from me to decipher my true meaning behind my subjective descriptions of experiences proved to be a frustrating experience and a waste of my time. I may be a 30–45 minute appointment in their life, but for me, this IS my life. And having an anxiety-based need for control, my solution was a lot of research and hours of pre-scripting conversations so I could better explain myself. If I could pre-script enough about each topic individually, then in a real-time condensed office visit, I would only have to work on transitioning between topics as I already had all my speaking points for each area sorted in my head.

Alice Just as a general comment, I've found it interesting that several of us didn't recognise our anxiety, or thought it was something else, some of us not until we were thinking about/had discovered PDA. Anxiety is a word you hear far more these days, I wonder what people mean by it?

Riko Ryuki I think their high anxiety is our low anxiety. I doubt many of them feel like the world is ending just cos they have to call a plumber. When my boiler was broken and they wanted me to try fixing it I felt like I'd rather slit my wrists my anxiety was so high.

That's why they think we're over-reacting, because to them it isn't a big deal.

Alice Absolutely great illustration.

**Sally Cat** I had an epiphany when my GP pointed out I was having a panic attack that I'd not noticed. I realised I'd been having them so often for all my life that I'd become blind to them, while NTs treat having one panic attack as a major issue. The health service recognises that prolonged anxiety and stress, which is the scourge of modern society, is severely detrimental to health, but PDAers have always experienced high-level anxiety, day in, day out, from the year dot.

And YET the health service is pretty much doing its best to deny the very existence of PDA in adults. If just our hardwired anxiety levels alone should be raising red flags for them, surely they should be doing all they can to support us to reduce our anxiety, not make our anxiety worse by refusing diagnosis and, therefore, our right to accommodations?!

**Alice** It's an interesting time. On the one hand we hear of health professionals and entire authorities denying that PDA exists. On the other there are people being diagnosed by using phrases such as 'ASD with PDA traits' by just as well-recognised health professionals. What a dichotomy within the profession! And why? In the end the rigidity is just causing more suffering. I can't understand why this isn't now official [Professor Elizabeth Newson first identified PDA in the 1980s]. Maybe I'm too simple but I wouldn't want to be letting down my patients like this. Am I an old cynic, or is it down to funding?

**Sally Cat** My sense is that lack of funding is a major driving force behind the current lack of PDA recognition. I suspect that they are afraid of the financial consequences of opening the floodgates to our existence, so it's easier to metaphorically sweep us under the carpet while metaphorically burying their own heads in the sand.

**Alice** That is SO short-sighted.

**Sally Cat** I also think there's ingrained ignorance in play. I'm reminded of the attitude of a senior health visitor when I told her I believed my 2-year-old daughter had female pattern autism. She told me, quite arrogantly and very dismissively, that she already knew 'all about autism in girls – and boys!' And that my daughter was NOT autistic.

Alice From what I've heard people say, here, mainly, I agree. Possibly the worst culprits are those who are very experienced and think they already know it all, forgetting that diagnosis is, by its very essence, an evolving science.

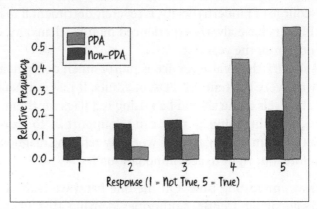

Graph 3: I feel anxious in life
*From a 'Quick PDA Poll' with 240 PDA and 145 neurotypical respondents*

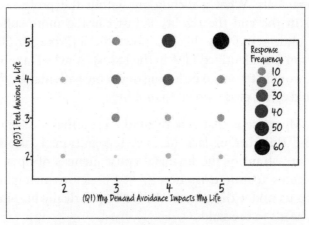

Scattergraph 2: Correlation between Graphs 1 and 3
*There is a moderate positive correlation between 'Demand Avoidance impacts my life' and 'I feel anxious in life'*

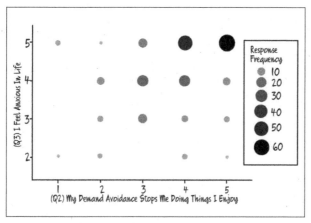

Scattergraph 3: Correlation between Graphs 2 and 3
*There is a moderate positive correlation between 'Demand Avoidance
stops me doing things I enjoy' and 'I feel anxious in life'*

# IS ANXIETY THE ROOT OF PDA?

From Riko Ryuki's blog

I've been doing some thinking (actually I never stop thinking, haha, my brain doesn't have an off button), is anxiety really at the root of Pathological Demand Avoidance? Or is there something else?

A couple of years ago, if you'd asked me if I ever felt anxious I'd have laughed and said, 'Nope, I never feel anxious.' Ironic, no? Not when you consider that for a long time I could only ever describe my emotions as either being Good or Bad. Even now I still struggle with feeling, describing and understanding my own emotions (alexithymia). It was only after learning about PDA and actually googling what anxiety feels like that I realised I was feeling it literally every day. It took a while for this to sink in.

The thinking around PDA is that Demand creates Anxiety which leads to Demand Avoidance (D=A=DA). What doesn't fit is when I cannot identify any anxiety around a demand; in fact, sometimes I don't have any feelings at all about a demand; it might even be something that is fine for me to do, but I have a knee-jerk reaction to avoid said demand. It's like it goes Demand leads to Demand Avoidance with no emotional reaction in between

(D=DA). These demands are often ones I try to talk myself around to meeting, this is then when I start to feel anxiety, sort of like Demand leads to Demand Avoidance then me trying to Comply which creates Anxiety which leads to more Demand Avoidance (D=DA=C=A=DA).

I'm not the only one here; other PDA adults have said they don't always feel anxiety when faced with a demand. So are we so used to feeling anxious that we only notice it now when it peaks? Or is anxiety merely a symptom of demand avoidance? Is our 'ausome' autism getting in the way of our noticing when we feel anxiety? Does anxiety only show up when we are either pushed to comply or when we know we'll struggle to meet the demand? Is anxiety what happens as a direct consequence of us being physically unable to do anything needed/wanted straight away?

From the start it's been noted how anxiety must be at the root of demand avoidance, why else would a person feel the need to avoid everything around them. So can emotions happen without a cause? Because often there is no real reason to feel anxious; why would picking up a book to read make me anxious? Why would going to the toilet, something I've done a million times before, all of a sudden make me anxious?

Some say it seemed like their PDA child was born angry at the world, that from a young age they avoided things. It would take a while for a child that young to develop anxiety around things, especially things they have no understanding of. So how could anxiety be the cause of their demand avoidance? Or is anxiety triggered by literally anything, even before we have any understanding of the things triggering it?

So many questions. Maybe if we were able to scan PDA brains in an MRI machine we would be able to tell if demands always trigger an emotional reaction or not. Maybe if I knew more about the way emotions and the brain/body works I would be able to answer some of my own questions. We may never truly know what happens at the point of demand avoidance, but for now, we do know that anxiety plays a large part in demand avoidance, and so we will continue to use strategies which work around anxiety, because it seems to help and it's all we've got.

# – 4 –

# PDA AND MASKING

» Individual prevalence of masking
» Reasons for masking (e.g., hiding symptoms of anxiety and hiding being a freak)
» Self-awareness of masking
» Stopping masking
» Meltdowns
» Overloading
» Having coloured hair
» Is it possible to permanently mask?
» 'Unobvious' meltdowns

---

Do you mask? Or do you not mask? Does this maybe tie in with social anxiety? And how do you express overload or meltdowns?

---

Ruth  I mask all the time. I catch the PDA me grumbling behind the mask on occasion and tell them to grow up.

Forever Young  'Mask' implies that I know what I'm doing. It's more like mimicking behaviors to see if they feel like the me that I haven't found yet.

Cara  Yes, I mask – I'm a master of hiding symptoms of anxiety. Carry bottle of water and chew gum to alleviate dry mouth, dark clothing and a cardigan and don't forget the super, super powerful deodorant, all to hide the excess sweat. Completely shut down when it's over. I need lots of recovery time.

Little Black Duck Yes, I mask. It's like my life played out with a backdrop of charades. Watching. Waiting. Pretending.

I didn't trust myself to know how to be. Hell, I didn't even know who I was, really. So I just played as myself. Keeping my darker, crazier, nasty, confused bits to myself. I didn't want to be that mean, angry girl. But I didn't want to be insipid, either. So I settled on kind of a semi-me.

Tony Enos I understand... But leave room for yourself to let your freak flag fly once in awhile, or it will find its way out at inopportune times! At least in my experience anyways.

Little Black Duck Yeah, my overwhelm and meltdowns are expressed when my mean, angry girl has had enough and breaks free from her cage of self-imposed exile, all hulk-like. Mostly it's a verbal lashing but sometimes she's REEEEAALLY pissed!

Julia Daunt I definitely mask. Always have and always will. I mask with everyone. The only person I can say I'm completely myself with is Paul [Julia's husband]. Everyone else gets a controlled or edited version of me. I don't really quite understand why I do it to such an extent. Most of it is social based. I mask so I can fit in and enjoy other people's company. If I was unable to mask socially I wouldn't socialise. I'd be scared that people wouldn't like me anymore. They certainly would be surprised. I'd be embarrassed too. My behaviour is very childish at times and I don't want people to think badly or negatively of me. Sometimes when I'm really comfortable with someone the mask slips a bit and some behaviours might come through but I'm always on the case and soon get that mask back in place. Masking is vital for my survival. It's vital for my enjoyment.

Alice I have masked all my life and been aware of it, as it was something I referred to as 'putting on an act' which I have done extremely successfully for many years. So much so that when I was in social work training and we were using role play, my tutor was quite concerned about me as I played a role so convincingly that she thought I might have the problems I was portraying!

I have latterly been less able to mask for such a lot of my life, the 'mask slipped' I suppose, and the recovery period got longer, which has resulted in this gradual discovery of possible PDA which made so much sense of all of my life.

On a funny note: 1 nearly ended up on the stage! 1 was very good at amateur dramatics and my mother, who was a speech and elocution teacher, wanted me to go to RADA [Royal Academy of Dramatic Art] – needless to say, 1 didn't!

Jarred M  don't know that I'm masking but 1 think 1 do naturally cos people think I'm social, even highly social, and I'm not.

But also my eloquence makes me appear charismatic. I'm just good with words not people.

Ruth  1 had to defend myself in court on Friday. 1 was lucky enough to have my mum with me for moral support. On the way, we'd been speaking for just a couple of minutes and she said, 'You're using a lawyer voice. Sound just like one.'

Masking also includes mimicking for specific situations when out of your depth and knowing the right language and tone is essential.

Vanessa Haszard  1 have been thinking about this a lot lately. 1 masked the opposite of what 1 tend to see others describe.

1 was terrified of my father seeing what a 'freak' 1 was, and that in itself caused great anxiety.

He was very much about what you presented the world, but somewhat angry and abusive himself behind closed doors.

Ironically, this meant 1 was almost so exhausted trying to mask there, that 1 had less energy to keep it up. And when placed with an adult that 1 had less respect for my behaviour was often pretty appalling.

1 had no less than 4 teachers refuse to teach me over my 11 years at school, one of which quit teaching (he really needed to, he was awful), after he pushed me in the swimming pool on my last day of school.

1 might not have been so pissed off if he hadn't thrown my towel in after me, but the spiteful fuck had to go that extra step.

They had to call Mum to get me to back off. 1 chased him round the school throwing water and whatever came to hand, swearing at him. We were both made to apologize.

Despite my efforts, conflict with Dad was pretty full on come my teens. When 1 moved away at 17 to university hostels 1 completely lost my way.

I didn't have anyone to mask or hold it together for, and ended up suicidal, thrown out, and sectioned. I tried through three marriages to be the 'right' person, and to be honest was mostly miserable.

Now I have more understanding of how and why I am, I actually bitterly resent masking, and mostly don't bother, but find myself in situations where it is more or less involuntary at times. I know I am exceptionally capable, but am acutely aware of the price I pay.

It is when I have to perform at a level for a sustained period that I am at a hugely heightened risk of spectacular collapse, and significant physical harm.

My daughter masks moderately well at school now, and doesn't need to at home. Very few demands in this house. Her behaviour up until 18 months ago was terrible at school (4 different schools could not cope), and I was concerned that the fact that we were not having problems at home meant she was hiding from me as I had my father, but when I began to get my head round masking, I realised that she simply has no need here, because of the almost zero demands, and I try and keep her anxiety low.

Lucy Clapham I masked constantly until I was about 12 at which point my mental health took a turn for the worse and 'outed' me. I wasn't aware that I did it back then. While I was unwell (severe depression, anxiety, OCD and a nervous breakdown) I had a tendency to act to hide myself. Unfortunately these acts were often copied from TV shows and my broken brain often tended to go for characters that were not very nice or were weird which kind of got rid of the point. Now I mask again but I am far more aware of it. I allow a certain amount of 'me' to show (I am no longer ashamed of my stimming, for example) but hide the more inappropriate side of me. At home the real me comes out and I am exhausted and ratty! I have always found it easier being 'someone else' when out in public. It definitely helps with the demands in life and the social anxiety. I pick better characters now though!

Nicola T After reading these posts, I realise why I was such a horrible child. It was the demands from my mother and schools, and although I masked as much as I could in school, when I was at home, I let rip. I try not to let myself get in a situation now where I have to mask, although work is one such situation, and I am slowly beginning to hate what I used to love, because it is exhausting. Hubby went to something today which I was supposed to go to, and I would have been expected to behave in a suitable manner around loads of crusty and boring old men, and their toffee-nosed wives, and wear a dress and makeup, neither of which I enjoy doing, as I also have sensitivity issues with clothes and makeup. I find those sort of things absolutely exhausting, and as I have work tomorrow, a day masking would have meant I was so tired tomorrow, that I cried off. I hate having to meet new people and behave in the *right* way.

Sally Cat I mask. Like others have commented, it's been a lifelong and unconscious thing for me. I never felt right in my skin. I wanted to be like 'normal' people and get along well with them. I was always gutted when I felt I'd made social mistakes (social anxiety).

The school playground was brutal. I longed to be an adult and have more compassionate peers, only to find, once adult, that I still misfit into society.

In trying to be who I wasn't, I was out of touch – terrified of, in fact – the real me. I didn't WANT to be Anxious or Angry, or Controlling. I wanted to be Mellow and Friendly and Nice. I repressed emotions I didn't want. They didn't go away though. My unwanted meltdown anger seeped out as overpowering snipey moods at loved ones. I hated myself for being so mean to them, but I couldn't stop myself.

I sought an autism diagnosis after coming across a female autism traits list and realising, after digesting it, that I fitted every trait on the list. The trait I identified most strongly with was masking.

I view masking as a necessary social interface to compensate for my autistic social blindness. I am unable to read the nuances crucial to neurotypical social interaction.

I believe I have a hardwired social drive to want to get on with people. My corresponding social blindness – and the social mistakes this causes – leaves me driven to try to assemble a social mask based on copied reactions. The masking process for me, I think, is unconscious.

**Sally Cat** Also, thinking about it, I suspect that my PDAer roller-coaster emotions would be a social issue even if I could read those elusive nuances: so we socially driven PDAers might also mask purely to conceal the intensity of our tsunami emotions.

**Tony Enos** Before my diagnosis I used to mask all the time. I relished time alone when I did not have to. In life the nail that sticks its head up is often beaten back down so masking was a way of flying under the radar, avoiding unwanted scrutiny or attention. I found early on that I was extremely good at interpreting what people thought of me and at playing to exactly their expectation.

When someone thinks they are smarter than you and has you figured out, they don't pay close attention to you and you are free to do whatever you want essentially out from underneath their microscope.

It had downsides too. I was constantly trying to convince members of the opposite sex that I was normal and worth dating. Not only did it come across as trying too hard, but it resulted in my living as though I had imposter syndrome. I knew I was an imposter in the situation because everything about me was putting on a show to hide what I was and try to seem normal.

Particularly perceptive people could pick up on that and sense my being disingenuous and it would cause them to distrust me even if they couldn't put their finger on why.

Since I have been diagnosed I have to a great degree stopped masking. There is a reason I am the way I am and that reason is not because I am defective, my brain is literally just wired differently. I am 6' tall, have a big bushy beard, wear overalls, rubber shoes, I look like a hillbilly or a dirty biker half the time. The clothes are comfortable, utilitarian, and best of all, NO ONE in the SF Bay Area wants to start a topic [fight or argument] with what appears to be a 6' tall hillbilly-redneck. The conservative bullies assume I am one of their own and leave me be, and the open-minded people in the area are just pleasantly surprised by my left-leaning views if they have cause to get to know me.

I spent my late teens, twenties, and most of my thirties escaping into the woods where no one would be around and I could just be myself. Now, I live in a cabin in the woods with my girlfriend. I talk to people online, I hang out with her, or the cat and dog. I am happy this way. Trying to mask for the world all the time is a quick track to burning out and being miserable for me.

Meltdowns for me can look like smashy smashy slam slam. It is hard on my belongings. I have learned to leave a situation causing me to boil over. I can control where I put my feet down so I am capable of leaving a situation before I smashy smashy the person upsetting me. Inanimate objects can get the brunt of it. I don't start trashing the whole place like Godzilla or anything, but the things I do touch I can be extremely rough with. Having dyspraxia makes things fall and drop all the time and adds fuel to my fire and my girlfriend says it is kind of like watching me spin up into a tornado, with everything I try to do resulting in my knocking three more things over. She has learned to suggest I walk away from what I'm doing and I have gotten better at taking her advice when she says that.

This system works pretty well for us and I verbally reassure her that she is not the cause of my frustration and she gets that. She says the things just plot against me and it is her way of showing sympathy for what I am going through.

People in the past have nit-picked or criticized me during a meltdown and that just makes me even more angry and gives me a target to verbally unload on.

C. Keech I didn't realise I masked until about 6 months ago. I thought I was just 'putting my best foot forward', 'faking it til I made it' or exercising 'self-preservation', all of which, I suppose, I WAS doing. It was only when I went into situations voluntarily, wanting to be open (such as seeking counselling) and was unable to switch it off that I began to question myself.

Around friends or in crowds when I'm in a good place my mask can be flawless. I'm able to achieve social 'flow' and for this reason, when the psychiatrist that referred me for assessment first suggested autism I protested wildly, citing my social skills as the reason why I couldn't possibly be.

It wasn't until months later, having read the literature he signposted me to that I realised (a) that mastering how to appear neurotypical was par for the course in most female autists and (b) that the reason I was so fiercely protective of my social skills was because of the years of painstaking effort I'd put into refining them!

Silva Forgive me if I just say a resounding 'Yes' to this. I could witter on for an hour otherwise. All my life and I just thought it was a 'coping mechanism.'

Tracy I mask all the time. I feel very vulnerable when people notice anything or ask anything or have any reason to believe anything is going on with me. Usually that makes it a lot worse, even with people who care about me. So I try not to let people know much. I mostly try not to let them know when I'm upset or struggling or feeling much of anything. I try to manage it on my own and just do the things I have to do to get through the day. I frequently feel that I just can't do it anymore but I don't really know how to do anything differently yet. When I try to do anything else – let people know or ask for help – I usually get in trouble or people get mad at me and get in arguments and that's so incredibly painful when I'm in that vulnerable open position that it scares the crap out of me and I go back to masking as best I can. Then at some point I blow up, unfortunately. Then when

I am able, I spend time reading or sleeping or doing nothing and that seems to help a bit. It's a bit of a mess really.

Meltdowns manifest usually as arguments or as a very strong desire to be left alone to do nothing. It's hard to say 'leave me alone, please' without others thinking you are mad at them, so it's counter-productive in a lot of ways. I try to communicate that's the way I can calm down, but...

If people continue to push me beyond that point I have been known to scream and I am scared at my anger. Or I get very, very tired and depressed and apathetic. Or I start crying. I hate it that sometimes I beg to be left alone but am not taken seriously until I start crying.

Sally Cat  When I'm overloading, I can't talk to people in a friendly, calm, reassuring way.

For me in the past also I've been scared of being alone and not taken time out when I've needed it, becoming very, very irritable and explosive as a result.

Tracy  I often hide my emotions when I'm overloading, hoping I can stop the situation from going out of control, but the voice I take during such times often sets people off – husband sometimes says he feels like I'm talking to him as if he were a child; he doesn't like it. It's when I'm trying especially hard to stay calm and be patient and find out how to get through...

I'm not at all scared of being alone, I prefer it. I'm scared of people getting mad at me when I ask if I can be alone. My husband often asks, 'Are you mad at me?' in a very pitiful voice. I hate it, it makes me feel so bad that I asked in the first place! So I say, 'NO, well, I wasn't anyway' (but now I probably am!) and then we fight.

Laura Mullen  I mask, didn't know it was masking. Just knew I couldn't be myself. Myself was way too much for people, too strange, too intense, too bubbly, too flakey, too deep, too all over the place, just too much. I am learning to be myself now, at 33. It's been hard and it drives a lot of my anxiety now. I have a horrible fear of rejection, but then again sometimes I don't even feel human, how could anyone understand that? I actually dyed my hair purple and teal to kinda make people stay away from me...they know I'm too much for them to handle so they don't approach. Whatever. When I get overloaded, I snap. I become very irritable, short-tempered, and start snapping at everyone, and then I start to cry. Of course, then people think I'm being manipulative, I'm not, I'm just so overwhelmed, I can't hold on anymore. I need time to myself after that, no one making any demands on me, not even myself.

Sally Cat As a very socially anxious teen, I dyed my hair bright colours and smothered on eyeliner as a way, I think, of taking control (and, maybe, expressing how I felt): if everyone was going to stare at me, it might as well be because I'd chosen to stand out. My punk image then became a mask. I wouldn't allow people to see me without my eyeliner on. I felt too exposed and vulnerable without it.

## Punk Mask

As a very socially anxious teen, I dyed my hair bright colours and smothered on eyeliner as a way of taking control

And, maybe, expressing how I felt

If everyone was going to stare at me,

it might as well be because I'd chosen to stand out.

My punk image then became a Mask.

I wouldn't allow people to see me without my eyeliner on.

I felt too exposed and vulnerable without it.

Laura Mullen I was a goth teen, still kinda dark in many ways. LOL, it's my comfort. But I also use my hair color not just to push away, but there are those who are like me that find that they can then approach me, which is kinda strange, but I like to comfort other people in the same boat as me. I hope that makes sense.

**Sally Cat** I remember in my mid twenties choosing to tone down my image so as to be approachable to more people.

My meltdowns have also taken the form of becoming short-tempered and snappy; of going on and on at someone (always when I felt safe) and unable to stop myself. Saying things I knew would hurt them – hating myself for this – but feeling out of control, like I was possessed. I didn't know why I was doing it. I was stuck. Since learning to spot and name my anger, I've ceased to have these meltdowns.

**Laura Mullen** I've learned a lot too recently about my anger. I suffered extreme PMDD. It sucked, I would end up in a rage and psychosis each month due to hormones. So even if I'm just cranky, everyone stares at me, waiting for that monster, even though it's been gone. So yeah, when I snap I get scared, and then really really overwhelmed, and then cry. I can't stop crying these days, it seems, but it's not depression; I literally cannot control my reaction now.

**Sally Cat** I think we PDAers have roller-coasting emotions (even if we want to act calm and happy on the outside).

**Laura Mullen** Yeah, I can't believe how much the PDA profile fits me, I wish I had known this sooo long ago. It would have helped me greatly growing up. Of course it looks so different and then my brother's ODD and I internalized a lot of it, but still I wish it had been recognized. Dropping the mask and discovering a sense of self has been hard. But I imagine the journey is that hard for everyone.

**Vanessa Haszard** I never saw anyone else say that about the punk thing, Sally Cat! I was a bit of a goth/punk crossover, and it felt like pulling on conformity, where everyone else was trying for non-conformity.

**Sally Cat** Historically, aged 13, my best friend – who was a year above me in school – became a punk and started hanging out with cool punk friends, all older than me. I idolised them, but they declared I wasn't cool enough to be a punk. I looked very young for my age as well. Aged 16, I decided to change and stop being the underdog. Shaving myself a Mohican and dying my hair was part of my emancipation, even though my friend had herself moved on from her punk phase. I wasn't interested in following fashion.

Rachel R I was the odd girl out at school really, the gothy/rock girl with hair totally over my face, band hoodies, chains in my pocket, spiky collar. No one else at school was doing it really but it did reflect how I felt too and I guess maybe became a mask for me. I lost that identity when I went to uni and had kids. Now I'm 31 and in a week in getting my hair dyed purple and turquoise...I'm sick of trying to be who I ought to. I'm going to live like me, maybe it'll keep people away, lol, sorry it just rang true of my experience so felt compelled to comment x

Dee Dee How do you know you're masking, Sally Cat?

**Masked Me**

In learning of the term Masking
I realise that I've always Masked
It feels like an unconscious, automatic process
It's like I'm always behind glass

It's how I've always been
It's so normal for me that I am often unaware of doing it
And I don't think I can ever fully switch my masking off

Sally Cat Good question. I related to having always done it when I first heard it described (in a female autism traits list). I can spot myself assembling what I think is the right expression and posture when I'm talking to someone and plucking out 'appropriate responses', but I can't tell whether or not I mask in all social interaction, say with my daughter. Sometimes it feels like I'm kind of behind glass and I can never directly interact with anyone. I'm always a step removed, if this makes any sense?

I think this is why I used to like drinking to excess and getting high: it broke the invisible barrier down between me and the other people (but I then tended to make a complete tit of myself, LOL).

Tracy  Yeah, I don't really feel like I'm being me most of the time. I'm trying to figure out how I'm supposed to behave, or what way I can behave that will cause people to leave me alone, and doing that as much as I can. I figured that was it?

Becca B  Nik [Becca's long-term partner] and me both mask in public and sometimes around NT friends. Less so usually when it's just the two of us or more understanding people, but it all depends on how we're feeling, how tired we are. All sorts.

I generally 'pass' better for short periods of time than Nik does, although again that depends on the situation. We both get the 'but you seem so normal!' response from casual acquaintances which I'm never sure how to take.

Sally Cat  Please remind me: Nik is PDA and you are non-PDA autistic, is this right?

Becca B  That's right.

Julia Daunt  I ALWAYS mask and I'm yet to meet anyone with PDA who doesn't.

Sally Cat  Maybe it's the extent of the masking? I think my masking restricts how I express my meltdowns, so I try to contain them. I get the impression that other PDAers let it all out?

Julia Daunt  I normally try to hide my meltdowns but Thursday's meltdown was too extreme. I couldn't contain any of it. I don't mask at all in front of Paul. He's the only person I'm 100% myself with.

Dee Dee  Do you think it is possible to permanently mask…not sure if I'm just over-thinking it or it's actually happening all the time… mmmm, I'm not sure.

Alice  That's an interesting thought. It has crossed my mind in terms of how long I can mask for, and it seems to be quite a long time, but the bigger the 'performance' the harder the fall afterwards.

Sally Cat I think I maybe do permanently mask, but I have to consciously adjust my mask when interacting with people I'm not familiar with. This is perhaps why I have had serial best friends: once I've learnt how to interact with someone, it is less stressful.

Tracy Personally I don't know what I would look like if I stopped masking. I even mask at home with just my husband around, or even most of the time when I'm alone. It's an anxious protective mechanism – I'm trying to find out how to relax. I'm scared of the possibility of people finding out what's going on underneath, and the possibility that I myself might not like that person I am when I'm not masking. I'm working with a therapist...

Dee Dee Is an observer a masker...like people watching and copying, mimicking and acting, Sally Cat? I'm an observer and an actor – is that the same thing? An oddball, really! It feels odd/awkward. Being a dick to compensate...

Sally Cat I think so, Dee Dee: observing others and mimicking them. I do this x

Dee Dee I'm a masker then, all the time. Different masks for different occasions. I have a work head, business head, mum head and a special head for my partner. I like heads better.

Sally Cat But, for me, not one specific person, just kind of impressions I've sponged up and odd mannerisms or whatever. I think it's an unconscious process for me.

Julia Daunt I don't just mask meltdowns but I also mask Demand Avoidance.

Riko Ryuki I suppose masking is the way many of us survive socially, especially as many of us were brought up with families who had little to no knowledge of autism, much less PDA, so we had to find ways to cope.

   It's hard to hide a meltdown, so even when masking if we reach meltdown we won't be able to continue masking fully so people might be able to tell we are having a meltdown. Most maskers would also meltdown once safe and, because they have held it together for a while, the meltdown would be worse than if they hadn't masked.

Sally Cat As I recall from your blog post description, you have extrovert meltdowns? From discussion, there is debate about whether Flight and Freeze responses can also be classed as meltdown, plus internalised Fight response meltdowns equaling self-harm. These 'non Fight response' meltdowns, such as myself and others have, are not obvious. Does this make sense?

Riko Ryuki I guess. I used to shutdown more. Isn't a shutdown the freeze response and meltdown fight/flee response? Would people differentiate between self-harm and self-harm during meltdown, as they might have separate causes? It seems like there's some overlap. And do we class panic attacks that involve lashing out as a meltdown?

Sally Cat I'm not sure TBH. It's hard for me to label things I've experienced my whole life and frequently come not to even notice. For example, my not noticing having panic attacks.

Waiting in outpatients at the hospital yesterday, I decided to tune into how I was feeling and spotted I was having a panic attack. My hunch – though I could be wrong – is that my melting down follows having repressed this beyond endurance (hence my tendency to flee hospitals).

What defines a meltdown?

Riko Ryuki  It is a bit confusing. I think a meltdown is where a person becomes unable to control their emotions/emotional response and lashes out either verbally or physically in any way. That's my understanding.

Sally Cat  Me too...I think...however, my uncontrollable drive to flee crowded and confined spaces, while continuing to mask, but unable to slow my pace and accidentally bashing into people often causing critical comments: I think this is a form of meltdown. I have no control. It's not a conscious act.

Riko Ryuki  Yes, that makes sense, that's def the flee action and it would be misinterpreted easily by others.

Sally Cat  So this would be an 'unobvious' meltdown?

Riko Ryuki  I think so, yes.

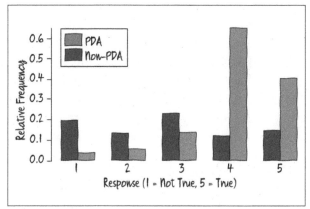

Graph 4: I mask
*From a 'Quick PDA Poll' with 240 PDA and 145 neurotypical respondents*

# MASKING

From Riko Ryuki's blog

You might have heard that autistic people have the ability to mask. They can adapt to the situation they are in by pretending to be 'normal' and hiding their differences. They hide their stims, try not to talk about their interests, try to make eye contact, pretend to care about small-talk topics, copy body language of others, use whatever slang everyone else is using even if it makes no sense, etc. Masking is exhausting and some autistics require copious amounts of time afterwards to recover from hiding who they are and pretending to be someone they aren't. Even when autistics mask they don't always pass fully as an NT person. I've heard that many autistics deliberately mask; they realise at some point that being themselves gets them unwanted attention or they get ignored, that being themselves makes them stand out in a negative way or they get treated negatively by others. They realise that they are liked more if they pretend to be NT, that they get hassled less or ignored less by pretending to be someone else. I've heard that some mask so well that they get refused an autism diagnosis because they no longer appear autistic; they get told even if they do have a diagnosis that they don't 'look' autistic or that their diagnosis is wrong. They get told they are 'high functioning' and so don't need any supports/accommodations or that they are 'fine', all because they can pretend to be someone else despite the adverse effect masking has on them. They get told when they stop masking that they are 'faking it' or they are 'ill and need help', they get told they are 'behaving badly' and they 'usually know better'. While masking can be helpful in some ways, it can be very unhelpful in others.

Not everyone deliberately masks. Not everyone can control their masking or even realise they mask at all. This is what my masking is like.

For years I thought everyone just became different upon leaving their house, like it's some strange magical door that makes me act like a different person as soon as I step over that threshold. I could be literally having a meltdown but the second I pass that line, I become someone else and the meltdown gets pushed inside me while outside a mask of happiness and calmness gets adopted.

Once I realised this wasn't normal for most people and that this thing is me masking, I realised I've been doing this for as long as I can remember, and I have no control over it.

There wasn't a point where I realised life was better if I pretended to be someone else, I've never had that ability of self-awareness; my deliberate acting skills are nowhere good enough for me to be able to purposefully pretend to be someone else. My masking is unconscious, an instinctive reaction to what my brain perceives as a danger; it's a coping strategy and one I cannot control. Trust me, I've tried. It's very difficult not to mask, to stop it from working. It takes more energy for me to stop myself masking than it does to mask in the first place. I'm so used to adopting a mask when in the company of others that it's a difficult process to change.

I know now that I masked my whole life. As a child my home life wasn't any better than school life. I masked in both settings. There were rarely times when I was just me. After leaving home I began to unmask when by myself, this led me to become more aware of when I do mask, because I was able to notice the changes.

I know I'm not alone in this unintentional masking. I know others who have said they masked from a young age and that they have little to no control over it. Some parents have said they felt their child masked even from being a baby. It's so important that people recognise that masking is possible, that it causes just as many problems as it solves. It might make it easier to fit in but it hides our difficulties so we don't get the help we need. Schools in particular need to be aware of masking and make accommodations to ensure life is easier for the individual and so they aren't so exhausted when they finally unmask. Professionals need to be aware when diagnosing that some may mask and they need to have the skills to see past the mask to the very real issues underneath, rather than relying on what they can see outside and presume they are 'fine'. Society needs to accept and accommodate autistics so they don't need to mask as much, so they feel safe enough to choose not to mask or their brains don't see the world as a danger they need to hide from. Only then will we be able to be the people we actually are, instead of hiding behind someone we aren't.

# INTOLERANCE OF UNCERTAINTY

» Intolerance of uncertainty as a motivator
» Its relationship to anxiety (is either the primary driver?)
» Responses to uncertainty (e.g. shutting down, disengaging, panicking)
» Sometimes thriving on uncertainty (e.g. having freedom to choose)
» Demand avoidance as the primary driver
» Are intolerance of uncertainty and need for control two sides of the same coin?
» Is pathological demand avoidance rooted in hypersensitivity to demand, or hypersensitivity to danger?
» Responsibilities aggravating intolerance (as opposed to appreciation) of uncertainty

---

What do you feel about intolerance of uncertainty? A recent study has shown it to be higher in PDA children than anxiety. Do you relate to this as being a major factor in your life?

---

Julia Daunt   YES! I hate it. I don't like it and will do all I can to make it go away. Uncertainty or a sudden and unexpected change sends my anxiety through the roof in seconds to the point where I often will have a meltdown that can last for hours.

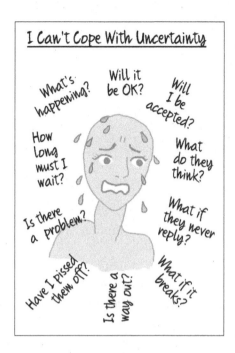

Jane  Yes, although I find it hard to distinguish from anxiety. I think I would describe it more accurately for me as intolerance of being uncertain of what might be expected/demanded of me, because it might be too much for me to deal with.

Ruth  I don't like uncertainty so I forward plan and anticipate as much as possible. I love horoscopes as they give me comfort as to what might be ahead and I'm always looking for opportunities so I feel more in control.

Ironically, demands associated with the opportunities can act against my intentions. But, the intolerance of uncertainty often overcomes it. This is why rather than bailing, I represented myself in court last week. The uncertainty of not winning was more painful than the effort required to prepare beforehand.

Sally Cat  I'm similar, I think – apart from boycotting horoscopes and astrology, LOL.

Miguel (9-year-old transcribed by his mum)  This definitely affects Miguel to a high degree.

If he knows what's coming next then things are easier.

This does not mean that his DA reduces; however, when the two are active together things are much more challenging for him.

Vanessa Haszard I don't know that I would separate it as such; it is the cause of much anxiety in my life.

Sally Cat Perhaps this is a key point? Intolerance of uncertainty triggering anxiety?

Mud Wildcat I was going to say, I think the first predicts the second.

Sally Cat I know I am very anxious when I don't know what's going to happen; what people are thinking; what they will do. I HATE being kept waiting in limbo.

I just have to KNOW. I want to know all about PDA. All about what makes me tick. All about all sorts of things (but so long as there's no demand that I do so: I want to know F all about recommended subjects!).

But I think I also feel anxious regardless of uncertainty. Like someone seems pissed off with me, then I feel anxious about that. I have, in fact, learned to soothe myself with this type of anxiety by reminding myself that I don't KNOW what the person in question feels about me, if anything.

So uncertainty can, for me, reduce anxiety.

Mud Wildcat That could be seen as uncertainty in interpreting the other person's attitude towards you leading to catastrophising or even just worrying about worse-case scenarios, hence the need to reassure yourself. Without that uncertainty your anxiety might never have triggered.

Sally Cat Good point...but, if so, how come learning that I'm NOT CERTAIN soothes me?

And my anxiety in these cases is over being thought badly of, not over uncertainty about what they feel.

Mud Wildcat Because the triggered fight or flight from the original uncertainty has you looking around for danger so reminding yourself that there may be no danger (logic head) brings you full circle to self-regulate? X

Sally Cat Head = now befuddled!

Mud Wildcat I'd say, especially when younger and less self-confident (painfully so) I would agonise over having MAYBE caused people to dislike me. This feeling was like a knife to my heart. Perhaps though the key word here is 'agonise' as in stew over the uncertainty of not knowing for sure. I used to want to know for sure, but was terrified too in case it did turn out that they hated me. I used to hope valiantly that they didn't. I recall meeting up with someone I'd stewed over like this and being relieved they'd seemed happy to see me then feeling panic halfway through our meet-up that they maybe hated me again. Oh, those happy days! (Please read last comment under 'sarcasm filter mode'.)

It can, perhaps, be argued that the newfound peace I've described has been through accepting uncertainty?

Rebecca B I'm starting to wonder if I'm PDA too, so many of the traits discussed in the group fit me as well as Nik!

Nik either panics about uncertain things or shuts down and stops caring completely if they get too much for him. He's fine with a certain low level of uncertainty or if someone he trusts takes on responsibility for sorting something out.

Tracy Husband has a lot of panic when it comes to uncertainty. It's the cause of a lot of our arguments. I'll start saying something and he'll get too anxious about not knowing what comes at the end of it to let me finish. Then he has a bit of a meltdown.

Kind of interesting, there's quite a lot of evidence that folks with his kind of birth defect in the brain and visual impairment have a lot of autistic symptoms [Tracy's husband has epto-optic dysplasia, a subcategory of optic nerve hypoplasia]. He's also very, very clumsy and has a hard time getting his body to do what his mind asks it to, but he attributes it to his vision. Given my experience as a yoga teacher (have taught him and others, and there is a significant difference), I think there's more to it than that.

As for me, when he asks me, 'What do you want to do for the day?' or, 'What do you think we should have for dinner?' it is THE. WORST. PART. OF. MY. DAY. I absolutely HATE planning this stuff. I like to be free and easy...

Riko Ryuki  In some situations I thrive on uncertainty. It's easier for me to go on days out or shopping if I have little idea of what's going to happen. If there is a schedule then this makes me more anxious as I then need everything to go exactly as planned or else I'll meltdown. As long as I have a basic idea of plans then I'm happy, no information at all or too much planning cause more anxiety.

Jane  I like this kind of uncertainty because it's freedom for me to decide what I'm going to do and when I've had enough I can stop. It's other people in the mix that makes me anxious. Like if I don't know what time someone's coming round, for example.

Mud Wildcat  I think uncertainty when one is in control of responses and directions etc. is different from uncertainty caused by the mandates or schedule or others.

Jane  Very different, yes.

Sally Cat  I like options for ME: things not being set in stone, but I do NOT like lack of options because the outcome is in the hands of another's whim. This, I think, ties in with the PDA need for control.
OR does the PDA need for control lie in the need for certainty?

Riko Ryuki  A need to control to ensure plans meet the person's level of demands, reduces uncertainty if they are in charge, less chance of unexpected change from other people, less uncertainty as to what the exact plans are? So many reasons for needing control.

Jane  For me it's about controlling the level of demand.

Riko Ryuki  That too.

Sally Cat  I think there is an observer's assumption that Demand Avoidance must be caused by Something. This Something has been anxiety (Demand Avoidance has been described as being rooted in an anxiety-driven need for control), but I have questioned this based on personal observation. Intolerance of uncertainty having been shown to be more prevalent than anxiety for PDA children suggests that anxiety cannot be the primary driver. I personally suspect that intolerance of uncertainty isn't the primary driver either. I think that Demand Avoidance is its own primary driver (and is based on hypersensitivity to demand) and that intolerance of uncertainty and anxiety are just grumpy bedfellows.

Vanessa Haszard Yes! I don't actually NEED to necessarily be IN control, as long as I have certainty about how things will go, it is just that often the only way it seems I can achieve that is to have control.

Sally Cat I'm feeling that intolerance of uncertainty and need for (personal) control may be two sides of the same coin.

Vanessa Haszard I agree.

Sally Cat Bollox, I'm going to sabotage myself now and point out that I also feel a need for control when DD is dominating my existence shouting, prodding, shrieking, waving, etc. to grab my attention. There's no uncertainty issues going on...or ARE there? Maybe my stress is caused through not having certainty of what will be happening next because she, not me, is holding the reins? Hmmm...

Sally Cat We have to sort this question out NOW! I cannot cope with the uncertainty!!! LOL.

Tracy I always want the freedom to be spontaneous and to change my mind without having to explain it to people. I have tried to be fair and extend the same freedom to others, but they don't seem to think that's a good trade-off. People have said they don't think that would be much of a relationship. Isn't it possible to be in a relationship with someone without putting them in a cage?

Sometimes I do wonder if I really am willing for them to take me up on it. Only my mother ever did, and I suppose she didn't really have much choice – I get really pissy when I have to 'check in' with someone for any reason. And I really am not that close with her, so...

Sally Cat So, to paraphrase, you want freedom to change your thought flow in relationships and you offer this freedom back to people, but they don't seem to appreciate this deal?

Tracy I think that's about it.

Sally Cat OK, question: can intolerance of uncertainty account for Demand Avoidance? Picking a random example: if I feel Demand Avoidance against having a bath because – in my head – this will use time I don't want to allocate to it, can this be explained as intolerance of uncertainty? I'm struggling to see a causal factor, to be honest. I'm not, though, discounting intolerance of uncertainty as being a major factor in my life. I just can't currently see it as the root of my Demand Avoidance.

Riko Ryuki Nope, it's not the cause. My first thought when I read the study was 'barking up the wrong tree' lol – they are in the right park but are looking at maple trees and not oak. PDA is a result of a faulty amygdala; this results in anxiety and intolerance of uncertainty [Riko expands upon this in her blog post 'Why Arrangements Don't Always Work' at the end of section 16]. Intolerance of uncertainty is probably more an autistic thing IMO but it shows up with us as a need to control because we don't do strict and regular routine.

Sophie I had a similar response to the idea of this study's result, Riko. I love your tree analogy.

Sally Cat Riko, I love your 'barking up the wrong tree' analogy and I agree that Demand Avoidance is a primary drive, likely causing our anxiety and intolerance of uncertainty.

I can't see the logic in assuming that Demand Avoidance is caused by either anxiety or intolerance of uncertainty. If this was the case, surely everyone would become Demand Avoidant when anxious?

Riko Ryuki Exactly. And anti meds [proponolol] would 'cure' the demand avoidance. Plus we wouldn't avoid perfectly safe and normal, predictable tasks like using the toilet or hobbies.

Sophie I see intolerance of uncertainty as yet another way to avoid possible demands that may occur but certainly not a more prominent trait in PDA than anxiety.

I wonder if an 'imbalance', for want of a better word, occurs in the brain when it is saturated/overloaded where a normal response to avoid unpleasant experiences (that keeps us motivated to be safe and healthy) becomes disproportionate and in some cases even confused/crossed over, similar to pain and pleasure responses apparent in self-harm behaviour. Not sure if this makes sense?

Sally Cat It does. I think it tallies with my idea that Demand Avoidance is rooted in hypersensitivity to a universal sense of demand.

Riko Ryuki Yes, it would have to be a difference from birth but that would make some sense.

Sally Cat Just like autistic babies are born hypersensitive to sound, light, taste, etc., why not demand as well?

Riko Ryuki Yep.

Sophie Definitely from birth but we are all born with varying degrees of hypersensitivity.

Sally Cat And a minority of babies are born with a majorly heightened sense of demand.

Sophie  I also wonder if a disproportionate perception of difficulty plays a big role in demand avoidance, e.g. a simple task registers a neurological and physical response in us akin to a much harder one.

I honestly wonder if it really is a minority though, Sally.

Sally Cat  Sense of difficulty makes sense.

Panic = 'I can't do that because it's way too difficult, therefore, I'll avoid it.' Then pressure to do it feels like an unjust demand.

Sophie  Then throw into the mix, subliminal responses to stimuli. I think fear/anxiety is always there even when we are not conscious of it.

Little Black Duck  I really don't understand (as in, brain just can't compute) how intolerance of uncertainty scored higher than anxiety. Just. Don't. Get. It.

For me, intolerance of uncertainty is a subset of anxiety. It's just one thing, among many. Anxiety is The Mothership and intolerance of uncertainty just a smaller, refuelling vessel.

Gillian Mead (mother of adult PDA daughter)  Spot on!

Sally Cat  Gillian, would you please expand?

Gillian Mead  She desperately wants to know what is happening in the family and what dates, etc., but when told, cannot cope with the anticipation and goes into almost constant meltdown and aggression until the event has been and gone! I am no longer allowed to tell her of events within the family beforehand!

Sally Cat  Who is disallowing this: her or the care home?

Gillian Mead  Social workers, care home and behavioural nurse in Gloucester.

Sally Cat  Ouch!

Barry  Hmmmm. I have actually lived much of my life as an expert in uncertainty (in the field of robotics/AI [artificial intelligence]. In many ways I love uncertainty and manage it well. But...I think this is when I am independent, and can react freely. When I am dependent on, or responsible to, other people, I can become very stressed by uncertainty of their actions/timing, etc., and of uncertainty of being able to meet obligations. I try to plan around this by at least having a lot of time for the unforeseen!

I am still pondering this. It's an interesting question.

Sally Cat I'm finding it quite challenging to pin down. My partner (DD's dad) has said he can clearly see she has intolerance of uncertainty and I can relate to having had it similarly as a child myself. As an adult, I have perhaps learned to cope with it better.

Lou Doubleu That makes total sense, Barry. I used to be young, free and single and was fine with uncertainty as I had no responsibilities. Now I have children I hate uncertainty. It's the uncertainty combined with the demand of being responsible for me. But also being dependant (I am a stay-at-home mum).

Barry But, how does that play out? If I think of my son, he really likes to plan things out, and doesn't like plans to change. But he can take joy in a passing insect, and get distracted himself from the plan without a care. Sometimes, later, he will be upset that a plan wasn't completed after such happy distractions. But...in the middle of being upset, the sight of, say, an okapi can pull him right out of it. The world is full of distracting wonders!

I find that embracing the distraction (the random, the uncertain) reinforces itself and brings more joy, while trying to stick to plans leads to more disappointment.

Is this true for me as well? I think so. But adult responsibilities, multiple children with different distractions, etc., make it so much harder to embrace the uncertainties. That is true, Lou! We just posted similar statements. But while adult responsibilities have made 'rolling free' harder, I think I was like this all along.

Little Black Duck And this is why I love this group. It sounds so obvious when someone else says it. Thanks, Barry and Lou... you've added another little bit to my understanding of myself xx

Sally Cat In thinking about intolerance of the uncertainty over how other people will respond, this was a major factor in my quitting Counselling Level 4. We had to find a work placement in order to complete the course. As soon as I learned of this stipulation in Level 3, I panicked majorly. What if no one gave me a placement? My anxiety about finding a placement rocketed. I made a few inquiries and was let down (by my local National Autistic Society branch, as it happens, who never got back to me after promising me one). The anxiety became so unbearable that I quit the course.

Alice Once I can get my head round the phrase 'intolerance of uncertainty' which makes me feel initially quite blank (!) I can unpack it a bit and yes, I am definitely affected by this. Quite how this relates to anxiety in terms of cause and effect, I'm not sure, but I have a very high level of intolerance of uncertainty/anxiety about many things that are out of my control even if the fact that it is out of my control is to reassure me! For example, if my hubby was to agree to ring someone to explain that I couldn't meet them that day, and to rearrange the appointment, all the while he was doing this I would be in a highly anxious state – heart racing, sweaty palms, walking about or rocking, etc. As soon as he would be able to give me an affirmative reply, I'd be relieved. I would be disabled from doing anything else until the situation was resolved. This same process occurs in any situation where I am waiting to find something out – always something important to me.

Sally Cat I can't cope with my partner being on the phone to sort out bills, etc. I can't cope with not knowing what's being said or being able to control exactly what is communicated. It's a no-win situation for me really because I can't handle speaking on the phone either. There are so many triggers. Being kept in a queue seriously erodes my patience and I have been known to meltdown before I've even spoken to anyone!

Alice Absolutely. Someone doing it for you does help, but don't under-estimate that it's only a tiny bit better than having had to do it yourself!

Sally Cat For me, it's a toss-up. Sometimes I prefer the stress of doing it for myself and remaining in control (of my side of the conversation, at least).

**Alice** I get where you're coming from. I tend to try to do it myself only if I have to. But I often fail and things become bigger and therefore more stressful – I think there must be a cycle here – rendering it totally impossible.

**Dee Dee** Uncertainty does my swede in. Tell me now, when, where, who, I want to know every detail first.

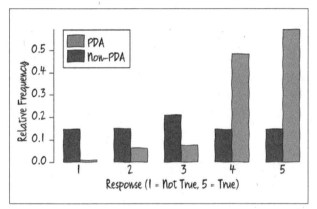

Graph 5: I need to know what's happening (I can't tolerate uncertainty)
*From a 'Quick PDA Poll' with 240 PDA and 145 neurotypical respondents*

## REASONS FOR AVOIDANCE

From Riko Ryuki's blog

There are many different reasons why a person will avoid something. Whilst most PDA demand avoidance stems from anxiety, the reason for the anxiety may be different each time. Knowing why something causes demand avoidance might help reduce anxiety by accommodating needs to ensure the reasons for demand avoidance are reduced.

Experience – having had a negative experience of something in the past will create more anxiety around the same thing in the future. A bad experience with using the toilet can mean the person will avoid having to go to the toilet even if that means making a mess elsewhere. The anxiety caused by having to do something that has negative connotations creates a need to avoid. At it's mildest this is seen in simple avoidance; at it's worst it can cause PTSD.

Intolerance of uncertainty – as with many autistics, the unknown can cause anxiety, this is why so many autistics prefer a set routine and tend not to deviate from it, because they are not sure what will happen when things change. If you go home from school a set way, any change from that will cause anxiety; the child may avoid getting into the car if they know a change may occur. If you're told there's a new boss at work you've never met before, you may become anxious and feel the need to avoid going in that day because you are unsure what will happen or how to talk to the new boss.

Can't be bothered – not to be mistaken for laziness. Often the idea of attempting a demand, no matter how small, creates an overall feeling of exhaustion. When you spend all day, every day, fighting to get things done and all the while your body is trying to stop you, you get a bit fed up of fighting. Sometimes it's easier to not try than to exhaust yourself doing yet one more thing. Laziness is when you have the energy to do something but don't want to anyway; 'can't be bothered' is when you have some energy, but know you'll use up what's left attempting to do something: it's a survival mechanism. Basically, you're trying to conserve the few spoons you have left by avoiding spoon-depleting activities.

Perfectionism – PDA tends to come with a big dollop of perfectionism; we like things to be perfect, preferably the first time around too. If we know we aren't going to get it right the first time around, or we do try and it fails to be perfect, we may avoid trying in the future as that discord between what we want/need and what it is makes us feel unpleasant, which in turn can cause anxiety about getting it right in order to avoid feeling unpleasant. Some feel that if it isn't done right the first time then it is a wasted effort and there is no point wasting time on imperfection.

Dwelling – dwelling on something that is about to happen or could happen can cause anxiety, often the wait for an event is worse than the actual event. One PDA strategy for kids is to leave informing the child about an event until just before it is about to happen. This reduces the chance of them avoiding the event because they have had time to dwell on it and for it to become bigger in their mind than it is.

Emotions – for some, even positive emotions can be difficult to feel, so they may avoid situations which will trigger certain emotions. Scary movies, praiseworthy events, being tickled, relationships, exciting events, etc. For some PDAers, emotions can be hard to endure, especially if they experience heightened emotions, are unable to control their emotional reactions or don't understand their own emotions. They may avoid anything that causes emotion.

Control – most PDAers are seen as controlling, although this is rarely the person's intent. Having control over their environment means they can ensure there are no triggers for anxiety. While this works some of the time, having too much control can also increase anxiety, because no one can control everything in life and having total control makes one fear losing that control and being swamped with anxiety. Similarly, having little to no control over one's environment means they are always on edge waiting for the next unpredictable thing to happen. Some may avoid situations that they know they cannot control or fear they may lose control over. Playing games with peers is a good example; many PDAers try to control the game as they feel they need to ensure everyone plays correctly; they fear losing control because then they will be in a social territory where they are most vulnerable. PDAers struggle in social situations. Having control over what's happening can make it easier for them to be included; there are rules and set patterns, so it's not a no man's land of foreign language and social conventions like most social situations. If the person knows they won't have control over the situation they may avoid the situation altogether.

Fear/phobias – fear is a powerful force. It can stop a person eating, it can lift weights you wouldn't think were possible, it can tear a person apart, it can give them great strength and it can make someone avoid. Fear keeps us safe but it can also hurt us. If you're standing on the edge of a cliff and fear overtakes you, making you leap back from the edge, that's avoidance. If you're standing in front of a bowl of cereal and seeing germs that aren't really there running around inside it and you run crying from the room because even though you're starving you can't eat something that you think will kill you, that's avoidance. If you see a spider and scream and run away, that's avoidance. Safety response, OCD or phobia, it all creates a need to avoid.

Processing time – autistics tend to have a slower processing time, especially when it comes to verbal instructions/requests.

Dropping demands on someone at the last second and expecting them to react/respond/comply immediately is likely to be met with avoidance. Often what is needed is a little time for the information to sink in and the person to work out how they need to proceed. Avoiding in this situation can sometimes be the person's way of getting time to process things themselves but to others it can be seen as refusal to act. It's usually best to allow people time to comply; that way avoidance can be avoided.

Executive functioning – some people struggle with executive functioning, the ability to self-manage, organise and act accordingly. This means that when faced with a demand they might not know where to start or how to start or what to do first. They may not be able to work out the things they need (toothbrush and toothpaste and water for brushing teeth) and so may become stuck. This can lead to avoidance, particularly if in the past they have gotten into trouble for not complying either straight away or correctly. Some may not be avoiding at all but are simply stuck, unable to start for lack of ability to organize; this can be seen as avoiding the task when really they are trying. Others may avoid trying if they know they won't be able to do it anyway.

Oppositional reaction – I've written about this before: PDA oppositional behaviour, where a PDAer's first reaction is to do the opposite of what's asked/demanded. This can take the form of avoidance, especially if the demand is to act and the oppositional reaction is to not act. Since not all demand avoidance from PDAers is due to anxiety but some inbuilt need to avoid or do the opposite, oppositional reaction seems the best fit I can think of for the natural avoidance of demands which don't fit under any other category.

# – 6 –

# CONTROL

» Need for control doesn't include wanting power over others
» Wanting control of own environment
» Environmental control rooted in feeling safe
» The difference between power and responsibility
» Lack of control causing trauma, anxiety and shutdown
» Environmental control accidentally spilling onto others
» Intolerance of being controlled by others
» The impact of having Chronic Fatigue Syndrome in the mix
» Choosing to allow others to be in control
» Disrespect for arbitrary authority
» Control as a means of understanding what's going
   on to avoid anxiety and uncertainty
» Control enabling choice
» Misperceptions of power and being a 'control freak'
» Control and theory of mind
» Employment issues

---

Do you feel the need to be in control? If so, is this because
you feel the need to have power over others?

---

Julia Daunt Don't know why I need to control but I do. I need complete control over my life but not over others (anymore). I've realised that it's not right or fair to control others. I control what Paul and I do as a couple or what I do alone. I only have input into what he does if it will have a direct negative affect on me. Like if he were to want to go on holiday for a month, with or without me, the answer would be no on both counts. I couldn't cope with being somewhere else for that long and nor could I manage at home alone for that length of time. Life is all about compromises. I use subtle control all the time. I love to plan events that I want to go to so that I can make them me-friendly. I love to host. That way I'm in control but in a good way.

Dee Dee My home and family, money, work, I need to be in control. I have no interest in the need of power over people, just material objects and me.

Riko Ryuki I feel the need to control certain things like DIY and decorating, arranging meetings and money. This is partly because I don't trust others to do it correctly and past experience has shown me to be right in my thinking. Things like hanging washing, putting clothes away, cooking, feeding the kids, dressing the kids, etc., I control because other people just don't do them correctly and it's quicker to just do it myself than have to fix other people's mess.

Rosie Bragg This too.

Nicola T I hate it when people do things in my house, because they rarely do it to my standard...like washing, ironing, etc., so my poor kids had no lessons in housework because I couldn't bear to teach them. All but one have their own house now, and they struggle to know how to organise themselves in it. I should have taught them how to do so much more than I did, but I couldn't. So no, I don't want to be in control of others, just in my environment, so it's right for me. I also find I have to do things in a certain order, otherwise I get terribly flustered and can't complete the task. I guess a little OCD creeping in?

> My need for control isn't about controlling OTHERS.
>
> It's about controlling my OWN ENVIRONMENT.
>
> To accept another's control is a DEMAND
>
> That I am HARDWIRED to AVOID

Sally Cat I can relate to this, except I don't do much housework either! LOL. My mum (likely PDA) was like this to me when I was a child. I'd want her to explain how she cooked things and she'd get all flustered and say she was too busy. Now, when PDA DD comes into the kitchen while I'm cooking, I have explained that I get put off and make mistakes if I get disturbed (I'll even accidentally cut myself with a knife), but sometimes she's so keen to help and learn and I remember myself as a girl and my own thwarted enthusiasm, so I force myself to find something for her to do (it hurts me!) and explain how I'm doing things. She gets so excited and happy, bless her. She's not learning much about housekeeping from me though!

Ruth Control isn't about power over others but about feeling safe. Knowing the likely outcome of a situation or reaction from a person means you can prepare. 'Manipulation' can help guide these the way that makes it predictably safe for us.

Felicia Control for me is needing to feel safe in my environment. I have found though that being spontaneous, especially with my kids, is much easier. I do things fast enough that PDA doesn't have time to come into play. But if I give myself time to think about it then it's not happening lol.

Rosie Bragg I have to be in control of my own life, choices, time, whatever, but I will absolutely avoid any situation where I have any responsibility over others' experiences.

Sally Cat I actually don't mind a bit of responsibility, but I don't like power. I volunteered to be the director of a postgrad whole-class multimedia project once. I was very anxious, but wanted to give it a shot. I spent nearly two of the project's allocated five days getting everyone to feedback how they wanted the project to go (I didn't input my own vision at all, I don't think) and then resolutely policed them all ensuring that the agreed plan was adhered to.

Incidentally, the interactive game we produced was a massive success and very well rated.

Rosie Bragg That's awesome.

I struggle desperately with feelings of guilt and shame at the basic fact that I exist. I tend to be apologetic if people have to interact or spend time with me; if I have made a decision about how we spend that time I feel like it's my fault if it doesn't go well, and that eats away at me for ages. I don't have many friends, and only one or two who I might see in person maybe once or twice a year. We generally meet up to go to events or gigs that we are all interested in, and they're the only people that don't exhaust me to be around – I don't take on the responsibility for their enjoyment either.

I really hate having to tell my son what to do. I'll never be a nag – it's hard enough just telling him once. Though to be honest, at his age it's more that we have a discussion about things, and I try and explain why he should do something so he understands and wants to do it for himself (I was a mess, on drugs. Severe PND, untreated ADHD, etc. Dad got custody of K as I had to admit I couldn't care for him at the time. Fast forward to kiddo being 12 and has issues so Dad kicked him out. He now lives happily with me). It has made it easier not raising him during the early years; I really struggle with feeling needed or depended upon. At least he is old enough to cook himself a pizza or something if I don't make tea.

C. Keech If I feel out of control everything goes very wrong, very quickly. Full shutdown, lots of tears, irrational thinking and genuine lasting damage because I traumatise easier than most (I've realised) and don't recover quickly but I'm not controllING...as in I don't seek to be in charge whatsoever and wouldn't have anywhere near the self-confidence, conviction or assertiveness to take on a managerial role, for example. I just need to feel in control of my own bits and pieces. Likely because they get very easily out of control due to near zero executive function.

A poem about my contrariness
I need control of my life,
And struggle to be free,
But control spills onto others
When I only meant Just Me.

And I'm hurt beyond endurance
When criticised by you,
But I criticise like crazy
The things that others do!

Sarah Johnson I control my life and circumstances to avoid pain, the need to mask and feeling the anxiety of being out of control. I don't control adults, but I do control my kids, my job, my dogs and my car. And my shopping. And my house. And my kitchen. And my washing. And my TV. And the household bills. And money. And who I talk to. And my time. But other than that...

Laura Mullen I would hate to have power over others but I do need to be in control. I think the two are very different. When it's tasks such as cooking, cleaning, doing school DIY [a homeschooling exercise Laura carries out with her children], crafts, experiments, I need control. Even driving I need control, though I never get it if my husband is in the car. Otherwise I am so anxious that I get overwhelmed and shut down. When it's school stuff, I panic because if it's not done correctly, will they learn what it is we are supposed to be learning? [Laura homeschools her children.] I wish I wasn't this way. I wish that I didn't feel this utter need to be in control. I wish I could let go.

Sally Cat I go mad if my partner cooks anything! I don't want to interfere, but I can't help myself if he does anything remotely different to how I'd do it myself. I can't bear it. It feels like a complete disaster to me, that the food will be ruined. Funnily enough, my mum (who I'm pretty sure is also PDA) is like this with me if I'm cooking.

Laura Mullen Yeah, we have an agreement. He doesn't cook. Period. At least if I am in the room and never for food that is for me. But I have to teach my kids to cook...so far it's just pancakes and scrambled eggs, but even showing them to make lemonade was hard. When it involves actual cooking, I'm standing there wringing my hands, panicking, and trying not to show it.

Sally Cat My partner cooks cakes and stuff with DD when I don't need to be in the kitchen. I don't like sweet things (shock, horror!) so I'm happy to leave them to it. Sometimes DD begs me to let her help with cooking dinner. I have to really steel myself to let her do something. It makes her so happy, but it frazzles my brain. I lose concentration easily too and make major mistakes cooking if anyone else is in the kitchen.

Laura Mullen I like sweet things. I can't eat them though as they often make me sick. But I used to love making cakes. But if my kids want to help me or do it themselves, yeah...I try, but I'm not too good at letting go of it all.

Pink I've learned when my daughter wants to do crafts then I get her dad (who is not overly craft oriented) to do it with her, because my daughter and I are empathic and we can feel the control of 'no, do it this way', even if it's not spoken.

Laura Mullen If I asked my husband to do that with the kids, he would have that 'deer caught in headlights' look. He has absolutely no idea how to work with his kids and it terrifies him. However, I think I found a solution: my oldest needs a new computer. He [their father] likes to build computers...

Sally Cat I'm very lucky that my neurotypical partner (DD's dad) is great with her and has loads of patience and tolerance to spend time with her as she gibbers on at him and tells him what to do, LOL. He has loads of patience and tolerance with me too and seems content to let me control everything DD doesn't.

But yeah, it's not about having power over him or anyone else (I hate this), it's about having control over our own worlds and this tends to inadvertently spill out onto other people.

Pink That's it put really nicely: the control inadvertently spills out.

Little Black Duck Zero interest in controlling others.

100% need to not feel smothered and snuffed out by being controlled by others.

Sometimes, the second encroaches on the first, inadvertently because where more than one person is involved, there needs to be a degree of compromise. I find compromising difficult at times. Certain things I cannot compromise (think that's the autism bit) and that can appear to be controlling, from the other person's perspective.

Sally Cat Good morning, Little Black Duck! Beautifully expressed, as always.

Little Black Duck Morning, darling.

10am Wednesday morning in Perth.

Sally Cat Nearly bedtime for me here: 3:28 AM.

Stephen Wright PDA doesn't have a schedule...it's like a 25-hour day? Maybe more? Little later each night for me till the all-nighter lol.

Little Black Duck But only *nearly* Sally, lol!

Think the 'schedule' is one of user discretion. Fluid or fixed or mixing it up, just for kicks.

Stephen Wright  Oh yeah...a guide for those who need to be guided. No one's holding our hands...so we need to step up. Make our schedule...then make them for the guided. That's PDA. Own it...chew it up...and spit out something beautiful at the closest selfish person. When you do that...you dont have PDA...you have the ability to change the world. Or not. But it will be your choice and now you have the ability to do it. Or something like that.

Little Black Duck  Yeah, something like that. Something like, 'I'm doing things My Way. Now, step off.'

Sally Cat  Little Black Duck, yeah, almost! (Bedtime, that is) xx
Right – half past bloody 4!!!! Nighty night peeps xx

Andrew  That's interesting what you say about compromise, Little Black Duck. I remember years ago with my ex, I had a habit of controlling what we did together but I hated sometimes how it felt like I was controlling her actions. It's like I didn't know how to compromise. I wanted her to fit neatly into my lifestyle yet at the same time I didn't want to be controlling her.
I think perhaps I'm better at it these days because of the awareness I have now. Like I might find it difficult but at least I know what it is that makes it difficult now!

Sally Cat  I'm a great believer in the positive power of self-awareness. If we understand how we tick and how our actions affect others, we can choose to modify our behaviour.

Andrew  Sally Cat, exactly! I've actually been thinking lately how self-awareness is like maturity, perhaps even the definitive version of maturity and not the 'grow up and get a well-paid job' version that society feeds us.

Sally Cat  It's highly valued in person-centred counselling theory. Developing self-awareness was part of the training I undertook to be a professional counsellor. I was told I have excellent self-awareness (yippee!), other students struggled, but my point is that it's crucial importance was recognised.

Riko Ryuki  I don't like having power over others, in fact it makes me ill because I think they will feel like I do when someone tries to control me. I want others to have as much freedom as possible.

Sally Cat  Me too.

Riko Ryuki  Although if I thought I could do a better job...lol sometimes I think it'd be better if I just did everything and ruled the planet, but the thought makes me ill and honestly, who has the energy?

Tracy  Yeah, I hate being controlled, but I'm coming to realize my trying to be self-sufficient is sometimes me exerting control too. Certain things in my environment I can't ask others to do because I need them to be done a certain way, and so usually it only works to do it myself. Even if someone asks if they can help and I provide specific instructions as to what I want, it does not work and frustrates both of us. Other things I do not care about so I can delegate. I often find there's more I need to control than I can really get done myself...so I tend to overburden myself in the absence of a better solution...then I meltdown.

Riko Ryuki  Yes, Tracy, I take on too much because I want it all to be done right, but I can't do it all alone. Lose, lose situation.

Sally Cat  Having Chronic Fatigue Syndrome doesn't help matters either. Even trying to do a bit of grass trimming to improve our pond edge, for example, quickly exhausts me if I can ever get over Demand Avoidance to do it to begin with. This leaves me out of control and dependent on my partner to do a lot of things. I have had to accept that I can't be in control. I don't like to nag him either. It doesn't feel fair.

Riko Ryuki  Yes, Sally. Some days just getting up exhausts me and other days I can do lots. Sometimes I get breathless from saying two words. My temp has been skyrocketing all day so I know I'm having a bad day. Running around after kiddie demands literally makes me ill and that's before I add in PDA lol. Actually I have no idea how I get through every day when I should have people helping me. I'm disabled ffs but I don't even get pip!

Sally Cat  That's so tough! I get dizzy within a few minutes of interacting with DD. I can't imagine how you cope with 3 special needs boys and no support. You are superhuman.

Riko Ryuki  I wish lol.

Tony Enos I need to be in control of things, but only so far as they affect me. I actually dislike being in control of others as their success and welfare becomes a demand. If someone else wants to be in control, that is fine with me – I will not get into a pissing contest and I have no time for trying to peck my way up some pecking order.

The only control I let someone have over me is whether I choose to go along with what they are saying or suggesting. I do not need to rally allies to my side in order to do my own thing. If I disagree with the person in control that is fine, I am just going to do my own thing.

Where this butts up against traditional institutions is when it comes to people in positions of authority. I do not automatically think less of someone in a position of authority, but I do not think more highly of them either. The latter can sometimes be a source of friction. I see those in positions of authority or control as equal collaborators who are fulfilling a different role. Depending on the ego of the person in authority or their need to be controlling, sometimes *they* have a problem with me as opposed to the other way around. I can respect the work someone is doing without bowing down to them or addressing them as though they are somehow superior to me; in my eyes, they are an equal with a different skill set that is fulfilling a different job than I am.

Leaders that value my opinion and give me a good 'why' behind their requests get much more out of me.

When a leader micro-manages me, it removes all demand relating to the outcome of the task from my shoulders and I simply stop caring about the result. They get what they ask for even if I see it is doomed to fail.

When a leader is insistent about doing something I don't agree with or don't see or understand a reason why, I will do my own thing – to me there was never any question that I was the one in control of me, but it shatters the leader's illusion that they had control over me and that does not go over well most times.

So I do not need to be the one in control of every situation nor do I need to have power over others, but I will absolutely retain control and power over myself. I will either agree with a leader or disagree with a leader but they don't have any control over me outside of what I agree to go along with. I don't know if that makes any sense but that's my take on it.

**Riko Ryuki** People have said that I comply with what people tell me to do; they don't know that I'm actually just letting them think they are controlling me. It's my decision to go along with whatever they say, up to a certain point of course.

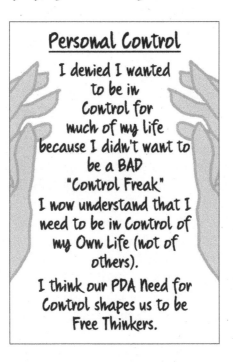

> ## Personal Control
> I denied I wanted to be in Control for much of my life because I didn't want to be a BAD "Control Freak"
> I now understand that I need to be in Control of my Own Life (not of others).
> I think our PDA need for Control shapes us to be Free Thinkers.

**Sally Cat** Nicely put, Tony. I'm going to post a separate question about social hierarchy in the near future. I think it's a common PDA trait not to be swayed by it.

**Daisy** I don't feel the need to control others, but I do have a strong desire to be in control of myself (to the point where, when a teacher told me to go to a different water fountain for some arbitrary reason I felt like shouting at him and cutting myself even though I knew it was irrational).

**Sally Cat** Hi, Daisy. Great example. I hate being coerced to follow arbitrary orders. I once had a job as a Sunday roast cook in a badly managed pub. The usual cook/kitchen manager was a kid who'd only previously worked as a pot boy and was loving the power. I got called into a staff meeting and told I had to take orders from him. You should have seen his smug look.

Next Sunday in the kitchen he delighted in giving me orders just because he COULD. I hated it! It made me want to spit and what little respect I'd had for him as a human being vanished.

Daisy Yeah, similar situation with that teacher, except he was incompetent and didn't like that I challenged him sometimes. I think he liked to 'put me in my place'.

Andrew I've absolutely no desire to have power over others. It's more so for myself.

Then again, lately I've been learning to let go of things and the concept of control is one of them. It's very difficult though because it's clearly a deep-seated neurological brain pattern.

Also over the last five years because I haven't been working or living within normal working hours, I've been able to get it into my brain that randomness is good for me. For example, some nights I don't get to sleep until very early morning, which means I wake up in the afternoon. However, once I've had a good sleep I don't mind that I'm getting up in the afternoon. I can still go about my day feeling in control. Ironically, from the outside, people view it as a COMPLETE lack of control! It's kind of upside down control lol but it helps my brain to not need control in a conventional sense. Does that make sense?

Sally Cat It does, Andrew.

Alice I like to feel that I am in control, which is different from being in control. When I talk about control it is not about power over others, it is understanding what is going on, so as to avoid the uncertainty or anxiety that this might otherwise cause me.

I think that my hubby thinks that I can be controlling; this is usually in areas such as childcare or other things where I am more experienced and can see that things will end in tears or sometimes be unsafe but I have learnt to dampen my need to control the process in these situations whilst ensuring a positive outcome.

Power is an easily misunderstood word, as it implies domination. For me, power enables choice.

Sally Cat I hate the phrase 'control freak'; it has so much negativity attached. I denied to myself that I wanted to be in control for much of my life because I didn't want to be a Bad Control Freak. I now understand better that I need to be in control of my own life and why. I think our PDA and need for control shapes us to be free thinkers. It's not all bad x

Stephen Wright People who don't have theory of mind can't trust others unless they prove themselves...once one becomes more aware of the world they gain empathy and can allow people in...if you're the only one in your world you need an aspect of control or you panic.

Things are so complex that get you there and you don't know why so you have meltdowns. That's just my perspective...there are many.

Silva Sally, I am much more comfortable when I am in control of myself, my surroundings and my life. It's part of why I hated being employed; much happier working for/by myself where I can control my efforts. I might want to work in the middle of the night one day and late morning the next. I agree with a lot of other comments; I do not want to control others unless their demands encroach on my space or activities. I usually just like to be left alone to do my own thing. Control makes me feel safe. I get anxious if I feel that an outside person or force is controlling me. When I was ill a while back and couldn't work, I hated having to accept benefit because it meant the government were in control of whether I got money I needed. Yuk! It would make me feel sick sometimes – affected my sleeping and showed in my health.

Sally Cat I've unfortunately had to claim benefits for most of my life because I can't be an employee and I don't have the business brain to be self-employed. When I signed back on the dole after finishing uni, I actually started dry retching. It's like my entire system was in mutiny against their control of me!

Silva Sally, I think I get that! It's only recently I've started self-employment after needing benefits for years following an accident that ended my nursing career and the long-term effects from that and a fight with the Big C. I did dog walking for a while as I could pick and choose what I did – I'm still doing that but working towards Health and Safety freelancing so I'm kind of part mature student, part employed, part retired. I also write. I do like variety.

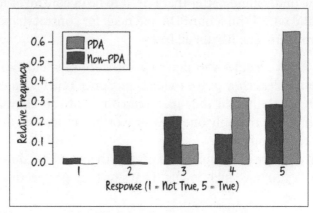

Graph 6: I need control of my own life
*From a 'Quick PDA Poll' with 240 PDA and 145 neurotypical respondents*

## CAUSING MELTDOWNS

From Riko Ryuki's blog

Meltdowns are awful things to experience, both for the person having the meltdown and those watching. So many parents try to adapt their parenting style to avoid triggering meltdowns. Those who experience meltdowns do everything they can to avoid having a meltdown, including avoiding triggers, shutting down instead, staying away from triggering environments, trying to ignore emotions, etc. It can feel like every day is a constant fight to prevent meltdowns, and not always a successful one.

There are times, though, when there is no way to avoid a meltdown. Parents have to enforce some rules, usually ones that involve protecting every person involved. Some activities can be dangerous, such as swimming in freezing water, playing with harmful substances, lighting fires, eating too much/pica, climbing furniture, etc. Parents may try to stop these activities to keep the individual safe, but this can trigger a meltdown, especially if the individual feels a need to do these things. At these times, it's safer to cause a meltdown than to allow the harmful activity.

As adults, we have to do certain things that may be triggering. These may be really important things like making phone calls or dealing with doctors, or they may be important to us personally such as attending an event or going to the cinema. We have to weigh up the chances of a meltdown occurring against how important/necessary the task is. A life-saving operation at hospital will outweigh any potential meltdown, whereas a trip to the cinema may not. People don't always make the best choices either; sometimes we under-estimate the impact a task might have on us, meaning we do something that causes a meltdown that could easily have been avoided. Sometimes we know a meltdown may happen but think it might not happen this time or have been lured into a false sense of security by managing before without having a meltdown. We may also decide the task/event is more important to us personally so we risk a meltdown; after all, we can't stay cooped up indoors where it's safe forever, missing out on all the fun things we want to do.

Sometimes the only way we can learn our own boundaries and the boundaries of rules is to try and risk a meltdown. This is true not just of children but of adults too. We can't allow a young child to run into the middle of a busy road, so we stop them even though we know it will cause a meltdown. The child experiences that meltdown and hopefully learns that they are not allowed to run into the road and that trying causes a meltdown. Hopefully the child learns to stay away from the road. Another idea may be to never let the child go outside, but that's not very conducive to a healthy and active life.

If a child has a meltdown when going to the cinema then the parents need to consider how important going there is. Surely the child can watch the same film at home at a later date? If it's important to the child then working around what's causing the meltdown may be a better option; for example, if it's the number of people at the cinema then going during quiet times would be best. It isn't worth potentially causing a meltdown if the child doesn't learn anything necessary to their life and if there are ways around triggering a meltdown.

One area where the issues are blurred is around school. For some kids, school causes daily meltdowns; the child simply cannot handle being at school. For some families, though, they have few options – some parents can only work while the child is at school and they may be unable to stop working as there are no other options available financially. Some feel the benefits of school outweigh the cost (meltdown). Some would prefer their child not to go but the child insists; despite the meltdowns, they may really enjoy school. For others, though, moving the child to a different school, insisting on accommodations or a reduced timetable, or home schooling are the best options to both reduce meltdowns and make life easier for all involved.

It can be difficult to know when to accommodate and avoid a meltdown or when to push and 'cause' a meltdown. Many factors are involved in the decision and sometimes decisions are made in the moment so aren't always the best option. With children, it can be helpful to explain why a meltdown had to be caused, a while after the meltdown has happened and when the child is in an emotionally safe place to discuss the causes. Helping a child to understand why a meltdown happened and why it was unpreventable can help them understand themselves where the boundaries may lie. The child may also have some useful ideas on how to prevent or deal with meltdowns in the future. With adults, reflecting on what happened and what can be done in the future can be helpful. Some adults like to put things in place to make meltdowns easier and get them over with more quickly. It's also important that everyone understands that meltdowns happen sometimes, that it can be no one's fault and it's best to accept them and move on.

# MELTDOWNS

» Triggers: being on time; being told no; changes of plan; injustice; sensory overload; being overwhelmed
» Forms: rage or depression
» What meltdowns feel like
» More about sensory overload and need for silence
» Is Fight only one of three meltdown possible expressions (along with Flight and Freeze)?
» Shutdown
» Detachment, bypassing meltdowns (but demands still triggering them)
» The need for time out
» Meltdowns diverted into self-harm
» How this connects to autistic stimming
» Meltdown perceived in observers' faces
» More about forms of meltdown
» Dissociation from experiencing meltdowns
» Possibility of assumed meltdowns being mania
» The difference between 'getting angry' and meltdown
» Masked meltdowns?
» Likelihood that Flight and Freeze are also meltdown forms

---

Do you have meltdowns? How do you express them?
What provokes them? What do they feel like?

---

Sarah D (mother of PDA son) Having the pressure to be somewhere on time. I can answer this one! X

### Please Just Walk Away

Please don't blame me for what I say and do during meltdown.

I cannot help it or control it.

I seek to avoid triggers, but once meltdown happens, control is gone.

It's scary!

Please just disengage from me.

Calmly walk away.

Please don't try to make me feel guilty

Or punish me

Or carry a lingering sense of being wounded by my Badness

(I feel bad enough as it is anyway).

I cannot help melting down. It's a hardwired part of my PDA.

Gillian Mead (mother of adult PDA daughter) What pokes the 'tiger' in Lee's case are the words NO! Don't! Wait! Criticism! Rejection!! Also sensory issues, expectations, and anticipation, and of course change!

Rachel R I have them daily. They seem to take one of two forms, rage or depression. I'm trying to pay more attention to triggers. Rage meltdowns happen suddenly and instantaneously from nowhere. They feel like there is a molten ball of lava in my chest. It feels like it needs to burst out somehow or I'll combust. I'll either scream, slam doors, or text abuse at my husband or mum, and I want to burn all bridges with everyone because they deserve it. I feel so riled I want to punch through walls or throw plates but I don't. Triggers can be husband texting to say he will be late home, change of plan, someone wronging me or injustice in some way. Also triggered by sensory overload in being touched or too much noise or being asked to do too much. These meltdowns are short-lived.

I also have depressive meltdowns. I collapse on the floor and feel so heavy I can't hold myself up. I 'just can't do it anymore'. It's an overwhelmingly heavy feeling all over and it feels like the end of the world. Like it's always going to be like this and there is no solution. These can last a couple of days or longer. I just want to snuggle under a cover and literally do nothing. Triggered by being overwhelmed by life or demands. I'll call my husband and tell him he needs to come home as I'm not doing anything and can't have the kids anymore. I want to run away and just cry. I've been known to shut myself in the bathroom with vodka and kids' building toys and sort them into coloured piles or build structures...

Martin Nightingale I feel you x

I used to think there was something wrong with my heart or that it was floating anxiety – only finding out about PDA explained why it was so situationally and environmentally dependent.

I never thought I got sensory overload, but as I have less meltdowns and feel more chilled, I am more bothered by noise – I wonder if it is because I was so filled with my own inner noise ('lava in the chest'! What a great description) that I couldn't hear the babble around me!

Rachel R I've only had sensory overload since having kids and being a stay-at-home mum. It's again something I only unpicked a few months ago. I'd get annoyed at the kids for screaming, etc., because surely they know they are causing physical pain to my ears?! How dare they be so cruel... My daughter's autism nursery nurse noticed I'd always respond as soon as they made a noise, etc., and I realised it's because it clouds my brain and it also hurts me. If she'd not come to support us I'd probably have never realised that ears don't hurt normally; people hear noise in their ears not in the front of their brain either?! For me this had always been normal. How could it have been abnormal? I swear that lava ball hurts inside and it materialises from nothing so fast and can't be put out (I'm trying by compiling a list of heavy but melodic songs that instantly soothe and 'melt me', only got one song so far though so it's kinda on repeat)... Rant rant rant...

Sally Cat   I love silence. Even my bloody neighbour and his mate (who's illegally lodging there) standing outside smoking and yap yap yapping with my neighbour's booming voice REALLY PISSES ME OFF and I get close to melting down and telling him to f\*\*king shut up. If he played the radio, I would be even more pissed off.

Rachel R   I'm very intolerant of stuff like that too, Sally. Sadly, now living in a flat with someone next door and down below, I have to get used to some level of noise. Thankfully it's just old ladies and they seem harmless enough...

Sally Cat   I tell you what did used to make me meltdown: neighbours playing loud music at night. I'd get more and more wound up until I'd storm round there TRYING to be civil but barely holding it together not to punch them in the face!

Rachel R   I'd like to think I'd punch someone in the face in that situation but I'm more likely to burst into tears because of the confrontation lol x

Sally Cat   Yes, I hate confrontation. I get wound up, but find it hard to challenge people...unless I'm defending someone else: then I'm like a tiger!

Rachel R   I wish I could be like that. I'm more pushy about the kids getting support, etc., than for myself and I won't let things lie but it takes all my energy away and still in meetings about the kids I'll end up in tears... Tears are and always have been my default position lol whilst taking a beating internally.

Sally Cat   I think 'Fight' is maybe just one of 3 possible responses to overload/meltdown, the other two being 'Flight' and 'Freeze'? X

Julia Daunt   I very rarely let myself get to that point now unless I'm caught off guard by something or I'm under extreme pressure/overload or if for some reason I'm unable to have 'downtime'. My meltdowns, when they do happen, are still very explosive. The usual – crying, shouting, swearing, hitting myself, thoughts of suicide/self-harm, throwing things, hitting things (not people anymore), panic attacks and heart palpitations. I manage/avoid meltdowns on the whole by managing my anxiety on a day-to-day basis. I keep the anxiety as low as possible by keeping day-to-day demands low, having short naps throughout the day to sort of recharge/de-stress and by allowing myself 10/20-second rants about things that I'm finding stressful. My biggest trigger is unexpected things...bad surprises, as it were! Oh, and hormones...

Ruth I swear very creatively I am told.

> Meltdown is an involuntary autistic response to excessive Overload.
>
> It cannot be trained out via Discipline.
>
> When I Meltdown I have no control over my words & actions.
>
> My best strategy is to limit Overload Triggers in my life so Meltdown doesn't occur.

Martin Nightingale I tend to shutdown more than meltdown as I've got older. Meltdowns feel like almost uncontrollable anger/ frustration/sadness/despair – but they are more/different than the peak of the anger cycle.

I've only once assaulted anyone when having a meltdown and never a loved one – on the one occasion I have chucked a chair at a French teacher who was going around the class getting people to say their father's occupation in French, then he got to me and made some kind of joke (basically he said 'dosser' in a French accent – my poor father was unemployed after having worked continuously since age 14) – so I told him to 'fuck off', to which he told me to sit in the 'idiot chair' (a broken chair at the front of the room) with my feet in the bin. I twatted him with the chair – pretty sure I was just in control enough that it was a choice.

Another time, as an adult, I was cut up for a parking space. I have never before or since had 'road rage', but I jumped out of the car, furious at the over-privileged tosser (it was a very large and expensive car), mostly because I was taking my daughter to a movie, running late, feeling under pressure and that I wasn't where I wanted to be, and the cheek of the man! So I ran over and told him that however rich he was, he should have some manners! It was my doctor. He explained that he hadn't seen me, offered to move, and asked how my blood pressure was... Oops! And as stupid as I felt then was pretty much as stupid as I always feel after a meltdown – everything gets out of perspective and the world seems wonk, but it's usually me in a meltdown situation responding to demands (real or imagined), not the world.

As a small child I was generally compliant and even happy at school – but I had a meltdown every Sunday – a kind of uber tantrum – because my mum and nana wanted me to go to Sunday School. I was a pretentious little shit – it wasn't the boredom, the people (I quite liked some of them!), or anything like that, and I quite liked the youth groups and stuff – it was the content. I hated the allegories, the Bible readings, the sermons, the Sunday School booklets, the lot – my head was always full of counter argument, frustration, alternative allegories, satire, etc., so much so that the cognitive dissonance made me feel sick and the thought of having to sit through it made me go batshit!

As I said, lately, I don't meltdown much. Partly because of Citralopram, partly because I've mellowed, partly because I have tactics – listen to punk so loud it drowns out my thoughts, withdraw, do something manual and/or mindless, etc. I really don't miss the sensation.

Martin Nightingale I still am reminded of the sensation every time a demand is made though – it is like a 'pull'. Holidays, other folk's schedules, being volunteered for something, situations where I'm not meant to say no, occasions when I over-extend myself when strong then feel I've set myself up when it is too much (or the unexpected has screwed the pooch!), all make me feel echoes of a full-on meltdown.

It is all a bit odd though. I was a social worker for a long time and have been in lots of high-pressure situations and not had a meltdown, quite the opposite; I always reacted coolly and calmly (probably a control thing). Likewise, someone is an arse out and I can usually handle it fine. Which leads me to observe that pulling a knife on me is probably perceived by me as less of a threat than inviting yourself around for a cuppa when I'm not in the mood, lol.

Rachel R  Martin, I was a social worker too pre kids... I had addicts try to attack me, went into a guy's house who had meat cleavers in every room and I managed?!? So odd...

Martin Nightingale  Yep, really weird. I used to do other quite dangerous things too – never bothered me. I also try and generally go out of my way to be helpful and get on with folk (even though I have a long list of things that other folk believe that piss me off!). Being asked to do something completely reasonable though, and grrrr!!! And that's just being asked, let alone told!!!

I do think that some of it is that I try to be awesome at whatever I do – it's a kind of perfectionist thing – other colleagues would cry, worry, come for advice, etc., and I'd be the calm one – but they were probably handling and processing things in a healthier way?

I also think meltdown is very last resort for me – if I can refuse, manipulate, subvert a situation, that's my go to. Mostly I could do that all through school, hence the limited meltdowns there. But when older I had to develop whole sets of new tactics. Uni, etc., was easy for me, but work (outside self-employment – and even then I hate tax return time!) and relationships are pretty damn hard and can take all-consuming energy.

Rachel R  P.S. Funny you wrote about shutdown because I'm experiencing that more now too, like complete 'whatever, don't give a damn, not engaging with you'. I have noticed if my husband or anyone asks me to do anything it's like I'm being stabbed in the chest or punched and it knocks me back. It's funny he tried some PDA approaches on me like 'please' at the start of the request and the difference was incredible lol. I also try to be too perfectionistic in stuff I do. If I'm into something I need to know EVERYTHING about it, or I need to be engaging with it a lot. I am trying to curb that but it's like this thirst for knowledge that is insatiable...

Sally Cat Shutdown is something else I'm trying to get my head around. I've been able to attach many descriptive labels to traits of mine (such as struggling with noise and bright lighting = hypersensitivity) since my autism diagnosis 3.5 years ago, but 'shutdown' eludes me still.

Rachel R I don't know if this is shutdown but a few months back I got so peed off and done in that I just got into bed and ignored the kids for two hours, I literally couldn't engage. The 2-year-old couldn't have cared less I wasn't there but the 5-year-old suspected PDA was screaming 'Mummy' solidly for like two hours at the gate I'd shut in the next room. Yet I just blanked it. It washed over me like a wave and I felt so numb and uncontactable. I don't think it's really happened other than that time and as I say I don't know if that's shutdown or what.

Alice Sally, my version of 'shutdown' is when I have nothing left to give; I'm exhausted and speechless and have to at least slow down or possibly stop to recuperate. I guess that it's the way 'meltdown' is different things to different people. It may manifest itself differently again in your life x

Rachel R Kinda feels like I'm a robot or a car that has run out of power I guess, maybe. I feel I'm always bordering on the brink of that or exploding or crying in a heap at the moment x

Sally Cat I detach. In learning more of my triggers and recognising my feelings and needs (plus gained self-respect, I think) I regularly remove myself from family and have quiet time. I feel I need this like water. I read or f**k around on Facebook, but I am disengaged from family. I have no energy or desire to interact or speak.

Rachel R I constantly disengage by using Facebook. I really need to try and stop x

Sally Cat Maybe you need this quiet time?

Rachel R I totally do but I feel bad for my kids most of the time. I think being on Facebook (esp these groups) is feeding my need to learn more about ASD and PDA. Constantly need to be learning more x

Sally Cat I'm learning to accept my invisible, but hardwired limits and feel less guilty for taking time out and having a messy home, etc.

Alice *Warning: mention of self-harm.* When I first came across PDA the meltdown aspect was something that I didn't relate to, which then put me off the scent as I thought that as I haven't had meltdowns I couldn't have PDA. However, I have gradually realised that meltdowns can be as unique as each one of us, and when I thought it through in depth, I realised that my expression of meltdowns was developed during early childhood. It was (and still is sometimes) frequently expressed to me that I was a difficult child, which puzzled me at the time as I was very compliant. I now realise that 'difficult' behaviour in my family's eyes was to step outside of the box even momentarily, e.g. cutting my own doll's hair was a punishable and dreadful offence. When punished, I was sent to my room and left there for a period of time. This led to the internalising of my feelings, as if I made a noise in my room I was punished further. I remember at the age of 5 or 6, using a sharp needle to write on myself, I picked scabs and basically learnt how to be angry towards myself as I had no other way of expressing it. This pattern has continued throughout my life, and I now see these instances of self-harm or intense self-loathing to be my expression of a meltdown. In its mildest form I will fume inwardly, and at its worst I have needed hospital treatment.

As I have got much older I believe that I have managed to mostly lose the physical self-harm. Now, meltdown in my life manifests itself as moodiness, grumpiness, irritability, most of which I internalise which can render me speechless. Triggers are usually my close family, e.g. hubby and 'children' (not so little any more!) or other people being totally unreasonable to the point of pointless communication. On one single occasion, though, I was so angry that I threw the remote control at my husband, which is very out of character for me, and I have to say it was incredibly effective as it broke into hundreds of pieces and his reaction of shock at my bad behaviour was so funny that I got the giggles and the meltdown left me! He loves his gadgets. But I haven't ever done it again, or even felt tempted to. I'm sorry that this post is so long.

Rachel R  Hey, I feel you with the self-harm. I think my meltdowns used to manifest in this way. *Trigger warning.* When I was a young teen I began cutting myself, stealing all the knives from the kitchen (Mum didn't even notice). I then moved on to scalpels that were in abundance in the house. One time I actually went too far and thought I was not going to wake up the next morning. I wrapped my leg in a bath towel and wrote a 'Goodbye PS This was an accident' note. It's shocking that I was too afraid to even go knock on my mum's door for fear of her husband. When I was about 16 I used to meltdown and slam my head against lamp posts or walls (only this week I've realised maybe that was a bit bizarre). I do still get bad urges, sometimes from depression but mostly anger now, but I can usually control it somehow. Hugs to you x

Alice  Rachel – and hugs for you too x

Sally Cat  Hugs to you both. Alice, I too used to be punished as a child by being shut in my room or sent to bed early. I used to internalise my anger too. I took it out a lot though on toy plastic animals. I'd punish them by slicing their legs off. I self-harmed a bit. Picking scabs is very engaging for me, but this might be an autistic thing rather than self-harming?

   And I used to take huge risks with my health – life, even – binging on drink and drugs.

Alice  Sally – hugs.

   Interesting thoughts; it's only recently that I have attributed scab picking and the needle scratching to self-harm. So you think the former might not be? Or might be an autistic trait? Hmm. I was aware that my mother did it too, so it could even have been copying her I suppose. I haven't used drugs at all except for a suicide attempt with prescription meds.

   I have used alcohol as a numbing thing, but I hardly drink at all now.

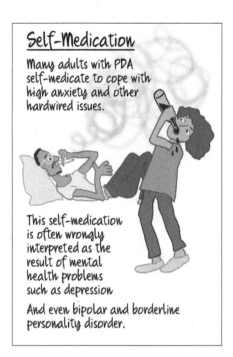

**Self-Medication**

Many adults with PDA self-medicate to cope with high anxiety and other hardwired issues.

This self-medication is often wrongly interpreted as the result of mental health problems such as depression

And even bipolar and borderline personality disorder.

Vanessa Haszard  A lot of the body-focused repetitive behaviours are debatable as to whether they are self-harm.

Personally, I have both many body-focused repetitive behaviours including scab picking, and I DON'T consider it the same as my self-harm, but others have often interpreted them as such.

I have come to the belated conclusion they are closer to a stim than self-harm.

Alice  Do you consider them to be autistic traits, Vanessa?

Sally Cat  Hugs all round xx. I'm not sure re autistic traits and self-harm. As children, both myself and my older brother used to like sliding needles full length under the skin of our palms (it didn't hurt if you did it right). As a younger adult I used to be very reckless with my health. It's like my body was an object that belonged to me, but that I wasn't really connected to in some fundamental way. I know that excessive drinking counts as self-harm. Maybe many autistics self-harm because of stress. Maybe it's expressive stimming?

Alice  Oh yes, I did that with needles too! I'd forgotten.

Sally Cat  Me too until this conversation!

Vanessa Haszard  Yes, I am thinking so now, Alice. They filled a need, both from the repetitive nature, and sensory input. While some sensory input is overwhelming, I actively seek other sensation.

Sally Cat  So stimming? (Stimming is another autistic trait I'm working on identifying in myself.)

Vanessa Haszard  For me, I have trich, amongst others, the urge to play with my bald spot, the sensory relief from running my fingers over it, even if I am not pulling, has a similar feel to the urge to jiggle or rock, both of which I experience strongly.

Alice  I jiggle, but not that much and usually when I'm on my own funnily enough.

Vanessa Haszard  Yeah, I am mostly on my own, have always been uptight and embarrassed about it, but have made a conscious decision I dgaf now.

Little Black Duck  I don't know. Partly because 'meltdown' is probably quite individual and, therefore, poorly defined. Partly because the word has been hijacked and minimised by Joe Public. And partly because I think my PDA prevents me from acknowledging that about myself.

But I think I probably do, purely from the look of shock and terror I can see on the faces of people in my direct line of fire.

For me, it feels like I'm clinging to my last shred of decency and moral code. I'm resisting the urge to rip someone's head off their shoulders. The effort that takes feels like my head is being pulled apart and about to shatter, irreparably, into a million pieces.

Sarah S  Yes. I have meltdowns of varying degrees. The worst ones are when there has been a strong sense of injustice used against me. I will, either unprovoked or provoked, become physical. When I was younger (or rather, pre-children) the meltdowns would be huge – and I would go on a rampage for a couple of days usually. I'd be looking for a fight, picking on the tiniest thing; the tiniest look someone would give me, someone queue jumping, someone accidentally brushing past me... I would shout, push, and even hit/assault them. Now I've had children, had CBT, and am taking medication which suits my issues, I don't attack people. I have too much to lose. I now use property to vent my anger and frustration. I will smash plates, kick or punch cars, throw neatly filed paperwork everywhere, and become very verbally aggressive to family or anyone who gets in my way. Despite being medicated, I still self-medicate with alcohol. If I feel the anger rising I have to calm myself down in order to steer clear of trouble. I stay inside my house, and get drunk. Very drunk. I may well become a keyboard warrior and argue with people on Facebook. I may order things off the internet, which we may or may not need, and may or may not be able to afford. I know I'm doing it, but don't feel I have control over it. Would I normally do it without alcohol? Probably not. But I'd probably end up in prison if I didn't get drunk.

C. Keech  Mine go one of two ways. Despairing tears and curling into the foetal position or complete shutdown where I don't know what to say and try to escape generally into reading (off my phone). I can even sustain fairly level conversations through text during this time but in the room be pretty much non-responsive. It's like an emergency hyperfocus back-up mechanism but can progress into an almost catatonic state if the trigger doesn't let up and pushes me into apathy.

I also have two pre-meltdown tendencies which can either turn into full-blown meltdown or not, depending on the kind of input I get from whoever is there to witness. At that stage I am still able to be affected by another person, whereas in full meltdown nothing anyone says makes a difference.

However, pre-meltdowns (characterised by either an angry or anxious disposition but both VERY wordy and manic) count on extremely specific responses which neither myself or the other person can predict. The reaction will be either positive (my state starts to let up) or negative (I transition into despair) and I won't know until whatever is said is said and I react accordingly yet unpredictably. It's exhausting for all involved.

I believe pre-meltdown is a desperate scrabble to avoid full meltdown but as my self-soothing talents are absolutely non-existent, I expect a lot from a very tiny group of people – the one or two I have allowed to see behind the mask. I am not very self-dependant emotionally at all. I refrain from using 'independent' as I'm not sure I believe I'll ever achieve it! xxx

Vanessa Haszard  Oh, hell, let me count the ways...

I experience what the professionals called dissociation, but I now am pretty sure is shutdown. I literally throw the stereotypical toddler tantrums, you know, crying and wailing on the ground, and have a long record of assaults, mostly police, and pysch staff, when cornered when in meltdown. I also used to break shit. A 'controlled' meltdown generally involves crying, hysterically rocking in a low protected corner or sometimes my dry bathtub, and may involve headbanging, biting, and an alarming amount of my hair being pulled in a short time (I have trich, but normally I only pull a little at a time).

Sarah Johnson I've been in a very bad mood all my life. I didn't know it was PDA until last month. I thought I was a nightmare. I'm not, I'm just a nightmare with a brain. According to what I have read I have one about 3 times a day. I call them intolerant, pissyfits when I am surrounded by morons. Apparently they're not – they're meltdowns caused by my inability to tolerate stupid behaviour. PDA or intolerance to assholes??? So non-PDA is a brainless desire not to rock the boat based on stupid behaviour?? According to hubby's behaviour he just doesn't get irate...yep, he lives his life NOT irritated. Ever. Unless they are irritating. I am always irritated.

Sally Cat My partner refused to believe our unborn daughter would ever annoy him. OH, how he laughs at his naivety now!

Sarah Johnson Saw someone in Lidl today whose daughter didn't stop crying in tantrum for the whole time. But as we were all old middle-aged mothers and housewives no one blinked. Apparently the daughter got a donut and then STARTED AGAIN cos she wanted more. I spoke to her olds outside. Hilarious!

Vanessa Haszard Frog [Vanessa's partner of 6 years] tells people 'Where you and I might not suffer fools gladly, Vanessa won't suffer a fool AT ALL.'

Dee Dee Overload – I withdraw and lay low for a while...less contact the better. Meltdowns – drinking, shopping, sex. Can last a few days...

Sally Cat Do you mean that your meltdowns involve drinking, shopping and sex? X

Dee Dee Yes x

Sally Cat Interesting – I want to mull this over. When I binge shop, could this be a meltdown?

Dee Dee I'm not me. It's like somebody is making me.

Silva Sally, re the binge shopping – I do that too. I even will order a ton of things online from somewhere like QVC or Amazon; then feel a panicky kind of 'Oh my God, what have I done that for?' and I'll go into my orders and cancel things. They must hate me in their admin. It's like a kind of release to buy stuff – or even, sometimes, like I'm trying to fill myself up somehow. Does that make sense?

> ### Dammed Meltdowns
>
> I never really had violent meltdowns
>
> I couldn't admit to being angry
>
> It scared me
>
> But my driving rage was still there
>
> And it came out twisted
>
> As a cold, snipey, hurtful tirade at people I felt close to
>
> I felt possessed
>
> I hated myself
>
> But my nastiness wouldn't stop
>
> I've learned to express my anger now and no longer do this.

Sally Cat    I struggle to pinpoint which of my episodes can be classed as meltdowns. Like Vanessa, I have had toddler-style writhing around on the floor tantrums, but only once or twice in my early twenties. Spaghetti Bolognese has ended up stuck to the ceiling after I've hurled someone's dinner plate. Mostly though, my meltdowns have been masked and splutter out as verbal assaults on a target I've not felt threatened by. The accompanying feeling is always that of loss of control, of having bubbled over beyond my limit. How do I differentiate between this and rage? I don't know. Maybe it's the scale of the emotion?

Sally Cat    A counsellor once had prompted me one time too many to try a particular therapy that I'd said I wasn't interested in. I snapped that I wasn't interested and that she should have done her job and LISTENED to me. I could tell she was quite taken aback by the 'volume' of my response. It turned out she'd been deliberately prodding me to get me to express feelings (my lack of emotional response/feeling-naming had been troubling her). She'd not expected me to react this strongly though. But it didn't feel strong to me. I was just being me. I have scored highly in an alexithymia (disconnection from own emotions) test.

Similarly, I used to be blind to my panic attacks and, I think, 'avoidance reactions'. Just kind of dissociated from my feelings.

And Dee Dee described shopping and bingeing as meltdowns. This interests me. I have run wild on many an occasion. What counts as melting down though?

Vanessa Haszard I hadn't thought about it, but the pizza, 1 kg box of fish fingers, and whole tub of ice cream binges of my youth had that out-of-control quality about them often too.

Sally Cat Dee Dee, would you please say a bit more about shopping being a form of meltdown?

Dee Dee I can't explain it, to be honest. It's like a reaction to fight. Maybe with my other head.

Sarah S Ah, that's interesting – that would describe mania.

Dee Dee Sarah, do you mind just elaborating a bit more please.

Sarah S Mania – I have cyclothymia, which is rapid cycling depression and mania. When mania rears its ugly head, I get hyper, aggressive, want to drink a lot, want to buy everything, etc. I don't do sex but if I did, I'd be doing that too! This can last from a few days to weeks at a time.

Sally Cat I'm struggling to grasp the difference between 'getting angry' and 'melting down'. Any pointers, please?

Sarah S The extreme reaction? Not being able to stop? Loss of control of one's self? Like someone has taken over your body and mind in such an extreme way that it's unlikely that anyone could get through to you...and the bit afterwards, when you're so physically and mentally exhausted that you can't move from a spot chosen by your body to wind down in, which could be anywhere. I don't know. I'm now wondering if there's a difference...you always make me question myself, Sally!

Martin Nightingale  I know what you mean. I think it is more instant – and in some ways not so much wanting the same kind of outcomes that anger is used for. I think the PDA reaction is more hardwired than learned, but I guess that isn't proven.

Sally Cat  In having learned to express my crossness, before I even get angry, I've ceased to have meltdowns (that I've noticed). I think there's some connection. Perhaps it's to do with how strongly we PDAers experience emotions, even if we're not consciously in touch with them?

Sarah S  Oh, and meltdowns aren't always as a result of anger. It can be down to sensory overload, which doesn't necessarily manifest itself as an angry meltdown.

Sally Cat  I get meltdowns because of sensory overload, say in busy shopping centres...but they tend to involve feeling REALLY PISSED OFF. Maybe this is just me?

Martin Nightingale  Yeah, my examples were often angry ones, but it is usually upset rather than anger that gets me, and that tends to be after having gone round and round for ages with the feeling of being demanded on and not having any route out.

Sally Cat  So is a meltdown a kind of emotional explosion?

Sarah S  That would make sense, Sally (the crossness bit). We encourage children to speak about their problems before they get angry. Why shouldn't we try as adults... Maybe it's a patience thing?

Yeah, my meltdowns can be triggered by shopping centre sensory overload too.

Sally Cat  It's worked for me, Sarah. I used to not admit to myself I was angry and get taken over by snarkiness I couldn't control. Since learning to say I'm annoyed, I've ceased to do this. Also learning to have quiet time has helped.

Re shopping centres, I get angry at lights, signs, adverts, noise and especially crowds (bastards!) LOL.

> When I meltdown, it honestly feels like I've been possessed by a malignant being that has taken control of my thoughts, words and actions.
>
> This being uses my memories and knowledge to hurt those around me.
>
> I watch on in helpless horror, shocked and ashamed I'm saying and doing such terrible, spiteful things.

**Martin Nightingale** Maybe – but then it is a bit chicken and egg – demands may cause a build-up of negative emotions, but then maybe sometimes demands skip the brain to meltdown in certain situations (usually situations out of our control).

**Sarah S** Hmm. Emotional explosion is good. Probably a better description of a meltdown than anything I've said. Again!

**Martin Nightingale** Hardwired or behavioural is the thing – I don't think my demand avoidance is learned behaviour (like a defiance thing), but learned behaviour could probably cause a similar response.

**Sally Cat** I agree: hardwired.

**Sarah S** What are you saying, Martin? That meltdowns are as a result of learned behaviour?

**Martin Nightingale** No, Sarah, the opposite, I think they are hardwired, not learned, but that it is probably difficult for outsiders to make a distinction.

I also think that anger and meltdown does feel different for me. Anger feels one way (and I have had a lot of situations that make me feel angry – turning on the TV will do it!), meltdown another (a bit dirtier, really, odd description as that is).

Sarah S  Do you, Martin? Interesting. Why?

Martin Nightingale  I think that is because I am usually rational when angry, and even in a flight or fight situation, the body symptoms are a certain way (breathing quickens, so control; assess; decide; act; etc., or just bloody panic), but meltdowns are very different for me, I know my PDA means I lack insight, I'm reacting badly, reason takes a break, etc., and that it is a bad move, but it also feels different (and more overwhelming).

Sarah S  Yes. I agree. (Though I can still be a little irrational when angry lol.)

Sally Cat  Interesting. I'm coming from a different place I think because I was out of touch with my anger most of my life and learned to recognise it at the same time as learning to recognise my autistic then PDA reactions (and trying to apply labels to them all).

And if one is rational, does this prevent a meltdown from occurring?

Sarah S  Oh, OK! Did you never get angry? Or did but didn't know it was anger? Something else? How would you have ignored anger? (Looking for pointers lol.)

Martin Nightingale  No, Sally, I think that's the point! You can't just use reason – now arguably you can't do that in an angry situation either, but you can learn to. Meltdown avoidance is a whole different skill set, I think, although being able to reason a feeling as PDA related is very helpful. Gosh, it's complicated!

Sally Cat  I never realised when I was angry and repressed it. All anger and meltdowns (well, nearly all of them) came out distorted and choked: as snipiness mostly. This, for me, brings in the question of overload.

Shopping centres, for example, overload me and then I get angry and meltdown. Are these two separate things? I don't know.

Sarah S Depends in what context...rational could be seen as succumbing to other people's expectations, to be the norm, to act in a socially acceptable way. In fact that would be a demand for me. I'm expected to act a certain way when getting angry, i.e. I'm expected to walk away or whatever. But in fact the fact that that's expected of me makes me even madder, at society mainly, of what's expected of me, even when I just cannot help it, I can't help whatever triggered me.

Sally Cat By rational, I mean being able to rationalise my own reactions: understand them... I think (getting confused!).

Martin Nightingale I hate shopping centres. I've never melted down in one, but have come close many times (speed walking to get away from the people I'm with and breathe). I tend to go alone and succeed most of the time (not all, sometimes I just leave) or make sure if it is a day out I go and look at something I actually like at some point (often a long way from the main drag or mall). But organised day outs are always going to be a big problem for me – if I haven't organised it myself I'm a right doom-monger.

So I guess it is PDA + a completely alienating environment. It is fairly rational to dislike shopping centres, unless you are super rich, and there's plenty of satire about it – so it isn't just us PDAers who see zombies everywhere.

Sally Cat See, this is what I do in shopping centres. I speed walk to get away from the crowds. I leave my daughter and partner (I'm conscious enough not to leave her alone, no matter how stressed I am) and just HAVE TO flee. To me this is a form of 'contained' meltdown. I have no control over my flee response, but I'm containing it so as to be as socially acceptable and non-aggressive as I can manage.

Martin Nightingale Yes, that's what I do.

Sally Cat So, perhaps, this could be explained as a masked meltdown?

Martin Nightingale Lol, I see it more as an averted one!

Sally Cat As you said, it's complicated!

But surely, Martin, if we lose control so that we respond with Fight/Flight/Freeze (in this case, Flight) is it not still a meltdown? Must a meltdown be Fight?

**Martin Nightingale**  I'm certainly not going to stick around when I feel like that and wait and see what happens if I don't speed walk away! I like science, but not that much!

**Sally Cat**  I just CAN'T stick around. It's not happening. I'm out. No volition involved.

**Sarah S**  Shopping centres for me are overload – meltdown. Not overload – anger – meltdown. (If I do have a meltdown, which is less frequent these days.) BUT that was one of the main things I had CBT for, to be able to go shopping without getting angry when I was having an overload. If I don't get angry, it's much less likely that I have a meltdown. The overload is still there, but the physical triggers as a result of that (panic, rapid breathing, rapid heart rate, etc.) are more subdued. I think. Maybe not.

**Sally Cat**  Must meltdowns always involve the Fight reaction?

**Masked and Unmasked PDA**

Some PDAers, such as myself, mask and hide our anxiety, meltdowns & roller coasting emotions

Others have no problem expressing their inner selves

These are the visible PDAers:

The "nightmare children" described in many PDA texts

Some PDAers fluctuate between masking and freely expressing.

It's easy to spot freely expressed PDA.

But this doesn't mean that we Maskers have a gentler ride

Containing ourselves is highly stressful & exhausting

Though different, we are all PDA

**Vanessa Haszard**  Me too, Sarah, but a small incident can kick it into anger. I avoid shopping centres as a rule, and even try to avoid the big supermarket here when I can, and never go alone.

Sarah S  Oh yes. Doesn't take much here either, especially if I'm in a shitty or stressy mood anyway.

Vanessa Haszard  I gapped it [left quickly] from the library last week in total overload, tears running, shaking, etc. Left my man to pay the poor woman at the counter, thrust the wallet at him and ran. When he came out he said she wouldn't take the $1, and hoped I was OK.

Too embarrassed to go back now.

Sally Cat  So, Vanessa, would you say meltdown can include Flight?

Vanessa Haszard  For me the flight is an attempt to avert a public meltdown.

Sarah S  I've never heard anyone correlating meltdowns with flight. Personally I would see that as anxiety and avoidance of meltdown.

Vanessa Haszard  I CAN'T have someone see that. Anger, yes, other emotion NO!

Sally Cat  Way I'm pondering it is that adrenaline causes Fight, Flight or Freeze. Does the term 'meltdown' apply to only the Fight option (and I can't have people see my anger... I'm learning to, but this is not easy for me...).

So meltdown is always the Fight response?

Sarah S  For me, yes. Just fight.

Flight and freeze is anxiety.

Sally Cat  As I have suppressed my anger for most of my life...oh, those snipy moods! OK, I'm getting some kind of handle on it (in more ways than one). Thank you. This conversation has been very helpful xx

Vanessa Haszard  For me, I guess I would define it as the point where I feel rational Vanessa has lost all control, and the emotion has become so overwhelming as to not allow me to regain that control.

Sally Cat  But, Vanessa, I have this when I flee shopping centres (I have no control over this decision).

Sarah S  I actually feel like I've let go and become the person I need to be to feel normal. I feel more normal having a meltdown than I do pretending to be a socially acceptable person.

Alice  Sally Cat, yes, I think that's a really good way of describing it. For me, meltdown can mean any of those.

Sally Cat  Alice, having slept on it, I've connected that my meltdowns in hospital waiting rooms where I've lost control and demanded special treatment from reception staff and nurses because 'I'm having a meltdown' has been as a result of my not fleeing. On one occasion, a nurse allocated me a quiet room to wait in. I was in such a state by this point that all I could do was stand in this room rigidly against the wall (freezing) answering her irritably and minimally and feeling completely overwhelmed by emotion, out of control and irrationally furious. Perhaps, as I think you say, all three reactions (Fight, Flight and Freeze) can be manifestations of meltdown?

Alice  That's how it seems to me, depending upon the circumstances.

Sally Cat  Some of us may default to Fight mode, others to Flight or Freeze. I think I default to Flight.
    But the Fight mode meltdowns PDAers have will be the visible, in-your-face ones and it might be easy to assume that all meltdowns must be of this type.

Alice  Yes, that's why initially I didn't think I had meltdowns.

Sally Cat  Also that, from what you've said, we'd both doubted that we could have PDA because we'd not had these aggressive meltdowns. I think it's maybe important for people to realise that PDA meltdowns can be expressed as Flight or Freeze or even perhaps as internalised Fight (self-harm).

Alice  Yes, definitely.

Sarah S  Yes, I agree it's important to figure all this out. The common assumption that all meltdowns are fight, could be harmful. In both your cases, you didn't think you were having them because you didn't fit into the assumed criteria. There are many manifestations of meltdowns, I guess!

Interesting that you said 'internalised fight', Sally Cat. Something I'm all too familiar with.

Julia Daunt Wow! What a few days I've had...and not in a good way either. Yesterday I suffered a 5-hour meltdown. Not good. I've not lost it like that for such a long time. I'm exhausted today. What happened was: I rang my new GP's practice on Monday to order my repeat prescriptions – all fine and yes they'll be ready Thursday. Thursday morning came and the phone rang...it was the doctor's...they said they couldn't issue my prescription for Methylphenidate (Ritalin) until they'd referred me to see a psychiatrist!!! WTF! Well as you can imagine I panicked and that triggered the mother of all meltdowns. I was sobbing uncontrollably down the phone but they still said no. I pointed out that I'd been taking Ritalin for 22 years and that I needed it to survive and that just taking it away wasn't advised medically anyway. Still no. I pointed out that I only had 2 days worth of Ritalin left. Still no. I was looking at a minimum of a 2-week wait! I was beside myself. Paul had to take time out of work to help. We were frantically ringing every service we could think of and nobody would or could help. There is a happy ending though – eventually the GP agreed to keep prescribing Ritalin until I'd had my referral! Hooray! I wish I felt happy though but I don't really – I feel more exhausted and scared. Exhausted from 5 hours of crying, screaming, begging, hyperventilating, heart palpitations and panicking and scared because what if the psychiatrist won't prescribe it...what then??? I feel drained. I'm also scared at just how quickly I was pushed over the edge. I really mean it when I say I lost the plot. I literally didn't know what I was doing and I remember very little about it now. That's scary...

P.S. – it's lovely to have Paul home.

Pink This was an interesting one for me to read the other day – I didn't think I had meltdowns particularly until I read other people's experiences!

I don't work with others very often, and when I do then I'm the one in control, so the only people I have to interact with regularly are friends and family. I have also learned to wing it in life so that I simply have zero expectations of how something will pan out.

When I have a strong idea in my head then it absolutely has to go that way or there shall be repercussions, and I guess this is my meltdown. I'll try and manipulate the situation, often simply having the words to explain why something needs to be done a certain way can sway it – and if not then that offers the other person the option of explaining why it has to be done their way. If I don't get my own way without decent explanation then I shall make damned sure everyone knows about it. Though I was brought up to be a compliant child, so it rarely gets to the point of breaking things or being violent, just gently seething and making a bad atmosphere for everyone around me, often long after I've remembered why I'm in a bad mood. Thankfully hubbie is really good at helping me get to the bottom of things, and picking things apart, because logic doesn't always come into the equation at the time.

Sally Cat Also, I used to create heavy atmospheres so everyone in the room felt awkward. It felt like I was exuding it out of myself like black smoke. I think these were Fighty meltdowns that I didn't feel able to extrovertly express.

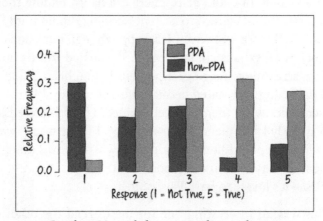

Graph 7: My meltdowns are always obvious
*From a 'Quick PDA Poll' with 240 PDA and 145 neurotypical respondents*

# WHAT MY MELTDOWNS LOOK LIKE

### From Riko Ryuki's blog

It's commonly known in the autistic community that a meltdown is nothing like a tantrum. It's a total loss of control, a need to get emotions out, to find some stability by exploding and getting rid of the pressure building up inside. Everyone knows you cannot reason with someone when they are having a meltdown; they are unreachable. Meltdowns don't all look the same though; every person's meltdowns look different.

My meltdowns involve me screaming. That's usually how they start, when everything just becomes too much that I have to let it all out and that usually happens through screaming. If that isn't enough though, I move on to shouting, swearing and letting out a stream of incomprehensible noise. During a meltdown I often lose my words; I can still talk, but the words don't come out right or nothing I say makes any sense. I can still have a conversation with people though, but I'm on edge and whatever I say will be hurtful and incredibly sarcastic. You don't want to get involved with me when I'm having a meltdown, it takes a lot for me to control what I say when I'm in this state (and yes, I do still retain some control, especially at the start of the meltdown, but if pushed I can quickly lose that thin control and this leads to a tirade of insults and nonsense).

When in meltdown I have this overwhelming need to destroy anything and everything. I can throw objects, crush them with my hands, stamp on things or just stamp my feet. I will hit things with my hands, kick and even scratch my face. It all depends on where the cause of the meltdown is coming from and what emotions I have inside me. If there are people around that I don't want to hurt then I may (unconsciously) change what I do. When I'm frustrated I tend to hurt myself more but when I'm angry I tend to focus on other objects or people. At the beginning of a meltdown I still have some control so I try to get my anger out without hurting or completely destroying things, but sometimes the anger is too great, or the meltdown has reached a certain no turning back point, or the meltdown comes on so suddenly that I can't direct my anger, and things get destroyed. I have broken phones, bins, plastic boxes, cups, toys, books. I have smashed my hands into furniture and on walls, I've bashed my head against walls, I've stomped my feet onto the floor and kicked walls and furniture, I've pulled my hair and dug my nails into mine and other people's flesh. I rarely attack other people physically and only attack others verbally if they try to stop my meltdowns or make it worse by mocking or insulting me. I prefer not to hurt others; I'd like to be left alone when meltdown strikes but some people just don't get it.

Sometimes a meltdown can be over in a flash. Sometimes it can last all day, seeming to stop and start. Other times there's no break and it just goes on for hours. Sometimes a meltdown leads to a shutdown and I become unresponsive, other times I return to 'normal' though more tired and on edge.

The most intense part of any meltdown is the desire to just destroy everything around me. It's like being possessed by a mad monster. No matter how much I destroy it's never enough, I always need to destroy more. I have noticed that if I do destroy things then the urge to do that again becomes greater, like the need gets fuelled, so for me, stopping myself from destroying things is important so I don't need to destroy as much in the future. This means adapting my life to ensure as few meltdowns occur as possible. This isn't always possible though and is a constant work in progress.

# — 8 —

# OVERLOAD

» Forms of overload: sensory; demands; social; physical;
  work; home schooling children; emotional
» What overload feels like
» Need for quiet time to recharge
» Different strategies needed to recuperate
  from social and emotional overload
» Triggers
» Spider hallucinations
» Calming overload through fresh air, space and (literal) grounding
» Overload causing either meltdown or shutdown

---

Do you overload? If so, what causes it? What does it feel
like? How do you respond to being overloaded?

---

Riko Ryuki  I get overloaded easily; many different things can cause
it. Sensory overload where I become too hot or too hungry or
too itchy and my brain starts to shut down so I can't handle any
more input from external sources. I have to remove myself from
the sensory issue or try to reduce the sensory attack in order to
function again. If not then it all becomes too much and I lash
out verbally or physically, shouting or throwing objects/hitting
objects. I can become overloaded by demands which make me
shutdown and become unresponsive. I'll avoid more and if

pushed I may lash out. I need to not do anything for a while in order to recover. If too many people are talking to me, especially when I'm busy trying to do something else like reading or people quickly change subjects, then I can become overloaded and my brain temporarily stops working. I need time for my brain to catch up and finish processing things.

OVERLOAD FOR ME FEELS AS IF MY BRAIN HAS AN ELECTRIC STORM CRAMMED INSIDE IT; A THOUSAND, MILLION TINY LIGHTNING BOLTS DETONATING CONTINUOUSLY ALL ACROSS AND THROUGH MY BRAIN SO I CANNOT THINK. I HAVE NO GIVE LEFT. THE WHOLE LOT'S ABOUT TO BLOW

Julia Daunt  Yes, big time. Often, but I like to try and keep on top of it. Taking short breaks, having a nap, changing task or just looking out a window are all helpful to me throughout the day. Oddly enough I don't seem to have a problem overloading other people, especially Paul. I tend to fire commands at him in quick succession and I don't take time to think he might not like the whole list all at once. I think it's a control thing but I also think it's a memory thing – if I don't say it all now I'll forget. My short-term memory is crap.

Silva If I'm in a situation where I'm surrounded by a lot of people – either in a social way or just in a crowd out shopping or on a busy beach or whatever – I get overloaded. My brain won't focus properly and process what's going on around me and if I can't remove myself, I get incredible headaches which, if I can't deal with it fast, quickly render me unable to function. Often I vomit. If at other times I feel overloaded by feeling pressured, I get extremely irritable, snappy and if it doesn't stop, have lashed out, shouting and making them stop. When younger I would trash rooms and smash objects, but I re-focus myself now and pre-empt that happening as I hated how it made me feel.

Jenny Penny Yes, I do get overloaded socially. Physically too, because I can't prioritise and want to do everything at once.

Dee Dee Work overloads me. I get home and hardly speak. Procrastination happens a lot.

Sharron Madderwords I'm always overloaded. I'm PDA, both of my children are PDA, I work nearly full time in a special school and I home school my daughter. By Friday I'm howling at the moon and sat rocking on puddles of my own pee! I take a lot of doggy walks and read a lot and try to spend less time with people for fun x

Vanessa Haszard I find sensory and emotional overload connected, i.e. if I am emotionally heightened the sensory stuff is more of an issue, and vice versa.

Silva Vanessa, yes! X

Sally Cat I am feeling overloaded right now. I've been dealing with a lot of social stuff. My brain feels fried. My head feels tight. I feel like I am kind of dried up mentally. Can't absorb much else (I'm not fully overloaded, just, I suppose, well on my way). It's like I'm out of resilience. No space left. If I got bombarded by anything now, I'd be likely to snap. I know myself well enough now, I think, to recognise the build-up, so I've been telling people in online discussions that I don't have much energy and cutting conversations short (politely, I think).

I think I get mental/cognitive overload (which is what I'm feeling now) as well as emotional, social and sensory.

Silva  Ah, Sally – take a break and nurture yourself somewhere you feel some peace, my friend. Hugs xxx

Sally Cat  I have learned in life to schedule in quiet time. I love my quiet time. Facebook is quite quiet time (very quiet compared to time with my lovely, demanding, bright, loud, noisy PDA 6-year-old!). I'm not good at being completely idle though. I like reading or messing around on Facebook mostly xx

Silva  That's good then. I think I'm addicted to reading – love books! Usually got at least two on the go at once. Bet you understand that.

Sally Cat  I can only cope with one on the go at once. I'm not great at switching styles. It takes a lot of mental energy for me. I have got to the stage though where I can watch a variety of TV shows (we watch one show per evening). I used to prefer binging on one TV series, but now we have several to pick from x

Vanessa Haszard I don't mentally overload from mental challenges, but find I lose my ability to think when in emotional or sensory overload.

Sally Cat Yeah, I don't know if the brain fog, frazzled feeling I get is caused by dyslexia, ADD or CFS or PDA (or some other TLA – three-letter abbreviations!) but it most definitely feels like overloading and I think of it as such (as far as I can currently think!).

I'm not sure if I get emotional overload...social overload, definitely.

But I definitely have a roller-coaster ride of emotions going on and this can take its toll.

Sally Cat [Commenting five days later] I think this is emotional overload. That I'm feeling now. One of the two baby bunnies we have, 10 weeks old. Has died. And I feel wrung out. Like there's a sea; an ocean of emotion and I am overwhelmed by it, it's like I keep shorting out. I am not sure whether I am shying away from feeling it because doing so feels like a demand. I have always struggled to process grief. And I also feel guilt (what could I have done differently?) and shame (I am a bad rabbit carer) and anxiety (what about his brother?) and it's all too much for me to process. I keep shutting down. Going slow. In my head. Kind of crushed. Kind of numb. But I think I might have a panic attack going on too that I can't process. My heart rate feels fast and I feel a bit sick and my mouth is dry. Does this make any sense?

And PDA 6-year-old DD is handling any grief with even more disassociation. She has been manically laughing and joking about the bunny's death all morning. I said that sometimes it can be hard to feel sad. She said that she sometimes feels sad, but she never cries.

Silva Oh, Sally I really feel for you. But please be kind to yourself, I think what you are describing is natural. I would feel all of those emotions too and I 'get' the overload – when I feel overwhelmed by emotions I react like that too. Like I can't process everything and the old saying of 'not knowing which way to turn' feels very, very real. When my mother died, I thought I was going crazy for a while. Emotional overload is traumatic to deal with xxx

Alice I get overloaded if I have too many events (even fairly small ones) too closely together. In fact my preferred state is no events in the diary at all. I get social and emotional overload.

If it's social I need silence and alone time to recover. If it's emotional it varies depending on what it is – I might need to talk about it to release some of the charge. I'm wary these days of overload of any kind as I find the recovery process quite difficult.

Sally Cat Social events frazzle me severely too. I do actually like them, but they need to be spaced out. I don't personally like a blank calendar (though I have far less issue with having one now – hurray! – than I did in my younger years when my depression felt rooted in my calendar being empty). These days, I thrive on having red letter days to look forward to, but I also know I need a lot of recovery time around events to maintain stamina x

C. Keech I overload pretty easily but my brain is very busy and works 24/7 regardless of my environment. This means I have a finite little area of space left in my brain for 'life' thus, if 'shit' happens, more often than not I crumble. As a free spirit with no job, no responsibilities and at the 'right' weight for what my insecurities deem 'acceptable', I can be really quite sassy, social and bold but now, as a single mother of three, unhappy with my weight and sole keeper of household, I am agoraphobic and chronically tired. It uses energy to keep my mood level and sometimes I just don't have it in me xxx

Sally Cat I find parenting exhausting. I developed CFS after becoming a mother. Being a single mother must be exponentially more exhausting xxx

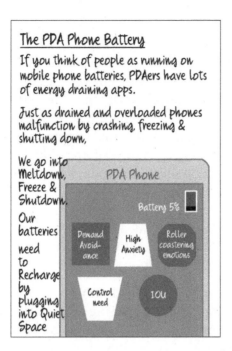

The PDA Phone Battery

If you think of people as running on mobile phone batteries, PDAers have lots of energy draining apps.

Just as drained and overloaded phones malfunction by crashing, freezing & shutting down,

We go into Meltdown, Freeze & Shutdown.

Our batteries need to Recharge by plugging into Quiet Space

PDA Phone

Battery 5%

Demand Avoidance

High Anxiety

Roller coastering emotions

Control need

IOU

**C. Keech** Home schooling too!! Sucker for punishment.

**Sally Cat** See, I just could NOT home school!!! Oh, I would if DD was really suffering at school. We discussed this from the year dot. Thankfully – oh, so thankfully!! – she likes school and is doing well there! I feel for you, C. Keech xxx

**C. Keech** I never sent mine and the school run is a bigger demand than just having them here now anyway! Xx

**Sally Cat** I am quickly overloaded in shopping centres and when kept waiting. Shopping centres, I think, overload me because of the crowds and bright light and noise and lack of natural air.

Being kept waiting overloads me, I think, because I need to know what's happening with my time. To have some control. I need to be free to do my own thing and come and go as I please. Not just sit there passively like a puppet. And it's not even just passive, because I have to hold myself in 'the zone' ready to deal with whatever interaction is going to happen at the end of this waiting.

This state of readiness is exhausting to maintain. I continually struggle when kept waiting to hold myself in from bolting and not lashing out at any available powers that be. Being kept waiting in a shopping centre environment is even worse! I, at one point, used a busy pharmacy in a shopping centre to get my regularly needed prescription drugs. They also – oh joy! – had a policy of saying the wait would be 5 minutes when it turned out to be half an hour. If pressed, they'd blithely inform me of additional waiting time without apology. For example, 'Oh, it's going to be another 20 minutes. We're busy.' They didn't seem to have any empathy for my experience as a customer trapped in an airless, bright, crowded environment with fractious baby. Visiting that chemist caused me to overload every time and go into meltdown. I hated it.

Elizabeth Mine comes from too much going on. It can be more socialising than usual, or having forms I need to complete, for example, but it tends to be a combination of things. I have physical symptoms like sweating, heart thudding, tiredness and vomiting. The latter doesn't come from my stomach though but through my throat contracting. (I'm one of those people who can't swallow pills without gagging and even brushing my teeth can do it at bad times.) I usually just have to stay in bed and wait for it to be over. I tend to make it worse by feeling bad with myself about it. I also have these hallucinations when I'm between sleeping and waking where I see a spider-like creature with extra legs on the floor or wall or ceiling.

Alice It's interesting what you say about your spider hallucinations – I had exactly the same thing, but only once. I thought it might happen again, but it didn't. I, too, was in that time between sleeping and waking. How do you feel about it?

Elizabeth When it first happened it got me really panicky as I'd just moved house and gone through a time when my panic about spiders had paralysed me into inaction. Now I know what it is I get what's happening which defuses it but I still get a moment of panic.

Sally Cat  I used to hallucinate crawly things out of the corner of my eye when tired.

Alice  Elizabeth, I feel for you – it really frightened me after I realised it wasn't real! I didn't mind if it was.

Sally, it's interesting that we three have all seen crawly things in these situations.

Sally Cat  I have put it down to having a hallucination-prone brain and tiredness causing me to invent details in my peripheral vision: slight movement gets translated into 'living thing scuttling'.

Little Black Duck  Yep. And most days. Sometimes several times a day.

It is, as the name suggests, simply Too Much! It feels like bombardment and harassment. My brain simply can't process all that's expected of it. It revolts under the strain and says 'Enough!' Overload creates confusion, sometimes out of nowhere, and can have me feel a bit disorientated. I need to stop or leave or both. And I need to do it now, before the panic sets in.

I usually need to get outside. The space. The fresh air. And the ground. For whatever strange reason, I actually feel grounded with my feet on the ground. Outside ground and not a building floor. Quite often I'll sit on the ground too, like on a street kerb. Not really sure what that's about but I've always been the same. If I'm home, I'll often lie down. My bed or lounge in my safe zone works the same way. I crawl into myself and wait for the fuzz to clear, so I even know what to do next.

Sally Cat  Nice description.

Silva  I also seek air and space when things feel too much, and yes, I am with you on the 'ground' and lying down too. Have you heard of earthing? A friend told me about it – simply, you go barefoot on the earth or grass – it is said to help you re-connect with source and feel grounded. I do that too sometimes x

Sally Cat  Like Little Black Duck, I tend to lie ON something (bed or sofa) if home, but I've noticed lying on the floor to please my cat has felt very soothing. I used to do it for mindfulness practice, but Demand Avoidance scuppered this. I've noticed a reduction in my Demand Avoidance lately as well (yippee) and I've actually enjoyed doing outside things like sunbathing for much longer periods than my previous zero minutes.

I relate, too, to desperately needing space and air if I get overloaded in a public space (or lack-of-space, as it were) like a shopping centre. This ties in I think with discussion in the previous 'Meltdown' section about whether the Flight response is a form of meltdown...

Pink  When I read this yesterday I was aware that I was overloaded, so hence leaving it until now to respond.

Daughter was doing her non-stop chatter and questions, oh so many questions... 3 hours' worth, as we sorted her new specs and wandered round town trying to buy some essentials. Got home and immediately got on to phone to recover. Somehow using my eyes and fingers to interact never has the same issues as using my mouth and ears...

And then got grumped at by hubbie for being on my phone instead of having some family time. Thing is, if I'd had the words I could have told him I was overloaded and he'd have got it, but I just didn't have any words left.

Alice  I'm overloaded now, I think. Hubby's losing his job with no prospect of a new one yet. I've got a chest infection and on antibiotics (about the fifth type in a row). Also on other meds. And a very close friend is having an operation tomorrow to remove a cancerous tumour.

I'm shutting down, I think.

Silva  Alice, in my life too, the pattern seems to be that everything comes along at once and I feel bombarded. Take all the time you need, my lovely. Your mental health is the priority, if you're to have the strength to deal with it all. And I promise that you will xxx

Sally Cat  Your current situation, Alice, reminds me of the proverbial 3 buses coming along all at once. Having ill health makes everything harder to cope with too. Sending you hugs xxx

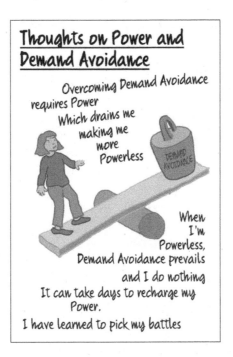

**Thoughts on Power and Demand Avoidance**

Overcoming Demand Avoidance requires Power
Which drains me
making me
more
Powerless

When I'm Powerless, Demand Avoidance prevails
and I do nothing
It can take days to recharge my Power.
I have learned to pick my battles

**Sarah Johnson** Children overload me. Or rather the modern parenting helicopter thing does. And their incessant need for feeding. Are they breathing – yes. Are they clean and warm – yes. Are they being educated – yes. So what's the drama??? I love 'em. They love me. Stop telling me I should do stuff with them. Their immature mentality means they bore me. I love them but let's not pretend they stimulate me!!

Oh, and when I'm overloaded I tell them to 'eff off'. They get that and do...bless them!

**Miguel (9-year-old transcribed by his mum)** M says he overloads. He says it's like a fuse.

Some things make the fuse burn steadily. Other things can make it speed up and then boom.

What comes next is one of 2 things, either a meltdown or M needing to completely withdraw himself. He is more likely to meltdown if he has more energy. If he is tired it's complete shutdown.

He gets headaches from overload and from tiredness.

He will then stay in his room and have his YouTube videos about scootering and cannot talk to anyone. He has to be left alone.

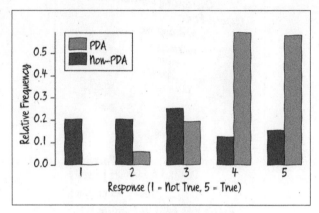

Graph 8: I overload easily
*From a 'Quick PDA Poll' with 240 PDA and 145 neurotypical respondents*

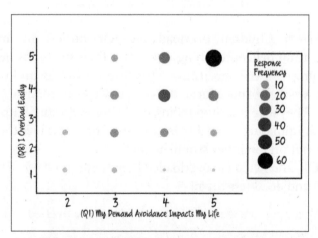

Scattergraph 4: Correlation between Graphs 1 and 8
*There is a moderate correlation between 'Demand Avoidance impacts my life' and 'I overload easily'*

# RECOVERING FROM BEING SOCIABLE

## From Riko Ryuki's blog

Being sociable is hard. It's tiring, mentally exhausting. My brain feels like it needs a break. This is common for neurodiverse people, not so much for neurotypical people. I've heard that for 'normal' people, being sociable is a way of de-stressing and recovering from the day's events.

For autistic people and especially for PDA people and even more so for those with comorbidities too, being in social situations is really exhausting. Maybe we are using our brains more than regular people and that's why it's more tiring, or maybe it's because our brains work in different ways and so we spend all the time attempting to understand and speak a foreign language. Whatever it is, it's tiring. So we need time to relax and recover from it all.

For many this involves spending copious amounts of time away from other people. For me this means sleeping, playing Nintendo DS games and reading. The time needed to recover depends on the time used in socialising and how much energy has been expended doing so. For me, an hour in extensive 'chit-chat' means I need at least two days to recover. It varies for each person. Sadly I don't get a lot of recovery time. In fact, having a family with young kids means my recovery time is almost non-existent and yet this is when I need more recovery time than usual.

Recovery time is important. It helps us stay sane, it helps ward off depression, it lowers our stress and anxiety levels, it gives us time to think and reload our engines. If we don't have time to recover then we may become less easy to be around. Our stress and anxiety levels will rise and we may become irritable, angry and emotional.

It's not us being selfish or lazy or unsociable. Just because some people need social time to recover doesn't mean everybody does. Not every person is the same. It baffles me how people can find socialising relaxing; for me it's incredibly difficult, it doesn't come naturally for me. Similarly it may baffle others how being sociable can be tiring; they may not understand why I want to be alone because for them that has a negative response. Most people don't like being alone. It doesn't necessarily make me introverted (although I am anyway), it doesn't make me anti-social, it doesn't make me a bore, it makes me different. And different is okay. After all, I'm fine with other people needing to talk all the time, so why shouldn't others be fine with me wanting to not talk? We are different, neither one of us is a monster.

Recovery is important, regardless of how we do it.

# 9

# PDA AND PEOPLE

» Lack of wide social network; few close relationships
» Need for alone time even in close relationships
  and exhaustion without this
» Serial best friends
» Having had obsessions/crushes on people – not being able to let go
» Driven to be popular, then realising this is unwanted
» The benefits of Facebook interaction and disliking phone calls
» Thwarted drive for greater intimacy
» *Trigger warning* major family issues: severed contact and abuse
» Having an affair when broken by a failed
  relationship (and the repercussions)

---

How do you get on with relationships (family, friends,
romantic, work, etc.)? Do you need time on your own? Do
you need people? Has this need ever been obsessive?

---

Catherine C  A comment was made by the TV programme announcer
the other night: 'All of your colleagues and friends will have
been talking about this today...' [Love Island – a TV programme
in the UK].

I turned to my husband, and said, 'I don't have any colleagues
or friends!' And we laughed and laughed!

I can't do working for other people very well, and the fewer close relationships, with friends/family, the fewer demands are put on me.

Laura Mullen  Well, I have been married for over 14 years. Don't think I could live without my spouse but he regularly gets on my nerves and I spend the hours between 11pm and 3–4am happily being alone. I have friends online but not IRL now. People are too much and I am too much for people so we just agree to be separate. And then my kids are with me all the time so I crave aloneness. I guess you could say the need to be alone, to be still and silent, to watch what I enjoy, read what I enjoy, has become obsessive for me.

There are so many demands on me every day, little demands: 'Hey, Mommy, look at this!' 'Mommy, do you think this picture is pretty?' 'Mommy, Emi is playing with my toy!' 'Mommy, I don't want to do that!' 'Mommy, my tummy hurts' and then it's 'Sweetie, can you make this for dinner?' 'Sweetie, can you go over this code, what do you think of this button here?' 'Should I make this dark or do you think the color stands out more on white?' 'Can you call and make an appointment for me at this doctor tomorrow? I won't have time and you know how I hate to make calls.'

So by 8pm every day I am done. Just done. I can't meet my own demands often and by then I am so frustrated that I just want to go hide. I feel utterly drained by demands and need to recharge. It took a long time for my husband to understand recharging does not equate to sleep for me.

Julia Daunt  I love people on the whole but it's got to be on my terms. That's why I like Facebook as it allows me to dip in and out of social stuff. I'm okay (with support) in small/medium social things but I really struggle, even with support, at large social things. Even though it causes me great anxiety I actually love meeting new people (on my terms) so I will actually plan and look forward to this even though it takes a lot out of me. I manage the anxiety about socialising the same way that I manage anxiety caused by demands. I don't like to be alone. I find silence unbearable...it's too loud. I like just being with Paul and I hate it when he's out.

Silva I need my space and time alone but am married and love to have him around too. It's a demand I think, to find a balance that suits us both. I cannot comprehend how people cope with having a lodger, for instance, or people who come to stay longer than a few days at most – and then only very close and trusted friends. I mask (I think; still learning terms) around the majority of people which leads to exhaustion. I often feel like a zombie for a couple of days after having visitors. I cope best with meeting up for lunch with people – a few hours is enough and I scurry home to sanctuary where I can re-charge. This is why I am best working independently – when I was employed, it stressed me out.

Alice I totally relate to your comments about lodgers and guests – also lunch!

Elizabeth I've had obsessions about friends, rock stars and lately somebody a lot more problematic. I'm a true crime junkie and this man is convicted of mass murder but has always maintained his innocence and I believe him. It's the miscarriage of justice aspect that leads to the obsession. I find murder cases interesting but I've never fixated on anyone who confessed/I believe is guilty.

Stella Girl I have obsessed over boys or men since I was a young girl. I would fall in love or lust and would not be able to get over this obsession until I had found someone else. Luckily I never crossed the boundaries into stalking but I probably came close. I had many boyfriends, lovers, partners, etc.

Sally Cat Me too!

Stella Girl Anyway…I became obsessed with sex after I was hurt really badly by a boyfriend who told me that I was not adventurous enough in bed.

I could write my own book about how I reacted to this mistreatment of myself. Basically I decided that no man would ever be able to criticise my sexual prowess ever again. I needed to be in control so badly that I became obsessed with sex and all that it entailed. It took me nearly 15 years to overcome this obsession and having kids certainly helped. I am now completely celibate and have been since my youngest son (7 years old) was conceived. Having 2 boys with special needs has kept me busy so I don't have time for anyone else.

Sally Cat  I had such an all consuming crush when I was 17 that it was tearing me apart. I couldn't stop thinking about the guy. Writing pages and pages in my journal analysing every tiny snippet of interaction I ever had with him, driving myself mad. I decided to go vegan in the end, just to focus my mind onto something else.

Sally Cat  I used to want to hang out with big, shiny groups of cool people, but I inevitably found myself bored stiff and annoyed!

Little Black Duck  People seem to get on with me, more than I do with them. I feel quite often like I'm peeling people off me. Needy. Demandy. Too much. The people I really care about think I'm awesome and are very forgiving of my ways.

Stef  I would say I was fairly successful at having a few close friends and lots of great acquaintances over the years, with my husband being my very best friend and doing most things together for the 14 years we were together (although we did both have some of our own interests, we kept mostly separate), but now that he is gone, I feel very lonesome...

Silva Stef, I feel for you. My husband is my best friend too – I married quite late, at 46. I have some close friends who are like sisters to me, and often think I have created my own non-biological family where I feel safe. I wish you peace and contentment xxx

Vanessa Haszard I have serial long-term, one-at-a-time friends that I eventually get pissed off with because of the lack of reciprocity of effort in the relationship, and tend to completely cut off, sometimes badly. Mostly now I have online friends; some I also know in real life, but our interaction is primarily online, and I have more or less decided real life friends are not worth my investment of energy and resources.

I have a great long-term partner now, and he is OK with running interference for me, and putting a buffer between me and the world, in a loving and uncontrolling way. My younger daughter and I have a good relationship, and I am in contact with my maternal grandparents and mother regularly.

I have finally stopped torturing myself over seeing my father, and stated clearly I will no longer contact.

My oldest daughter, who I left with her father at 3, but lived next door, and always tried to do right by, including giving her and her father the house and smallholding my parents bought us, has not had the challenges her sister has, but blames me for everything that she doesn't like about her current situation, (17, unemployed, feeling sorry for herself, and Daddy is struggling to sell the half-million dollar property I signed over to him, and she wants to move YESTERDAY), so I have temporarily backed away there too.

Dee Dee I talk myself, well, at least try to, out of relationships...my other half says 'stop pushing me away'...what is wrong with me...

Alice I don't think there's anything wrong with you, it sounds like the DA is kicking in. It happens to me with my husband, I find it very frustrating.

Dee Dee  Do you then have an interment cuddle, kiss or even sex to make it better? x

Alice  Dee Dee, a what cuddle?

Dee Dee  You know, a cuddle into his belly.

Alice  Oh, right – TBH I don't necessarily try to make it better at all.

Dee Dee  I feel compelled to make it better coz it makes me really sick otherwise.

Alice  It sounds like you're nicer than I am – I just can't.

Dee Dee  We avoid conflict in different ways...how interesting! How does everyone else cope with relationships?

Maybe coz you have been together forever and know each other inside out you don't need to. I've been with mine for a year now.

Alice  Good point – we've been married nearly 27 years.

Dee Dee  Alice, what's your secret then? 27 years. How? Xx

Alice  I don't have a secret! It hasn't always been plain sailing – far from it. A lot of tolerance from both sides and picking your battles are two strategies that seem to have helped.

Dee Dee  See...with me any sign of sinking, that's when I'm swimming away... I'd rather swim away than drown in battle... I'm such a wimp....a baby.

Alice  I've thought of that many times – but when I've let things simmer down, and considered the options, I've stayed.

You're not a wimp or a baby. I don't think many people like conflict. My hubby is one of the least confrontational people I know, which although that comes with huge frustrations, has helped too because it has given me the time to simmer down.

Dee Dee  He's a keeper.

Alice  So far!

Dee Dee  I'd be happy with 27 years but sadly ruin everything... sighs...

Emily Cool I think for me if I feel I'm failing or not doing well enough at something, I don't want to talk about it, and seeing family members, even if they don't actually say anything about it, adds pressure. For example at university, I struggled to get out of bed, get to lectures, and hand in work on time. I felt my family would think I was lazy. Well, I felt as if I was lazy and useless. I didn't want to have to address any of it. If I'm finding things particularly hard, communicating is an added difficulty on top that can be just too much.

Pink I have recently had the opposite. Since getting a good understanding of PDA I think I've seen my mother in a different light; I think she also has PDA...

Sally Cat I think my mum has PDA too.

Alice I have been married for 26 years (!I know! How did that happen?!) and have two children who are young adults living at home. I have a small number of close friends, one of whom I see most weeks, the others less frequently. I used to be more sociable. I have a wide group of acquaintances who I see rarely. I have an older brother and I see him and his family about once a year, although we text more often. I'm expected to see/entertain hubby's family from time to time which can be very difficult. Both my parents died. My relationship with my mother was very complicated.

I don't work any more due to physical ill health.

I have a quiet life these days, I can't handle any more than that. I am alone much of the daytime and sometimes late at night. I need time on my own every day, particularly if I have been out or socialised and need to get over it. However, I wouldn't want to live on my own, so the balance is quite good for me currently. My children have lots of friends so they come over, but at their ages they rarely need me to be involved.

The relationships I do have are okay, I think. I worry about my effect on my children, and I could put more into my marriage. It would be fair to say that my husband could too. We muddle along. At present nobody knows about my PDA journey.

I have had obsessions or even 'crushes' on people over the years; each one has petered out over time. I've never been sure what this is about, so seeing that it fits the PDA profile is reassuring.

Pink  The obsessive thing is interesting for me – I've realised that everyone I've been drawn to has had something to offer me to help me grow as a person, and I see the same in those who are compelled to be around me. Once we've learned what we need to learn from each other we often move on and out of each other's lives, sometimes coming back when there is more to learn. I've learnt it's best to be fluid and let them go – holding on to them will only make the journey back harder.

  I often need downtime to ground the energies I've picked up from those around me; it all gets too much sometimes. I've learned socially that alcohol helps with that, and I'm trying really hard to not fall into the booze trap in order to be around people I'm not so comfortable with. Sometimes it works, sometimes it fails.

Sally Cat  I am drawn to people, but don't intuitively know how to successfully interact with them. I think this is why I mask.

I used to have obsessions about people and it would drive me insane, especially as I would be too painfully shy, self-conscious and socially mystified to be able to interact with them. But I couldn't let go.

I used to long to be popular too. I used to love going out to pubs and clubs and would get drunk and/or high so as to have the confidence to talk to people. I've had serial best friends (who have sometimes been a boyfriend) who have acted as a social 'interfacer' for me.

I gradually realised that I didn't actually want the ramifications of popularity because most people irritated me and I didn't want them around me. I've also come to realise that I need a lot of space and downtime. Socialising exhausts me.

I like interacting online, on Facebook, because I can dip in and out of it as I choose and don't have to worry about what I look like or how I sound. I hate phones and video chat is even worse for me. I need time to consider my replies without being in the spotlight.

I'm happy now living in a village with my mellow partner and our less mellow PDA daughter.

I wish I was better at instigating meeting up with other people, but I do see girl friends from time to time for lunches, which I find very enjoyable.

Silva Sally, your dislike of phones/video chat resonates very strongly. I have friends who nag me to use Skype and I shudder at the idea. I also like FB because of it's freedom to come and go xxx

Tracy Yes, like Sally says, I am drawn to some people, I have STRONG crushes (not romantic usually). It doesn't happen very often, though there is usually at least one person in my life at any given time who I am crushing on, and usually I don't really even know them, though I want to. As far as friendships and relationships go, I usually am dissatisfied with what most people think of as friendship – going to a movie or out to eat or shopping together once in a while – seems often pretty boring to me and I usually want to go home long before it's over. So I'm not very good at keeping friends. As far as close friends or close relationships, I want to be more intimate than I actually seem capable of. It's kind of a push–pull. I attempt to reach out and draw closer, to let people into my experience and listen to theirs, and then maybe I get triggered and snippy when something makes it clear that the other person is not relating at all to what I am saying, or I don't know how to respond to them. And then we get into these awful painful fights. So I feel quite sad and lonely sometimes when I think about that. I'm trying to work through it with therapy, but it's always been this way, and I don't really know if I've ever had a GOOD relationship. I'm even quite distant with my parents and my brother, and I don't know anyone anymore (other than my family) who I knew when I was a kid.

As a kid, it was easier at least to make relationships, but I got quite badly hurt often because I would always have just one friend, who I thought the absolute world of, and then I would be absolutely devastated when the relationship broke off or I realized they actually did not like me very much, or found me difficult and eventually didn't want to be my friend anymore. And I pretty much ended up feeling like I was not worth knowing, or that I must just be some kind of incomprehensibly annoying person nobody could get to know or understand, so I eventually just decided to come up with things I could give people, and that's my main strategy now, to try to be useful to people, so that they will at least tolerate my presence and I can interact when I need to, because although I like being alone most of the time, I get lonely too, for connection.

Eventually the only relationships that mattered to me was just seeing my cousins for a week a year, who I really connected with, and I was, again, just devastated when they had to fly home, across the country, and I would be alone for the rest of the year. And I know eventually I just stopped connecting with people like that, and I've been alone ever since, even though I try, and I pretend I feel connected in that way, but I really don't, not even with my husband (though he gets mad when I say that). Even though I know that's not the right way to deal with it, I just can't be hurt like that again.

So no, I don't get on very well with relationships, although I make a good show, and I don't think anyone really knows how lonely and inept I feel.

Sally Cat I am not close to my family either. I've not spoken to one brother for 30 years and the other one has stopped speaking to me. I think we're all on the spectrum, likely PDA. I recently cut my mum out for 2.5 years coz I realised she'd been severely undermining me and had started upsetting my little daughter too. I couldn't work out whether she was being deliberately emotionally abusive or not. I saw a counsellor specifically to try to figure this out. The upshot was that I cut my mum out completely, which was about the hardest, most painful thing I've ever done. My counsellor said from her experience my mum had been deliberately abusive, either this or she was psychotic. It was as our sessions drew to a close that I came across a female autism traits list and sought diagnosis.

Tracy I'm so sorry about your mum. My folks are oblivious and distant, but they're all right, especially now that I've grown up. My brother too, though he was a bully when I was at home.

I am worried though about my husband. He is trying really hard and in therapy but frankly we can't seem to have conversations anymore without one or both of us feeling badly. Sometimes it's really awful and he doesn't always respect my boundaries. He feels bad about it after, but it's happened multiple times and I feel hurt and scared. I don't know what to think.

Julia Daunt Thankfully I get on quite well with most of my family and I'm close to them. I also get on well with Paul's family. Family, to me, is important but so are friends. It's hard to maintain all the relationships (demand) but I do try to give extra effort to it. It's so easy to just get caught up in life and before you know it, it's been months since you said hello. I do have a bad (or good) habit of being able to cut people out of my life when we have a falling out or they let me down big time. I'm very black and white in this area. They wrong me or we have a misunderstanding and I get angry and upset but then I let it go and move on. Almost as if it never happened. It might take a few weeks. This I know isn't a PDA thing necessarily but is perhaps more of a learnt self-preservation thing. People can be so hurtful. I think because I have enough going on that I need to be able to move on quickly when things have gone wrong within relationships. Relationships are hard work but I think they are worth it.

Silva On 'family' – I have a sister 11 years older than me and a brother seven years older. I think my sister is a narcissist and my brother is, I believe, on the spectrum (as I think our parents were). I cut my sister out of my life for several years after Dad died; then after Mom passed away we built a bridge. It didn't last. Her daughter (in her forties) is also narcissistic and a fantasist. Her manipulative behaviour caused me endless problems so it's better this way, and my life is happier without their toxic influence. My brother had also cut them off (long before I did). He and I get along great but we live at a distance. I have no kids and he lost touch with his adult son (who is also on the spectrum, but more so than my brother), years ago. My bro is happily married to his second wife though. I am also happy with my husband. I recently found out that my sister was not my father's child (blood groups make it impossible). Mom gave birth to her just past her nineteenth birthday, after marrying my Dad at 6 months pregnant so there's a story there, but it's too late to fathom it now as Mom has gone.

I had a fraught relationship with both parents – with Dad we resolved a great deal when he was terminally ill, with cancer of the pancreas. Mom and I grew closer after both building bridges and working at it and became very close for around a decade after she was widowed, before she too died. At my age, there's a lot to look back on – I am sure a lot of our family dynamics were due to PDA or spectrum issues. Knowing nothing else, as I grew up, I just thought this was 'normality' for everyone. We didn't know about the spectrum or autism back then where I grew up.

C. Keech Mine's just fallen to pieces! I've blocked him and his whole family and am holing up, feeling like I don't want my future. Don't know what else to do so I'm not too good at any of it! Xx

Riko Ryuki I don't really have any contact with family; my kids are the only family I see regularly. I've always masked around family members so being around them is exhausting. I feel like my kids are the only ones who see the real me. I can manage friendships but not close friends, more friends by circumstance, as in we work together or go to the same groups. Most of my friends are online and it's far easier to communicate and be myself with them, but it does get a bit lonely not seeing friends face to face, even though it's harder that way.

Laura Mullen I grew up with my mom having to completely cut out her family. I know all about the process she had to go through and I experienced it from the angle of a child having parents cut family members out. I also have had to cut my brother out of my life. For my mom and myself it was due to abuse in childhood and refusal of family to believe it was abuse or saying we were lying. Plus just being toxic. TBH, I guess it should be harder than it has been to cut them out but it is a relief.

Sally Cat I've cut my brother out for 30 years. It has always, at the base of it, felt like relief, but the ramifications of family and social pressure to 'just get over it and get on with him' have been undermining and exhausting to me.

Laura Mullen Sally, thankfully because my mom had to cut out her own family there is no pressure on me to 'reach out.' She gets it...he just thinks I am throwing a hissy fit and should grow up. But I didn't chase him with chainsaws or hit him or emotionally abuse him. Now my parents understand that, they don't even bring it up.

Sally Cat That's great (apart from the toxic relationship you previously had to endure) x

Silva I have had to cut out my sister and her two (now adult) children. My sister is a woman almost 70 now, but she has been in a relationship with someone else's husband for 40 years. Our moral compasses are worlds apart. She likes to 'stir' – she deliberately keeps in touch with the person I once lived with (I will call them 'G') who was so very toxic to me and psychologically abused me over 15 years. When I was having cancer treatment, just after leaving G, G started a relationship with an 18-year-old who was of course easy for G to manipulate. G was 40 at the time. My sister is in close contact with them and their 3 children. Sends cards, has them round at Christmas. My niece is a narcissist, very self-absorbed. Example – when I married, my niece was a bridesmaid. I asked her to keep an eye on the tiny bridesmaids (as she was in her thirties) for me and she flew into a rage, saying it was 'her big day and she would be centre of attention' so why was I ruining it for her by asking her 'to babysit'? My nephew, her brother, abandoned his 2 tiny children when he cheated on their mother. He married the woman he cheated with and had 2 more kids but ignored his first 2 girls, saying he wished they'd never been born. Anyway – enough! To me all 3 are toxic and I have cut them out of my life. Sorry this is so long (again). I guess in my mid fifties there's a lot of 'past'.

Can I just add that having not talked about these things to anyone for years, this is actually stirring things up in my head but in a healthy way – like a catharsis. So thank you for that, Sally. This feels like a safe place where no one will say, 'But she's still your sister…!'

Vanessa Haszard In a methamphetamine-facilitated acting out of my ongoing patricidal urges, aged 20, I set fire to my parents' bed, with nail polish remover as an accelerant. The house was completely gutted, and I had no contact with either of my parents for a little over a year.

All four of my grandparents attended my first wedding which was some four months later (he proposed to me in the visitors wing of Mount Eden Prison!) I can't remember who reinitiated contact between Mum and me, but that led to renewed contact with Dad as they were still together at that stage.

My second husband-to-be and I moved 600 km away about three years after the arson.

Mum and Dad divorced about the same time I divorced number two, eight years post arson, and Dad makes less than no effort to contact me (the only time I hear from him is if he wants me to do something for him that is geographically convenient to me).

I have made the effort to facilitate a relationship with his biological grandkids, and sent my daughter to stay, etc., but he makes zero effort himself.

I can remind him three times about a birthday, including on the day, and he still fails to call her and say happy birthday, send a card, whatever.

I finally emailed him saying no more a few weeks back, following an unfortunate call to my grandmother to see how she was, which found me on the phone to him when she insisted we say hello. He triggered hell out of me as he mostly does, and was then totally confused as to why I was upset. It upset my grandmother, sadly.

I actually regret not having given up years ago, but it is just a reflection of my pig-headedness.

I have a much better relationship with Mum since she and Dad divorced, and we talk several times a week. I had a weird experience with my maternal first cousin a few years back.

Having drifted away as people do as they age, he initiated contact with me, having cut contact with his parents (who are amazing, and are more like grandparents to my daughter, than great-aunt and uncle, partly, sadly, because they haven't really been able to grandparent their own granddaughter, which is a whole other issue in itself...), and more strangely, our maternal grandparents.

I never managed to establish what his reasons were, and in 2010, when losing our second baby destroyed my third marriage, he involved himself in my husband's breakdown, which was partly caused by me being under section, and unfriended me on Facebook, sending a message that said something along the lines of not wanting this sort of shit in their lives. He hasn't said a word to me since.

He now has some contact with his parents, but the miserable cunt emailed my grandparents this year requesting they stop sending birthday and Xmas cards as they haven't opened any in a decade!!!!! I messaged him via Messenger prior to blocking him so that photos he had me tagged in would no longer be tagged.

The message was fairly pointed, and not polite.

I have warned my partner of the probable need to restrain me in the event he shows up at their funerals.

I said to him repeatedly...'FFS your fucking aunt was speaking to me again within 18 months of me torching her house! What the hell is so bad you can't get past it?' But never had any reasonable explanation.

This same man brought his best friend and his Mrs to my grandparents decades ago, and they embraced them as honorary grandparents as they had new babies, as their parents were deceased!

This man is ostensibly normal!?

It confuses me.

It has meant his parents have treated me and my kids very well, and his loss is our gain, but I see how it hurts people I love very much.

Ruth Very close to my family and still am, thankfully! Pretty sure my Nan and my Mum are PDA. They would antagonise one another but Mum never cut her off. Very close to my Mum as we are so alike (although that can often drive people apart!). Was brought up in a very understanding, loving household and I know how very, very lucky I was! Anything other than that and I would be a hugely different person.

Nat I cut both of my parents out at different times for different reasons. This is going to be a long one!!

My father had some kind of major mental health crisis when I was 6, which left him very different from the loving but slightly odd man I'd known til then. I'd get glimpses of that man, interspersed with abuse. Eventually, when I was about 11, the neighbours called the police and my mum and me were moved into my grandma's house. I waited for a long time to see if he'd 'recover' with treatment, but even medicated he never did. Despite everything, we kept in touch with a few letters a year after I moved away. Then, finally, when I was about 20, I just stopped answering. The last time he spoke was a phone call, where he called me a 'wriggly arse worm he spunked out into a dead badger'. On reflection, I should've cut him off sooner, but I suspect there was some Stockholm syndrome going on there.

My mum was, and is, more passive. She's a people pleaser who chooses terrible people to value. I know she isn't happy and she hurts herself with what she does, but it was definitely necessary to break away from her for a while. She is well aware of the abuse I dealt with from my father and from her mother, but feels that can be brushed aside and insists we were always close. She will lie, manipulate and generally do anything in her power to keep her mother happy even now and it makes things difficult. I'm also estranged from the string of 'stepdads' she chose – all awful people, from pedophiles to rapists, mass-scale smugglers to violent drunks. I don't know what it is in her that makes her seek out people to victimise her, but it's taken a long time to realise I can't put myself in the way for her.

My grandma (mum's mum) has narcissistic personality disorder and I was the target. I had irons run over my arm, public humiliation, physical and mental torture. You name it. She tantrums like a toddler to get her way and was happy to blame me for anything and everything. She's the matriarch of the family, so at this point I'm not in touch with 99% of the family or childhood friends. She's convinced everyone I'm a terrible, spiteful child who moved away to hurt her and my mum who'd never done a thing to me.

My father's family occasionally send a card. They know what he's like (his sister wrote that he raped her in her suicide note) but they prefer to sweep it under the rug as much as possible and I'm an awkward reminder.

My boyfriend, a PDAer also, was estranged from his whole family, but is now back in touch with his mum, stepdad and sister. It's a difficult relationship and not always positive, but they're working on it from both sides. His father essentially decided to dump the 'weird' son and start a new family with another woman. His loss.

Sally Cat Thank you for sharing. It's truly awful what some of us have had to go through growing up. I'm so sorry you experienced this living hell. My mum, when I last saw her, criticised me for praising my little 6-year-old PDAer: 'You don't want to praise her too much!' I retorted, 'Having PDA is hard enough as it is, I think she needs all the confidence she can get.' My mum (passive also, but veiled aggressive) was in a funny mood that visit. I could feel it, but she masked it. I've not heard from her since. I know that her funniness was her issue and not to do with me. Before cutting her out recently for 2.5 years, I always blamed myself for her weird moods and suffered extreme confusion and anxiety for it. This was why I'd had to cut her out: so she stopped negatively affecting me.

Ruby I've had major issues in relationships because, I think, of low self-esteem and naivety. I've been taken advantage of and put up with shitty deals where I've been treated like a second-class citizen. I have felt deeply wounded when people I've loved have discarded me. Being powerless is very hard on my PDA because I need to be in control of what happens to me. Maybe this is why I have been obsessive?

I've failed to understand how my actions would impact others (and not just in being obsessive). I've been a complete bastard without really realising it at the time. I've seriously betrayed people who trusted me (and I feel terrible for this). Once when broken after a boyfriend dumped me (and by broken, I mean BROKEN like I'd been mortally wounded and so anxious and pained that I didn't know how I could go on living) I ended up falling in love with a friend's boyfriend who I'd connected with and who had proceeded to pursue me. I'd fended him off saying it wasn't right. I knew this as an abstract social construct and, as well, I knew this as I didn't want to betray my friend, his long-term girlfriend. But this man kept coming back and I enjoyed his company. We bonded really well. He said I was his soul mate and he was in love with me and convinced me that his relationship with my friend had died. And I, broken in two as I was, found I'd fallen in love with him. I am not proud of this, but we had an affair. I was aware that I was betraying my friend, but believed she'd not really mind because her relationship was dead. I even fantasised that we could all live together happily (they had kids: ouch!).

After a few months, this man decided (crying) that he couldn't see me any more because he had to put his kids first and stay with his girlfriend. I was gutted, but healed. Then someone I'd naively confided in told a bunch of people what had happened when she was drunk and all hell broke loose. I was demonised (not him: he lied to save his own skin and relationship and made out nothing had really happened and he'd been preyed on – just once – by me). I was so anxious, PDA anxious. I was too terrified to face all these people hating me and I slipped away. I gave up this entire social group that had meant the world to me because of this anxiety and because I had no idea how to ever explain that I'd not understood how wrong what I'd done had been in their terms. I could now see that my behaviour had hurt my friend; that I'd betrayed her trust. I have continued to have nightmares in which I want to make it up to her, but am lost for words and too fearful to face her, but feel so very bad. And in waking life, it saddens me deeply that I did betray her and I cannot make amends.

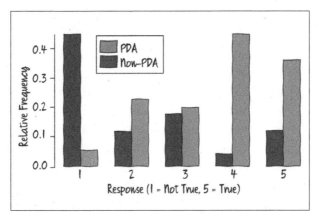

Graph 9: I have had obsessions about people
*From a 'Quick PDA Poll' with 240 PDA and 145 neurotypical respondents*

# OBSESSIVE BEHAVIOUR FOCUSED ON PEOPLE

## From Riko Ryuki's blog

Most, if not all, people on the spectrum have obsessive behaviour. What this means is that they are keenly interested in one particular thing. A particular subject. A particular film. A particular type of toy. Particular objects. My eldest (PDA) son is particularly keen on marine biology; he knows more about this subject than his peers. For PDA people, often the obsession is focused more on one particular person as opposed to a subject or object.

Many people dislike the term 'obsession'. An interest in something that makes them more knowledgeable than their peers, in neurotypical people, is usually seen as expertise. But when that same feature is seen in autistic people it is labelled as an obsession. They make it sound like a bad thing.

PDA people tend to appear more sociable than other people on the spectrum; this may be because they often have more of an interest in sociability. Or maybe it has something to do with control. I'm not sure. Either way, PDA people have a tendency to become overly attached to one particular person. This attachment includes a want/need to know everything about the person, a tendency to treat that person differently from others, an almost possessive preference for that person to focus solely on them and no one else. Some people have said how their PDA child would prefer one parent or sibling over the others, even to the point of excluding the others and becoming aggressive when anyone else would try to include their particular person.

Some PDA people flit from one person to another, becoming obsessed with one person, finding out everything about them and going out of their way to fit the person into their lives before dropping them and moving, sometimes quickly, on to another person. This might seem normal to the PDA person, that once they have gotten everything out of the person that they want, then they are 'used' to the person or have become 'bored' and so go looking for a new person. This can be puzzling and hurtful for the chosen person as they might not understand why the PDA person has moved away from them; they may be left wondering what they did wrong.

Some PDA people can be overwhelming in their obsession and the person chosen may feel smothered. Some like the one-to-one they receive from the PDA person and that they can quickly gather information about the person and are willing to help them in any way.

Not all PDA people will be 'obsessed' with anything/anyone in particular. Some may flit from one interest to the next, becoming highly knowledgeable in them and spending copious amounts of time and energy pursuing their interest, before moving on, sometimes forgetting a lot of what they have learnt to make room for new information. Others will spend years on the same interest, gaining a fair bit of knowledge as they do. Some may not seem to have any interest in a particular thing; this may be because they haven't found anything that interests them yet or their interest doesn't seem unusual enough to have been picked up on by others or it's an interest which isn't easily noticeable such as daydreaming or studying people.

One of the reasons why autistic people are known (stereotypically and not always correctly) as having one particular obsession which they become experts on is because of the time and dedication people on the spectrum are able to give to certain subjects. If neurotypical people were to spend a similar amount of time, energy and dedication to one subject then they too would seem like experts and the idea of autistic obsessions would not have become such a prevalent 'thing'. There's nothing wrong with having one particular interest or flitting from one interest to the next; however, it can be troublesome for others when the interest is in the form of heavy or unwelcome attachment to a person. This is when the PDA person needs to learn how to use boundaries. This may not be easy for the PDA person, especially if they don't know or understand where they are going wrong or are unable to control their impulses. There are times when the PDA person may require some help in understanding how to allow other people space; this is even more difficult if the PDA person is very young as they won't have the ability to understand. Clear instructions delivered in an understanding and compassionate way may be more likely to garner a positive response. However, if both parties are happy with a close attachment then there may be no problem at all, as some people do prefer to have one close friend.

# 10

# HIERARCHY AND RULES

» Rules must stand up to reason and personal ethics
» Respect given where due, not because of arbitrary authority
» Belief in equality
» Respect for necessary rules (although Demand
  Avoidance can scupper this)
» Following own moral compass rather than society's
» Criminality
» Protective of the weak
» 'Demandy' wording likely to trigger the avoidance reaction
» Avoidance of rules
» Dislike of hierarchical formality in language

---

What is your attitude to social hierarchy? How about rules?
Do you respect rules laid out by other people for you to
follow? Do you expect other people to follow rules?

---

Dee Dee  As long as there is a valid reason and logic and I understand why, then I don't have a problem.

Sarah Johnson  I'm classic PDA. I want the rules, analyse if they are ethically right, argue and then give in because I have to. I give in to get along only and because I have the emotional reaction but not the fight. If I could I'd argue being a parent of under 5s is, by definition, being disabled. Do I have the money to take that to court...no? But I would if I could. I get on my soap box. Then everyone yawns and tells me to take a chill pill. So I give up. I toe the line – but in my time (i.e. when it gets tricky or I have to pay out – then I back down, but not without a lot of moaning). War is illegal, old age sucks, parking fees are wrong, not all homeless people are idiots... I could go on...

Plus – I know a lot more than most. I hate incompetence – you wanna tell me what to do, I gotta trust you. There have been about 4 people in my life who I truly am impressed with, role models if you like (one of them died – bastard). The rest talk shite, or don't know stuff. I get on with engineers or relaxed, knowledgeable people who can back up their argument with facts and good examples.

Riko Ryuki I respect someone's position if I feel they've earned it. I don't see people as deserving respect simply for having a 'top' job, but if they can prove they actually deserve the job and my respect then I will happily give it. But I'll still not take their advice or respect them if they try to control me beyond what I feel is reasonable for them to do so. For example, if I am seeing a doctor about a problem and I feel they are a decent and knowledgeable doctor and they have shown that they are able to give correct advice/medical help then I will go along with what they say and respect their authority as far as it pertains to their profession. I will ignore them if they go on to try to tell me what to do say, for example, in my fashion choices outside of medical practice.

I believe all people are equal. No one is better than another person, especially not based on gender, race, religion, age, disability, etc. Some people may be more knowledgeable, more skilled at, quicker, a natural at, etc., but that doesn't make them better overall, just more useful at certain things. Although I would see some people as being better than others or worse than others based on their actions, if you have the ability to do good but choose not to then that makes you worse than those who don't have the ability to do good but try anyway.

I'll follow rules if they make sense, are explained and/or are ones I agree with. I expect everyone to follow these rules too unless there are specific exceptions. For example, if there's a fire I expect everyone to follow the fire procedure but fire people are obviously an exception to that. I tend to challenge any rules

I don't understand the reason for or disagree with. If there isn't any obvious reason for a rule or no one has explained why the rule is there then I will ignore it, even if logically I know there is a reason but it just hasn't been explained yet. I won't wait for an explanation, I'll just ignore the rule and blame the rule maker for not making the reason clear.

Sarah Johnson  Well said!! I agree...

> I ALWAYS QUESTION RULES
>
> NEVER JUST BLINDLY FOLLOW
>
> I RESPECT RULES THAT ARE
> THERE FOR A REASON
>
> AND SERVE A GOOD PURPOSE
>
> BUT IGNORE ONES CONTRARY
> TO MY OWN ETHICAL CODE
>
> AND ONES WHICH ARE
> SCREAMED AT ME AS DEMANDS
> WITHOUT EXPLANATION
>
> THESE I JUST WANT TO FLOUT

Alice  I'm a stickler for equality and fairness. However, I also respect authority earned by knowledge.

I am very honest (maybe too honest on occasion) to the point that if I am overpaid in change, or have an apple too many in the bag, I take it back.

I've a fair amount of experience of hierarchy, having worked in a 'lifers' prison and also with the army, where I constantly challenged the rules! For example, I was co-leading some play schemes for the army in Berlin and because my equal co-leader was male, the army insisted that they spoke to him about important matters – this really angered me. In the end I got them to understand my way of thinking. I imagine it's different now.

I'm the first to challenge what I see as a pointless rule, however I'm pretty good at keeping rules myself and try to create fairness and equality if organising something myself.

In social settings I see all people as equal and try to ensure that this is the way I behave towards them.

I do expect people to follow rules, particularly if they are about safety. Rule abiding in general creates a peaceful society as long as those rules are fair.

Riko Ryuki Of course, sometimes I agree with the rules, am fully committed to adhering to them, but then demand avoidance comes along and ruins it.

Little Black Duck I'm OK with hierarchy and rules...*to a point*.

I am willing to follow these rules if they are sensible and fair (by my gauge). I am willing to acquiesce, if they have jurisdiction.

I have a HUGE issue when these rules are neither sensible nor fair. When I feel they are over-stepping their remit.

I will usually tell them so, right before I ignore them or leave. If I can't leave (say giving testimony in court or being detained by police), I will sulk. One teacher put in my report I was 'surly' and that's pretty accurate.

Little Black Duck I have different degrees of sarcasm too...on a scale from humorous to go fuck yourself in severity.

Like when a judge made a comment about something I said, on a matter of law, I just went, 'I'm sorry. Being a non-criminal, I'm not that familiar with courtroom etiquette.' That's the sort of shit I do. I will have my say, on most things.

Silva I am almost puritanical about the rules I feel are right and fair – equally I get incandescent about things I feel are unfair. My pet hate is disloyalty or breaking of trust. If I see no point to a petty rule I will ignore it. Laws are different because I believe in fairness and think if we all started breaking laws it would be unfair. As to social hierarchy – I ignore that too and treat everyone as if they are equal; having said that, in a way, I have my own 'hierarchy' in my head – compassionate people, loving people, advocates for weaker souls and animal lovers, are at the top. Shallow, attention-seekers are near the bottom. Right at the bottom – cruel souls. I don't recognise Society's heroes – I have my own and I loathe the modern obsession with celebrities.

Vanessa Haszard  This is going to sound arrogant as all hell, but I have a better orientation on wrong or right on my moral compass than the society I live in, and the legal framework it imposes.

I have little concern for legality, other than in the context of its relevance to my freedom. I try to keep a low profile as a rule, but leave alarmingly large blips on the radar occasionally (the only one that made 6pm national news was in 2014).

I am very much head down at the moment as I have an active suspended sentence for another 6 months, I think.

I do, however, expect others to follow some set of rules. Few comply with my framework, but I gave up expecting that years ago. Most are too lazy to even give it the consideration it requires, so laws are kind of essential for people management, but it doesn't necessarily make them a good indicator of wrong and right.

Sarah Johnson  Yep. I only toe the line to avoid prison – that was instilled in me as a child. Getting into fights, pissing people off, getting followed, people attacking me, me running... I've had all those. But I've been lucky. Plus being a nurse stops me from getting a record (before 16 was another story). My bro is PDA – and he's a copper. Why? Cos the rules are either to be beaten or joined...

Vanessa Haszard  Yeah, the record it turns out makes life itself just about untenable. Unemployable, uninsurable, and therefore just about unable to secure accommodation, it is problematic. However, I decided, having made 40, suicidality was over-rated, and I am in fact going to live to 120 as a burden on society and the taxpayer just because I fucking can!

Sarah Johnson  You's an old duffer now, kiddo. Wouldn't have the energy if you tried. I say to the old tattooed boys in hospital (I'm still a rebel there too) – sign of a misspent youth. They giggle then I get their history. Love 'em. But they're tired and philosophical now. Go and talk to people who need to hear you, Vanessa. Volunteer and have some groovy chats...they're out there and waiting for you to make them laugh. X

Vanessa Haszard  That too, believe it or not, is problematic, won't let me anywhere near children or elderly even in a volunteer role as I have violence convictions (almost exclusively assaults on police officers, I don't randomly assault people!).

You bite a cop or two and they get all excited about that sort of thing.

Sarah Johnson  FFS!! That gets my PDA all in a twist. Good example of the world of bollox!! You could be making a difference to those old beans. What about the streets?

Vanessa Haszard  I do what I can on my own iykwim, help out a couple of community sharing and support groups from the shadows... lol.

**Invisible Rules**

I am judged via the benchmark of Social Rules

That I often don't understand

Though I am often driven to try to follow them blind

And, perversely, when I do understand them,

Demand Avoidance often pushes me to break them

'Rescued' a young borderline from about 300 km away, had her here for 3 weeks, made her a weight blanket, and put her on a bus. I met her in a group on here. She tells me it has made a huge difference to her, and has declared so rather embarrassingly publicly. She is a lovely young woman.

Probably scared her into getting her shit together!

Sarah Johnson  Lovely! Now that's making a difference. Saw a paranoid schizophrenic yesterday at work and I'm like so 'what's the start, auditory or visual, what's the worst?' They were so relieved that I understood. He was in so much pain. There's me, trotting about doing shit. Just do shit, Vanessa. X

Sally Cat  I don't automatically follow rules; as others have said, I question their validity. As a child, we were very poor and I was repeatedly told by my parents that I could not have stuff I wanted. These things were almost always things my peers had, and I felt an overwhelming need to have them too. My mum got stressed by my stress and angry when I begged for stuff, as if my wanting it was a crime. The more she told me I COULDN'T have these things, the more my PDA drove me to avoid the demand of NOT having them. In retrospect, I think I was also hit with unrequited peer pressure. My life felt like a bleak, bereft desert. I wanted the things I couldn't have more than anything else in the world. In desperation I resorted to shoplifting. I found the stealth and danger thrilling and addictive, but maintained a moral code. I decided that it was ethically sound to steal from big business chain stores because they could afford the loss, but vetoed stealing from small businesses.

Mud Wildcat  Yeah, in Glasgow we call that 'The gangster Code', Sally, LOL.

Sally Cat  I was a gangsta by heart as a kiddy wink, LOL.

Vanessa Haszard  Isn't it funny, I was pressed to steal a pick'n mix lolly and went back and returned it, but thought nothing of pounding on someone who teased me about being fat.

Sarah Johnson  I was stealing (in my knickers – melted chocolate, nothing worse) from the age I could go into the shops (around 7). But if I saw a nice person who gave me love...I couldn't. The co-op? Easy pickings...getting arrested at 15 stopped me, but not because it was wrong but because I wasn't prepared to take the consequences. Now I don't steal because I know most of my victims or I don't want to get caught and I have money for things I really want.

**Mud Wildcat**  Hmm. I would nick food when I was wee if I was hungry – no guilt but I saw red if someone hurt animals. One big girl was always picking on me but one day I was hanging with my cricket friend in the bushes. The bell rang, my cricket hopped off and she smashed it. I have no idea what I did to her but she was terrified of me after that. I'm a bit unpredictable to this day if I see innocents being threatened, but I don't get violent I just snarl. Why does anyone follow pointless rules? Surely that sort of thinking is dangerous.

Equally, why do they ignore vital natural rules? What nonsense.

**Sally Cat**  Oh, I get VERY tiger-like defensive of helpless animals!

**Sally Cat**  Also, I think the way rules are communicated is important. For me, there is a huge difference between a sign saying, 'KEEP OFF THE GRASS' (Why should I? You going to stop me?) and a sign saying, 'Please do not walk on the grass' + small print = it is easily eroded by feet' or something to this effect. I'd be much more likely to comply in the latter instance.

Rule-Breaking

My automatic response to rules and directions is to break them...

KEEP OFF THE GRASS

Vanessa Haszard Those signs just about make my feet itch with the need to feel it lol.

Sally Cat They represent personal challenges to me to defy them, ha ha.

Julia Daunt It depends on the rules! Laws yes but 'keep off the grass', no! Lol. I'm very stuck in my ways but like to think I'm a very moral person. I'm not a fan of hierarchy at all. It's not that I don't like it but I don't really understand it. Why are certain people afforded respect or special treatment just because of who they are or what they do for a living? Crazy! To me everyone is equal and everyone deserves to be treated with respect. If you are disrespectful to me then I will be to you. Simple. Most 'do not' signs piss me right off and make me want to break the rules...so I do just put a toe on the grass! Lol

I also like to modify things such as recipes. I find the demand to follow them to the letter too much so I adjust them slightly... PDA-style.

Beth I don't mind rules if I agree with them but if I feel they are stupid or pointless then I won't follow them. On the other hand I get really annoyed at others who don't follow the rules!

I'm not good with hierarchy. I believe we should all be equal and I won't give respect to someone just because I'm told I have to. I could never be in a job where someone demanded respect or where I had to call them Sir/Madam! I also get annoyed if the school calls me and tells me that my child has broken a rule. If I think the rule is stupid then I tell them and then get branded as an unsupportive parent!

Sarah Johnson Saying Sir is easy. Maybe you mean in a position of subservience is what you don't like? As a nurse saying Sir or Madam is easy – as I may be keeping them alive post op...

Beth Yes, I mean in terms of subservience. I always say that if I met the queen I would rock up my leggings and Ugg boots and greet her the same as I do any of my friends.

Sally Cat I have learned Turkish and, confronted by their informal and polite versions of the word 'you', decided to address every-one, including the village mayor, informally. It just didn't feel comfortable to me to 'speak up' to them. I could get away with it because I wasn't anywhere proficient with their language.

One of the things though that made me fall in love with that Turkish village was their hierarchical gaps. The mayor would invite me to sit on a stool in the street and share pide (local pizza) and the chemist, for example, would invite me to drink tea. I loved this.

Beth I love what you said about the Turkish village, I would love it there. People should be treated on how they behave not what their job title says!

Sally Cat Although – boy! – did I clash with their culture when I was informed I couldn't have a second villager boyfriend because I was 'used goods'!

Beth Omg I would not have accepted that either! How rude.

Sally Cat I think I was quite an education to them!

Beth Lol, yes, I can imagine.

Sally Cat A later boyfriend I had there (and, yes, I had more than two, so HAH!) once accused me, when I was wearing a lovely silver mini dress one evening, of looking like a prostitute. I think he regretted his words, LOL. I spent the entire car journey back to the village (we were with others too) going on and on, 'oh look, there's a red light! Shall I get out and WORK?'

Then, the next day, I sprayed my hair pink, back-combed it, donned some skin-tight, plasticky trousers, an Ann Summers chain-fronted top, a chain joining my nose ring and earring; plus loads of black eyeliner (obviously, this had been essential packing for a visit to a central Turkish visit in winter, LOL) and strutted through the village centre to the restaurant he worked in and said, smiling sweetly, 'Do I look like a prostitute now, Ali?'

Beth Lol I love it! That sounds exactly like something I would do!

Sally Cat I did feel very anxious and, in reality, quickly scampered back to the guest house I was staying in, washed the pink out my hair and put on (slightly) more normal clothes. BUT apparently this incident went down as kind of local legend!

Our relationship didn't last, sigh.

I think perhaps the killing stroke was when he told me I'd have to obey him and stop going out if we got married. I literally fell off the bed laughing!

Pink  Rules badly worded drive me crazy. I was on holiday recently and there was a rule that said 'gentlemen must wear long trousers in the dining hall' and I got told this was why I was not allowed in wearing a bikini top. Almost all of the men in there were wearing shorts... I think the rule should have been no swimwear in the dining hall...? Sadly the language barrier that probably created the bar rule also stopped me being able to argue it to closure, so I took great satisfaction in going and putting my skimpiest non-swimwear clothing on instead and heading back in... The poor girl on the door looked incredibly grateful, bless her!

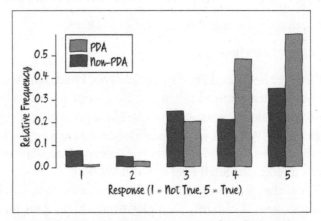

Graph 10: I respect competency rather than rank
*From a 'Quick PDA Poll' with 240 PDA and 145 neurotypical respondents*

# IT'S NOT YOU IT'S ME

From Riko Ryuki's blog

Behaviour. It's a bit like that saying: 'Why worry about what others think of you? They're too busy thinking about what everyone else thinks of themselves to even notice you.' When it comes to behaviour, often people are too busy focusing on themselves. Most people's behaviour is based on what they are thinking and feeling, it usually has little to do with anyone else. Even if someone else has set them off, said or done something that triggered a response in them, the person's behaviour is usually self-centred.

A person could walk up to me and punch me for no apparent reason. The person who punched me would be being self-centred in that their action (punching me) had everything to do with how they were feeling and very little, if anything, to do with me. My reaction, although based on what someone else did, would be self-centred. I'd feel confused, hurt, angry, a bit disorientated. My reaction to the punch would be based on how I felt. Any bystanders watching would react to the situation based on their self-centredness. If they were angry they might react by shouting, attacking the person, swearing, calling the police. If they were shocked and afraid then they might move away or be frozen to the spot. If they got a secret thrill from the punch they might shout with glee, cheer and make rude comments. However they act it would be based on how they feel.

It's safe to say that all humans are selfish. Sure people can (and do) regularly display acts of selflessness. But humans are inherently selfish; we have simply grown to become more than that. All animals have a basic drive to survive. They wouldn't be able to survive if they were going around helping and protecting others. They do sometimes though, usually once their own basic needs have been met. Humans do this on a more frequent basis though and that's because we have the intelligence to understand selflessness and how it is culturally pleasing to be selfless. When a child is born, they are only aware of themselves, their own needs and wants. As they grow they become aware of the people around them and they become aware of their feelings. They feel pleasure at other people's happiness, pleasure at helping others, satisfaction at doing good. These feelings are further validated by those around us. 'It's good to share', 'you should always help others', 'stop being selfish', 'what about George, does he want some too?' etc.

For people with ASD (Autism Spectrum Disorder) and/or PDA, understanding other people's emotions doesn't come easily to them. They can struggle to understand and recognise their own feelings and so struggle to see similar emotions in others. They might not understand how someone feels in a particular situation if they've never experienced it themselves. This means that ASD/

PDA people might seem more selfish than their peers when, in fact, they simply don't have the skills and awareness to be as selfless as people without ASD/PDA. Many people find that, once they do understand, that they are in fact just as selfless (if not more so) than their peers. Of course there are many ASD people who feel emotions more strongly than their peers and so they will hide their feelings as a way of coping and fitting in. This may make them appear uncaring but in actual fact they care so much it hurts to show it.

# – 11 –

# FANTASY AND ROLE PLAY

» Daydreaming and immersive reading as role
  play/fantasy life attributed to PDA
» Immersive serial daydreaming ('Life Dreams')
» Pretending to be animals in childhood
» Role play not coming naturally and being
  instructed by other children
» Aphantasia and lack of fantasy play
» The square circle
» Role playing as a coping strategy
» The relationship between masking and role playing
» Pre-scripting to prepare for interactions
» Running internal conversations
» Role playing characters from books
» Using role play to avoid demands
» The connection between social role play and 'Life Dreaming'
» Role playing a costume character to reduce
  demands of social expectation
» Using role play in work during customer calls
» Professionally writing role playing games
» Role playing to survive: an extrovert version of
  'Life Dreaming'? Auditory daydreaming
» Dislike of playing characters defined by others
» Dislike of school drama classes

» Post-apocalyptic fantasy scenarios
» Childhood difficulty in distinguishing fantasy from reality
» Being unable to role play on demand

---

Being comfortable (sometimes to an extreme extent) in fantasy and
role play are considered to be common PDA traits. Has fantasy
been a significant part of your life? How about role play?

---

Alice  I have always had a rich and enjoyable fantasy life, I was aware
of this as a child and still use 'daydreams' now to self-soothe.

I have also read voraciously all my life, definitely to escape
from reality sometimes.

As a teenager and young adult I became very involved in
amateur dramatics and played some amazing parts.

I often played 'make believe' with my children. All these
aspects, I believe, are part of the role play/fantasy life attributed
to PDA.

Sally Cat  Daydreaming was a major, major part of my childhood.
I had a series of intense fantasy scenarios – each one lasting
for a year or two – that I used to escape the unpleasantness of
my real world. I was always popular and powerful in my fantasy
world. I dubbed this my Life Dream as a late teen. I continued
to dip into Life Dreaming until very recently. I have noticed I
am more driven to fantasise this way when I am under a lot of
stress and/or depressed.

I don't really relate to using role play though. I've noticed my
PDA daughter using it though, for example, pretending to be a
horse when tackling a steep hill. I used to like pretending to be
various animals as a child too. Perhaps this counts as role play?

Vanessa Haszard  I didn't, but Thea was almost always a dog, cat, or
horse for literally years!

As a child, I had a rich fantasy world which I preferred to reality

I never told <u>anyone</u>

Nicola T  I used to spend hours as a kid lying in bed, playing different characters in *real life* happy scenarios. I would have a few characters, all with different voices, and would often fall asleep during these *plays*. I loved it as it was an escape from the real world.

Sally Cat  This sounds very much like my 'Life Dream' serial, in-depth fantasies I had. I always, always fell asleep to them.

Sarah Delderfield (mother of PDA son)  My son's imaginary cats were so vivid. Nearly once had a car crash as one of them 'escaped' out of the car and we had to stop immediately for the cat to catch up with us x

Riko Ryuki  My 4-year-old likes pretend play and involves us. Recently we've had to be Pokemon and fight each other. He also pretends to be a robot and has acted out PJMasks (a cartoon).

Jenny Penny  I have spent a great deal of my life in fantasy because the reality was awful. However, I can tell now that my imagination is not that great; it's very repetitive.

**Sally Cat** Jenny, my fantasies would be very repetitive, but I do think I've got a good imagination…

**Macushla** Role play did not come naturally to me. I shall be forever grateful to a bubbly little 5-year-old who took me under her wing when I started school. During one wet playtime she ushered me into the 'Wendy House' and thrust a large doll into my arms saying, 'This is your baby you have to undress her and put her to bed.' When I continued to just stand there looking mystified, she grabbed it out of my hands saying 'Here, like this' and proceeded to demonstrate how. After which she showed me how to iron the baby's clothes, and sweep the floor. I didn't quite see the point as it was not real, but I dutifully did what she told me, and gradually during that term began to understand that 'pretend play' could be fun.

**Sally Cat** What a gorgeous story – and great memory.

**Silva** Macushla, your story warmed my heart. The power of a simple act of kindness, and your willingness to try!

**Sally Cat** Incidentally, Macushla, I can remember, aged about 9, in school, being told off by another girl for picking a baby doll up by its head. She scolded me for not having been gentle with the doll.

**Vanessa Haszard** It is the one trait that confounds me. Thea certainly fit it to a T, but absolutely not for me. I didn't even 'get it' as a child. In fact, to be honest, unstructured play didn't appeal. I like DOING things, making things, arts and crafts. I loved board games, and the idea of D&D thrilled me. I had a basic set and some books, but no one would play with me.

I have struggled to 'play' with my kids too.

**Vanessa Haszard** I am also aphantastic, so I don't know if that might be a limiting factor. Thea is able to visualize.

**Sally Cat** It might impact. I have very strong visualising ability, and have effortlessly conjured up fantasy worlds in my head (not that I'm trying to show off or anything!).

**Vanessa Haszard** I have some spectacular 17-way conversations with myself, and can think somewhat mathematically, i.e., I can plot a circle mentally, but not see it.

**Sally Cat** Conversely, aged 19, I had a boyfriend who'd done a philosophy degree. He was most impressed by my untrained ability to intelligently debate with him. He was not impressed though when I said I could visualise a square circle. He'd told me it was an accepted philosophical basic that imagining a square circle was impossible. I guess the philosophers who came up with this 'universal law' hadn't taken PDAers into account!

**Vanessa Haszard** Hahaha a square circle!? My OC traits and penchant for maths scream at me even reading that...lmao.

**Sally Cat** My then boyfriend was outraged, LOL. It's easy, I told him, I can just SEE it in my head, no problem! LOL

**Vanessa Haszard** Hell, even writing the words next to each other is cringeworthy.

**Sally Cat** Not to me! Ha ha. A square circle is a mighty fine shape IMO.

**Vanessa Haszard** Lmao...it is 7am, you will fuck me for the day if you make me think too hard about this.

**Sally Cat** How about a round square?

**Vanessa Haszard** That's it, my day is going to be a mindfuck! Lmao

**Sally Cat** Vanessa, I've made you a picture of a square circle, just to brighten up your morning xxx

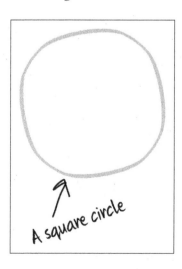

A square circle

Silva Massive, massive, massive part of who I am, Sally. I used
to drive my friends mad as a child making up characters and
wanting them to join in with my desire to act out roles. Very
active in amateur dramatics at school but not a major part
of curriculum then – was an 'after school' drama club. I have
even, when in unhealthy or difficult relationships, taken on a
character and role played her (or him!) as a way of surviving. I
once house shared with a childhood female friend for years –
(I was avoiding coping with man–woman relationships due to
suppressed issues from child abuse). She said she was 'in love'
with me and threatened to kill herself if I left her. I couldn't deal
with all that as well as a stressful job (the bitch ward manager
was then too) so I would adopt characters in order to cope. Just
thought I was weird. That's what she used to call me – amongst
other things like freak, bitch... Maybe I AM a freak? X

Sally Cat I've been wondering if role playing is the same, or similar
to masking.

Silva That's such an intriguing question. For me, the lines are
definitely blurred.

Tony Enos Masking and role play can often be one and the same for
me.

Sally Cat This is what I've been suspecting. I think, personally, my
masking is more of an unconscious process: an ensemble of
mannerisms, phrases and gestures amassed through experience,
whereas role play is perhaps a more conscious act?

Vanessa Haszard I don't know why but your comment immediately
brought to mind something I wrote decades ago:

All I need
Is to cry
Is to scream
And mourn every passing of each
Broken dream
As I stumble
Through life without

Stageplan nor script
I adlib as I go
Trying to make
The lines fit.

Tony Enos  I would agree to that. Role play can be a more deliberate act, sometimes as a means to an end (that end usually being avoidance of some demand) whereas masking can seem to be more of an anxiety-driven process to avoid ridicule...

Vanessa Haszard  Nice!
    And yes, while I said I don't do imaginative role play, ironically I do pretty much feel everything anyone sees of me is something of a role.

Sally Cat  Hmmm, maaaaaybeee. I'm not convinced that masking's only purpose is to avoid ridicule. I think I use it for additional purposes (although I do fear ridicule). Mostly I just want to communicate effectively, I think.

Vanessa Haszard  Hence my need to pre-script interactions a million times, then get thrown when it plays out differently in actuality because people are so fucking contrary, and unpredictable. Other people do that, right? Run discussion scenarios ad nauseum prior to engagement, so you feel you have some control in the situation?

Tony Enos  Hmmm... Role play can also be a form of escapism for some, while I don't think anyone would see masking as a form of escapism... Role play is not a form of escapism I use as an adult but perhaps I use the technique as I mask? I haven't entirely distinguished the two yet...
    Vanessa, I totally get you about pre-scripting. I spend a ton of time pre-scripting my ideas so that in real-time conversation, I have the ideas locked and loaded and I can spend more energy just trying to transition from pre-scripted idea to pre-scripted idea. Sometimes I may be doing quite well and then I am thrown a conversational curve-ball and boom, social awkwardness becomes suddenly visible lol.

Sally Cat  Vanessa, I have no idea, TBH, but I recently took part in a Cambridge University autism study about masking that sought to gain data on how many autistic people mask unconsciously, and how many pre-plan their social interactions (as you described, I think).

I guess both role play and masking serve as a means for us to interface socially in the absence of in-built, in-depth social reading ability. When people react unexpectedly, we are at a loss because we have no stored responses at the ready.

Vanessa Haszard  I have always been acutely aware of the 'requirement' of effort to appear 'normal'. I grew up thinking it was a given, and I needed to try harder.

Mind you, that was very much the message my father imparted. It was a little at odds with his 'question authority' message, which was of course at odds with his 'never question my authority' message...lol.

Silva  Vanessa, I do the practice/role playing of an imminent scenario if I'm about to do something I've never done before, or for official things like interviews.

Sally Cat  Yeah, I think if I have something like this coming up, I do run through it in my head imagining how I'd respond.

Alice  Vanessa, I practise or rehearse some conversations or encounters when I'm worried about them.

Tracy  I also replay conversations a lot afterwards.

Sally Cat  I think I maybe used to do this more.

Nicola T  Yes, Vanessa, all the time. I thought everyone did.

Little Black Duck  More so as a child but I think that's fairly typical. I think I've worked hard to train myself to be more pragmatic.

Masking, I do see as a form of role play. It's role play with a pragmatic purpose. That of being a socially acceptable person and not being seen as weird.

I'm almost certain my nursing career was built on acting like a nurse, rather than feeling like I was one, legitimately and authentically. I coped by playing the part. Then came home to resume life as me.

Silva Little Black Duck – OMG – lightbulb moment. I think I probably did the same thing. I was a psychiatric nurse.

Vanessa Haszard I definitely daydream, but of conversations, dialogues or multilogues. I think in words.

Sally Cat I run dialogues through my head a lot. I remember as a kid my stepdad praised me for my skill at transcribing imagined conversations. I had little praise as a child so this stuck with me.

Tracy I hear conversations in my head all the time. A lot of them don't make any sense, some of them aren't even in English, I don't know why.

Julia Daunt A big YES, for then and now. I'm just a big kid really. I love fantasy and love to imagine my life differently when life is too much. I'm a big fan of fantasy TV such as The Walking Dead and the Vampire Diaries. I love the escapism and get totally engrossed in the storylines, so much so that I often forget that it's not real. I give names to all soft toys and sometimes a background like where they were born. I talk to and for my cats and I have different personas who sound different from me. I talk in these personas throughout the day. I only do the above with Paul. I don't do it when other people might hear.

Ruth I once played six characters simultaneously in an online role playing game. Other than one other person, no one realised that they were all me! I now write and the ability to easily step into other characters, their body language, speech and mindset fulfils my fantasy needs hugely.

Sally Cat This reminds me of when I was really into reading Lord of the Rings. I took to standing part-hidden by city centre trees and role playing being an elf on watch.

Ruth Sally, I am massively influenced by books, films and television. My favourite characters are usually the odd ones on the edges of society, or paranormal in some way. I identify with that hugely.

Sally Cat This group's great, isn't it? We are normal within it.

Silva Ruth, I write now too and also can easily put myself into a variety of characters/situations and environments. I just see/feel it. It's as if I am that person. Have you ever 'dreamed' as a character? I do that too sometimes – I'm writing a novel and the protagonist is under pressure at the moment – I dreamed a possible 'next step' for her, from the inside, if that makes sense?

Alice  Silva, wow!

Ruth  Silva, that is exactly what it's like for me, writing. Often the characters tell me what they're going to do as if it was nothing to do with me at all. I hear a lot of writers do this, however. I just think we're naturally very good at it x

Silva  Ruth, yes – they go off in directions I hadn't planned. I've also had my characters bring in new characters I hadn't initially thought about. Thank you.

Pink  Copying characters from books I'd been reading was great as a child, but I hated performing in front of people from a very young age, probably because I could feel them wanting me to do it. As a teenager I drifted into what Sally Cat refers to as Life Dreaming. I had an ongoing story going round and round my head, that I continually added to, about a guy that I had a thing for...probably occupied a couple of years of my life.

I do not like dice-rolling role-playing games because, yet again, the performance aspect creeps in, though I enjoy watching others play. Before I realised I was PDA, I described myself as an introverted extrovert; I like to perform on my terms, not anyone else's!

I've got the Life Dreaming thing back again in a more productive way, as I've recently decided to write a story, loosely based on some of my experiences, so the characters are gradually forming in my mind.

Sally Cat  Yes, my Life Dreams comprised ongoing stories, lasting about 2 years a piece. I have contemplated writing a book based on a Life Dream scenario, but never got it together to do so. It's great that this is working for you.

I too haven't really got into RPGs. For me, I think it's because I resist the demand of buying into a fantasy world created by someone else. I like to be in control creatively.

Pink  Yes, I see something and instantly see how to make it better. Although I may not be able to find the words to describe how!

Sally Cat  I was like this when I tried guided meditation. My mind immediately rebelled against the scene I was guided to imagine: it felt woefully lacking in creativity and intricacy. I refused to engage.

Pink  Grin. The guided meditations I've found I can't engage with I've put down to them not being the right one for me at the time. Hurrah for YouTube, basically. It's not unusual for me to go through several before I'll find the one that works for me. Sometimes it's the voice, sometimes it's the music, sometimes it's the words used, but sometimes there's no obvious reason why one works and another doesn't.

Sally Cat  I can't get my head around how role play can be used to avoid demands. Any ideas, anyone?

Riko Ryuki  I know you can use role play to cope with demands. Maybe some avoid demands by becoming a character that refuses to do certain demands?

Silva  Maybe by becoming someone else, you can find alternative coping mechanisms? I do that. If I'm anxious about something, I will 'pretend' to be a particular confident and capable character. Like a stronger version of me.

Riko Ryuki  My son sometimes says 'I can't because I am a robot' in a robot voice; he even moves his arms up and down like one lol.

Sally Cat  Perhaps like my daughter pretending to be a horse to motivate herself to walk (trot) up our steep hill?

Silva  Sally, oh I like that! Bless her.

Riko Ryuki  I keep imagining there's a ghost in the house watching me and judging me which makes me behave better lol. Am gonna freak if I'm right though.

Sally Cat  I used to imagine, not through conscious choice, that I was being constantly observed and judged by a small crowd of people that no one else could see...

Riko Ryuki  My imagination can be a bit too close to reality sometimes.

**Martin Nightingale** In so many ways. You can construct your own worlds and live in them – you are in control in there and you make the rules – and probably with your acute sense of social justice and need for control, that's satisfying. You can socialise in a defined space – it's a game, ludus, and you can be whoever you want in a safe space. You can make cartographically correct worlds or be existential. From retreating inside your head to expanding your mind, it is kind of your choice.

**Sally Cat** Martin, your description is interesting. This sounds very, very similar to the fantasy scenarios I invented and mentally occupied, but without REAL players having been involved. Perhaps a similar social need is fulfilled?

**Francesca** My daughter uses role play to control her circumstances and therefore avoid being controlled, iyswim. So she'll go into one of her scenarios, say being a mum, and then gradually get more and more specific about what I should say in response to her, the tone of voice I should use, etc. Of course there's no point asking her anything while this is going on, like to finish eating or to get undressed for bed or anything. We have to get to the end of the scene first or else she can't cope and we have to start again.

Also she explained to me yesterday that she role plays with her toys to correct things that don't go according to her plan at school. If her best friend is being a bit dominant she'll replay their game between her toys so that it goes the way she wanted and she gets to tell off her friend as much as she wants. She says if it's been a good day she can go straight on to her iPad, but not if things haven't gone her way at playtime. Clever girl, being aware of this and willing to share it with me when she's only 7!

**Sally Cat** DD liked role play from a very young age. She confused the hell out of me when she was one and could barely speak, pointing at me saying, 'Baby!' Then at herself saying, 'Mummy.' At first I thought she was critiquing my parenting skills! Then I realised she wanted us to switch roles for a game.

**Tony Enos** As far as how to use role play to avoid demands: when I would mask all the time I was clean-cut. Short hair, clean shaven, would try to wear my nicer clothes (not to say I wasn't a walking fashion faux pas).

Now, I wear a large bushy beard, my hair is almost shaggy. I wear overalls all the time and rubber shoes that don't lace. I deliberately make myself look like a hillbilly or a hick or one of the 'big dumb ones' because it lowers people's expectations of me and reduces my perceived and actual demand from others. I give the impression to look at that maybe I'm a farm hand or a logger or a janitor or something and not the shining brightest of the profession either. My clothes are comfortable, but let's just say I wouldn't dress like this if I was going trying to meet someone in the dating sense. To look at the image I project, it's a one-dimensional caricature of a person, but it allows people to look at me and put me in a non-threatening box in their mind, and generally dismiss my presence. So by role playing this caricature, most of my conversations and interactions with strangers are highly predictable and limited in depth. Those who know me more closely know that I am intelligent (enough), articulate, fairly perceptive, and anyways I hate tooting my own horn but you get the idea.

Riko Ryuki  My memory is so poor that I struggle to keep role play and fantasy going for a long time. I forget which character I am and what I was doing. I'm constantly starting new daydreams or coming up with new characters because I can't remember old ones.

Silva  Riko, that amazes me – the way you must cope with that every day I mean. X

Dee Dee  My fantasies are too rude or to weird to put on here...my job is role play on the phone, my customer. I can imagine what they look like and their personality. They love talking to me and one asked if I would have his babies because I gave him a discount off the price! I probably am completely wrong but I do enjoy my job but not the complaints part; then I imagine evil thoughts, wishing they were dead!

> ## Being Comfortable with Fantasy & Role Play
>
> Is considered to be a PDA trait.
>
> I definitely relate to the Fantasy part.
>
> I daydreamed a lot in my younger life
>
> I don't relate so much to the Role Play part
>
> I've not got on well with Role Playing games because I don't like someone else dictating my bounds
>
> And I don't especially act out roles of my own devising
>
> But my Masking is perhaps unconscious level Role Play

Martin Nightingale 66% of my work now is professionally writing RPGs. As a kid, I loved them. As an infant, my imagination was very active (over-active). I am not your typical geek in some ways, but I am a geek.

I love books and comics, because of the worlds they conjure and the insights they give me – always have done. I like playing, because ludus is not just leisure between work, but play for the sake of it – and that feels undemanding.

I wish I was in a space to write more.

I escape into fantasy. Sometimes, I wonder if I'm role playing to survive.

Sally Cat I used to fantasise to survive, but it was all contained within my head.

This, to me, suggests that PDA fantasy and role play maybe fulfil the same needs, but perhaps in introvert and extrovert ways.

If these are the correct terms.

Joan Watson Pencils and paper role play is my #1 favourite thing.

**Louise** Role playing to an extreme extent?? Is it possible my PDA ex is taking on the part of Hitler?!

It's not factual! Maybe the effects of being in a relationship with suspected PDA make the person feel like they are dealing with Hitler?! My ex though did make me believe for the first year of our relationship he was younger than he was!

**Heather** This is the most influential 'trait' (?) of why I think my husband and son are both PDAers.

My son's extremely rich fantasy play is one of the things people point to as a reason to disprove his autism diagnosis.

My Asperger's diagnosed husband has been role playing since he was a young boy. It was always about superheroes and D&D type stuff. Then, close to four years ago, he began role playing on a site called Elliquiy, and that pretty much ruined our relationship. Not only was he role playing fantasy as fictional characters, he was role playing as a 'modified' version of himself with the women he was already role playing with as fictional characters.

Like, he would give out his real name, where he lived, yet change the facts of his home life, and his personality was always of a typically neurotypical and romantic emotionally driven man. I often think that 'version' of himself is maybe the person he wishes he could be? If a girl walked up to him in real life, he would have a panic attack and flee for sure.

If any of that makes sense...

**Heather** I should also note that my husband was heavily into drama club, and our son is a total ham and performer.

**Vanessa Haszard** Interestingly my mother's online MMORPG total immersion that my father blames for the breakdown of their marriage. He seems to overlook the fact he is an arsehole.

**Sally Cat** I dabbled with LARP (a friend was involved). I enjoyed being crew and playing different roles. Loved it. I recruited loads of new crew, including my current partner. But on being offered free slots as gamers, I think I pissed the organisers off by writing characters with backgrounds outside their predefined bounds and expanding their constructed world, in a slightly tongue-in-cheek way, to have new bits for us to fit into. I think, on reflection, this behaviour was quite PDA.

Little Black Duck  In high school most of my friends picked Drama as an elective subject. They saw it as easy and fun. NOT ME! I just thought Thank God it's an elective because I elect No Bloody Way!!!!

I panicked at the thought of it. Dismantling my mask to participate and be vulnerable and exposed was not just scary but impossible to conceive as being possible. Terrifying. Truly.

Sally Cat  Interesting! I wished my high school had Drama classes. On moving to a new area and a new school aged 14, I was excited, very excited that they had Drama. It was an option already decided in the previous term though, so I had to beg to be allowed to try it. I found that in reality I was too self-conscious and anxious to be anything but wooden in my acting.

However, as a young adult, a friend prompted me to go for an extras role in a touring theatre company's major production of Roald Dahl's The Witches. I was selected and absolutely loved the experience of performing on a big stage to huge audiences.

Little Black Duck  No. Just Stop!

Sally Cat  I got a certificate that I was a witch and everything, LOL.

Little Black Duck  When I was at uni, I'd go every week to the comedy improv thing. It was research and inspiring. I'm not sure I've seen anything braver than that in my life.

Sally Cat  I got into going to a weekly drama workshop near where I lived. I really enjoyed it, although the team-worky bit (and general social anxiety about performing) was a major challenge for me. I put my hand up to volunteer for a major role on the few occasions that the leader called us to come forward, but somehow he never allocated these roles. I was suspicious that he continually failed to allocate roles because he didn't want to have to pick me. The company then moved to a location two bus stops away and I stopped going.

Little Black Duck  I am so self-conscious that I often feel like I'm performing to an audience in real life...when there isn't one! An actual audience, sitting in judgement of my performance? Yeah, No thanks!

Sally Cat I commented about having experienced pretty much exactly this earlier on in this thread. I used to feel that there was an invisible audience of a few people constantly sitting in critical judgement of me, assessing my every move. I'd even smile and smirk towards them in my dealings with people, hoping 'they'd' approve.

During this same period, I noticed that I assumed 3D recorded music played in headphones had bands playing BEHIND me. I only realised my assumption on realising musicians were recorded so they sounded like they were playing in FRONT of the audience.

Little Black Duck And that makes your dip into drama all the more courageous.

I sort of instinctively knew it was probably exactly what I needed for personal growth...which is why it had me bolting the other way. I'm a chicken shit, lol!

Sally Cat You are, from what you've disclosed through posts here, IMO, phenomenally courageous and strong. You had a nursing career. Weren't you manager? I could never have done this! Big kudos to you! X

The only time I felt super anxious on the big stage was when I knew my friends, mum and little brother were in the audience. The audience then felt 'real'.

Little Black Duck I was in charge on my shifts and was like the manager for them but wasn't the actual manager of the facility.

Being responsible for other people's welfare and lives doesn't scare me as much as performing on a stage. Go figure!

Sally Cat We all have our own fear walls, I suppose. For us PDAers, anyway. I think that to achieve anything, things that non-PDAers consider easy, are major victories over anxiety for us. But who notices? Who respects? Fellow group members here, if we share. This is one of the many reasons that I love this group x

Riko Ryuki I hated drama. Thankfully we only had it once a week for the first 3 years of school. I would never have chosen it for GCSE.

Silva  Little Black Duck, sounds like your role was similar to mine –
nurse in charge but not Ward Manager?

Little Black Duck  Not really, Silva, I wasn't overseeing other nurses.
I was running the nursing home on the night shift, as the only
qualified member of staff. I was responsible for everything. The
65 residents, the three carers and their work, the building itself.
You know, just generally keeping the whole thing afloat.

Silva  Little Black Duck, totally hats off to you! I worked on an acute
forensic psychiatry ward in a unit within a general hospital. It
has closed now – was part of the care in the community thing.
It was 'full-on' but at least we had the entire general hospital
at our fingertips if we needed medical support. I know from
friends that when you were doing what you did, it was largely
just down to you with little back-up. I worked for a couple of
years on a long-stay dementia ward (we had those then) which
was heavy and full-on in a different way. 33 beds. The thought of
coping with double that...leaves me with my mouth agape. Well
done, Little Black Duck! It's a fantastic thing to have done xxx

Riko Ryuki  Most of my daydreams are set in fictional fantasy or sci-
fi worlds. I like to play a singer in some. I love singing but in
reality I'm tone deaf and have severe stage fright. I also like to
imagine myself in post-apocalypse worlds or on planets with
strange creatures. I get bored quickly though and I can't keep
them going for more than a day or two because I start to forget
the details and the story.

Sally Cat  Post-apocalypse worlds have been favourites for me. I
have sometimes had dreams – of the being asleep variety – of
post-apocalyptic scenarios which inspire a new waking fantasy.
I don't daydream much though now. I think it's because I'm
happier in life.

Tracy  You know, I never used to think I daydreamed at all, until
I realized I daydreamed literally all the time. It's one of those
things I just didn't identify as such. I read fantasy novels to
escape reality and I vividly imagine myself within them. I am
often surprised (and disappointed) to look up and realize it was
just a story.

I was always far too self-conscious and scared to do my own role plays, either alone or with friends. I suspect it feels too revealing of what I actually think and desire. For the same reason I do not write or draw or act, though I often wish I could. It feels quite dangerous to envision anyone (even myself) having the opportunity to know me that well.

As a kid, I also had difficulty distinguishing dreams from reality. I still have memories that I don't know if they actually happened or not.

Silva Tracy, I can relate but not to such an extent. When I was a child I recall adults saying I lived in a 'world of my own'. I think maybe we just have a rich imaginative streak – and I would suggest to you, without pressure, that you give writing a go. I find it a great outlet – I think I'd get overwhelmed if I couldn't express myself by writing, even though I am selective about what I share – some of what I write is just for me.

Tracy Just realized that the fact that I always have music playing in my head – either made-up or remembered or tweaked-remembered – is a separate kind of fantasy. I suppose I didn't realize that probably counts!

Sally Cat I often have music playing in my head, often sounding like it is played by an orchestra/sung by a choir, but I am not so much in control of it. At least, I can't make it go away, but I can control elements of how it's performed.

Tracy Sally, I can influence it but usually not control it. Kind of like dreams actually, and there's also sometimes hidden relevance to unconscious thoughts, like in some dreams. Sometimes the same song for days (that gets annoying!!), or sometimes a mashup or a fugue that will play variations for hours. Most of the time I find it amusing and calming, helps me to focus. There's almost always something going on if I pay attention, but sometimes I forget to notice!!

And I often get orchestras as well, playing songs I'm not sure whether I've heard before or am just making up...

Sally Cat There's a name for this, I can't remember what it is, but when I posted about it in this group before loads of fellow members said they experience it too. I wonder if it's caused by a kind of latent creative mode that can also tune into daydreaming, if this makes sense?

It's called musical hallucinations, or musical ear syndrome, I think.

Tracy  I know they're not actually happening, it's in my head not my ears! I get it though...

Before I got braces I used to unconsciously whistle parts of the fugues through my teeth...can't do that anymore, and I miss it... Auditory daydreaming...

Sally Cat  I like that phrase.

Tracy  Sally, actually I think I do tactile daydreaming as well, again under my influence but not my control. I feel stuff or imagine feeling stuff on my skin that is not actually there...does anyone else have daydreams that involve other senses than visual??

Sally Cat  Yes, it makes sense. I think/suspect PDAers as a whole are highly creative and that this may express itself in diverse ways.

Tina  My daughter role plays when she feels???? I don't know what I can call it. For example, we had an appointment with a psychologist for the first time. My daughter was terrified; she was white in colour, shaking, arms folded, and head down, leaving me to do the talking. I usually make a deliberate mistake in the conversation to prompt her into talking, as nobody can really tell what she feels, only herself. Anyway, as soon as I get something wrong, her head comes up, and you can literally see the switchover happen. But...with things like public transport, which she just refuses to do, if I can't take her somewhere, like college for instance, she just won't go. If I say to her, well, why don't you just do the role play thing to catch the bus, and be somebody else, she shouts at me and say's I don't understand, it doesn't work like that. I wish I could understand.

Riko Ryuki  Maybe she can only use role play when she's in a more positive mood. I know I struggle to imagine or pretend when I'm feeling sad/anxious/unhappy/scared/etc.

Sally Cat  And I don't think I'd want to do it if it was suggested to me.

Tina Possibly...I hadn't thought of that! Maybe it's because I'm with her on most things, but she would be alone if I couldn't take her somewhere, so the vulnerability might play a part. Thank you for the suggestion... I understand her a bit more now.

Tracy Maybe she can't do it deliberately; it just happens when it happens. It's like that for me.

Francesca I'd imagine if it becomes a demand it becomes impossible.

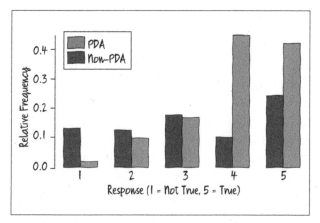

Graph 11: I have (now or in the past) daydreamed a lot
*From a 'Quick PDA Poll' with 240 PDA and 145 neurotypical respondents*

## FANTASY AND ROLE PLAY

From Riko Ryuki's blog

I've hesitated to write about this subject much because for me some parts are rather personal, however the subject can be an important part of a PDAer's life and the lives of the people around them. In this blog post I will be sharing my fantasy and role play and how I use it in my life.

### Fantasy

From a young age I have daydreamed fantasy worlds and stories based on those worlds. I can have quite a vivid imagination and especially enjoy taking worlds from TV/films and books and adapting them to fit my own creative scenarios. One of my favourite worlds is the Star Trek world. I would use the existing characters and include my own characters, making sure I kept the original characters and world as true to the original as possible. Often when reading a book I would stop and imagine myself or a character I created to barge into the story and save the characters or fix whatever was happening in the book. I guess I wanted to be the 'big hero' but I also don't like watching characters I like struggling. I quite like creating new worlds but it takes me a while to imagine up it all, especially since I prefer it to be as realistic/plausible as possible. It is often easier to use an existing imagined world that others or I have created and just adapt that to what I wish to imagine happening. Due to my memory problems, I would constantly have to start over with stories because, while I am able to recall the world and characters I have created, I struggle to remember when in the story I was up to and what was happening.

I have certain worlds created for different purposes. There is one world which is just me and a therapist in a therapist's room; this I use for problem solving. I can discuss ideas and problems I have here and pretend I am getting advice. Sort of like using an ideas board to bounce ideas off. This helps me as I am far better able to communicate in a daydream than in real life, and often the answer we are looking for is one we already have but just need time to come to terms with.

As far back as I can recall I've always daydreamed about being rescued from my life. I would imagine some distant relative appearing with a house all set up for me and lots of money. They would whisk me away from all my problems and make my life all better. As I've gotten older this type of dream has changed a little (now I imagine some distant relative has died and left me with a big house with servants and money), but the overall idea has stayed the same. Another daydream I have is that every other person on the planet disappears one day and I'm left alone, able to do whatever I want with nothing to stop me and no one to force me to do anything. While I don't actually want my family to disappear, I do need a fair bit of alone time and I guess this daydream reflects that.

I also have a specific daydream where I have a bunch of friends in a specific world where I look the way I would prefer, I can act myself and no one judges me. I can be myself and these friends accept me and are themselves a little quirky. I daydream fun and fights, arguments and other bad things happen but this is good for me because in this world I am in charge, I am safe. I can say what I like and I don't get hurt properly; I can end the story whenever I want to. It's a way of exploring my feelings and desires in a safe setting where I am in charge; I decide what the other characters say and do, everything is predictable and erasable, unlike in real life.

Sometimes I create imaginary worlds and vastly different characters just to see what I can do with them and to explore how far I can push my imagination. I love to create new worlds and different stories. Taking time to escape from reality into a fictional world is a healthy hobby; that's why books, TV programmes, films and games are so popular.

## Role play

Many PDAers use role play as a way of managing demands and their life. They pretend to be animals or they believe their toys or imaginary friends are real. Parents can use this to their advantage by asking 'Tommy the teddy if he can help Simon to get ready for bed' or telling 'Emily the elephant that it's time to brush her teeth (and maybe Jess will brush hers at the same time).' As a child I had many toys and teddies which I believed were real and had thoughts and feelings of their own. This is fairly common in autism [see http://adultswithautism.org.uk/autism-feeling-sympathy-for-objects], with many believing objects have feelings. Even though, as an adult, I know this isn't actually possible, I still emotionally believe that objects and toys are alive.

As a child I pretended to be a dog. I used to act like a cat too. I actually believed I had the same traits as a cat and would lie in the sun sleeping and walk on all fours in a delicate way just like a cat would. I had numerous plastic toy animals who all had personalities and my teddies all had names. While on some level I believed they were alive and existed in their own little world, I never used them to avoid demands, which some children do.

My role play mixes with my fantasy world in that I daydream I am being filmed for a TV programme on a particular topic (chores, uni work, how a PDAer manages their day); this type of role play, where I play someone being filmed, helps me complete demands as I the character I am playing (often myself) have no problems meeting demands. Sometimes I imagine I'm an alien who has to pretend to be human and do all the usual human things to 'fit in'. This does actually make completing demands easier. I have role played on trains that I'm on my way to a book launch, I have role played that I'm an undercover agent pretending to be a uni student who is actually monitoring other uni students, I have role played a gardener who is competing for a prize in a gardening competition. Anything that needs doing demand-wise can be helped along by a little imaginative role play.

# WORDPLAY

» Loving wordplay
» Word preferences
» Never calling children and pets by their real names
» Is the drive to make up new names rooted in demand avoidance?
» Memory issues: making up new words when real ones are forgotten
» Loving puns, double entendres, alliteration and rhymes
» Making up songs

---

Do you enjoy wordplay? Puns? Rhymes? Making
up new names for things or other people?

---

Mark  Totally!

Julia Daunt  I love wordplay. Paul and I use many of our own words
for everyday items and activities and most don't actually make
any sense but they do to me! Lol. He's had to learn it so that
he can understand. Can't beat them, join them, I guess! Lol. I
love puns, so long as I'm making them! Lol. I don't like sarcasm
because I find that the line between wit and hurtful is very thin
and most people mess up sarcasm and take that wit too far and
piss me off or upset me. I know I'm not the only one but most
people suck it up I guess, whereas I don't.

Jenny Penny  Love it! It's one of the few areas where I can bond with
my son in hysterical laughter. I love rhymes, alliteration, puns
and euphemisms.

Alice I love wordplay, word games, not so much puns but definitely the sense of the ridiculous in word use.

My family has many names for things, largely initiated by me. I have lots of nicknames for my children and they continue to evolve and come to me. I have also made up rhyming songs about their names.

The same goes for our pets; they have names that are similar to their names so they respond e.g. Tilly becomes 'Tiddly Diddly', etc.

I love making words up. I also love certain words and loathe others! I was very interested when I saw this PDA trait. I thought I was just a bit odd with my wordplay!

Silva I thought it was just me too. I hate certain words and love others.

Sharron Madderwords I never call my children or my pets by their real names; it just seems weird. My daughter and I have words and phrases that only we understand. Anyone listening would think we were crazy.

Sally Cat You should hear myself and DD! E.g., 'Your name's Hallibagger, is this OK?' 'It is! And your names Flibbity Flobbity Wingy Woo.' 'What a great name! Come along then, Hallibagger, time to flimbity flob your ningle plop!', etc, etc.

Sharron Madderwords We add random endings to words and sit making silly noises at each other. Bloody hilarious we are.

Sally Cat Many of the names myself and DD invent involve odd sounds, which I can't convey through typed text!

Sharron Madderwords I'm showing my daughter this and she's all 'see, Mum, we're not weird!'

Sarah Johnson My kids are called Banana, Boy, Shmoo and Beff. I also gave them names that could be shortened. Annabelle, William, Elizabeth and Amelia. My husband calls Millie Dave. She doesn't like that. The dogs are Roo and Bobbalish.

My dad is the best at wordplay. We giggle when we invent new names. Is that a release for a PDAer? Giggling at our silliness? I think so...

Sally Cat I've wondered whether my wordplay, re-naming drive might be rooted in avoidance of having to call people, pets and objects by their customary names, coupled with PDA creativity.

Sally Cat I have always felt happily compelled to re-name people. I remember this backfiring on me aged about 8, when I gave two girls cards (Christmas cards, maybe) calling them Karen Parrot (instead of Garrett) and Zebra Sofa (instead of Deborah Soper). I'd assumed they'd be delighted by the names I'd invented for them, but they were deeply insulted and angry with me.

I called my secondary school friend Omelette. Older still, lodging with the single mother of a 2-year-old in my twenties, I felt compelled to call my friend's daughter Bottle. She reflected when she was older that she'd hated this.

Thankfully (very thankfully), my PDA daughter loves me inventing silly names for her. I have lost count of how many names I've given her. Now aged 6, she likes making up silly names too. On reflection, she hasn't always liked the names I've given her. Aged 2, she once objected, 'I'm not a fluffy, little pancake and I'm not called Margery!'

**Alice Haha** my daughter who's called Bethany objected to 'Bethanothanoth' which was a shame in my view.

**Stephen Wright** I call my friend Russel 'Russel sprouts'...I can't tell how he feels about it yet lol.

**Silva** Sally, your 'Omelette' comment made me smile – years ago I called my friend's son Colin 'Collywobbles.' He is now 35 but I still think of him as Collywobbles.

**Riko Ryuki** I'm not so keen on names. As a child, few of my toys and teddies had names. I tried as a child to create my own language but I struggled to remember the words I'd used and what they meant. I like words to tell a story but I'm not keen on rhymes and poetry. I do like using unusual names for story characters though and sometimes it can be interesting to find out what a word means or where it originated from.

My brain is slow to respond so I'm really crap with wordplay, although do appreciate it eventually! I often accidentally use wordplay without realising it though, and people think I'm making jokes...good when it goes down well, I guess.

I often make up words for things when I can't remember the real word, and sometimes they stick.

**Silva** I love wordplay, even puzzle type books and crosswords. I write poetry and have done for decades. I have a lot of 'alternative' names for things too but there is logic there somewhere. Like my husband enjoys single malt scotch whisky, and I'll ask him if he'd like an 'Andy' which is my word for scotch. It's from Andy Stewart (you need to be British and a certain age I think – he was a TV character who used to do the New Year's Eve Shows on TV). He was a small man and a Scot. So an Andy is a little scotch. Our dogs are 'Baddy Bumptious' and 'Doozylittle' (not their actual names – just what I call them). I often call my husband 'Dilly Dally' or 'Fuddlepip.' No idea why.

**Martin Nightingale** Yep, I love wordplay, puns, double entendres, swears, silly rhymes, some poetry (but nothing high-brow), nonsense and improvised foolery.

**Silva** Martin, do you like Ogden Nash's poems? Make me giggle: His 'Ode to a Goldfish' is said to be the world's shortest poem – it goes: 'Oh wet pet.'

**Martin Nightingale** Yes! And some Milligan, Ivor Cutler, Attila the Stockbroker, Lear, Lewis Carroll, Benjamin Zepheniah, John Cooper Clarke – but anything too literary and I bow out! I prefer very angry or very silly (or both).

**Sally Cat** My PDA daughter composed this, aged 3: 'Oh, the clack we had! With buttons and bushes. Clocks and quocks. Yo, ye, yow.'

**Stephen Wright** More recently I've realized that sometimes a way to see what a person knows is to talk in code...if they understand... you can tell which level of understanding they have achieved. The art is in making it rhyme and making it funny too...then you can extract even more meaning.

In a good way! It is good to know who you are talking to...

**Little Black Duck** Words seems to be an area where my brain is very flexible. It just does its own thing and won't be locked into the English language. Nonsense words are joyful to my soul.

**Sally Cat** And to mine and my daughter's.

**Little Black Duck** Yes and J's [her son's] too. Like you and your daughter, we also connect through our secret cache of words and meanings. It's like a secret club. In true PDA style and form, J has dubbed his own version 'Jackanese'. How do you not love it, right?!

Sally Cat  That's so PDA-cool.

Little Black Duck  And Dr Seuss has a special place in my nostalgic heart.

Alice  Agree on all counts, Little Black Duck.

Stephen Wright  Just listening to you guys talk normal is soothing to the soul.

### A PDA Poem

You may think I'm selfish, lazy,
Overwrought, perhaps quite crazy.
I rarely wash nor dress up dressy,
I'm stay at home, but still so messy.
I put things off or just refuse:
My only acts are ones I choose
And I choose to help and give and share,
Although I'm stubborn, I deeply care.
I'm driven by heart and not by money,
I'm off the wall and – yes – damned funny!

Ruth  I have been called out on my pun obsession in another group to the point I refer to myself as a pundamentalist.

I have books I wrote in infant school with pun-filled stories (e.g., A dog woofing outside Barklays Bank) and just today I remembered a pun I made aged 8 or 9 that my teacher quoted years later.

I love wordplay, puns, writing limericks and anything where there are rules with words that I can exploit to comic effect. I think it's one of the major advantages of a PDA mind.

Sally Cat I love puns. I get a high from pulling off a really apt one. For example, I visited Hanging Rock when I was in Australia and delighted in asking a trekker I passed, 'How's it hanging?' (a clichéd Aussie phrase) – oh, it makes me smile and feel sooo good just to recount this!!

I'm also collecting a photo album (in a slow, Demand-Avoidant-friendly way) of carrying out activities in punnily named places. For example, I have a photo of me drinking beer in Beer, south Devon and my daughter in her robe by a full bath in Bath. Very satisfying!

Ruth It's that opportunity to make connections. Sort of like matching but a good pun/gag just clicks neatly and if good is usually socially acceptable and well received. Same with my poetry which is usually comic and rhymes.

Tony Enos Rhyming, alliteration, puns, my girlfriend and I can go back and forth all day. Wordplay is one of the things we really bond over. It's wonderful to have that in common.

Beccy B Seriously starting to wonder if I might have some PDA traits now! Nik and me are constantly rhyming, have nicknames for each other, pets and friends and have songs which we make variations of for different situations. He's singing one right now to remind me we're out of dried fruit bars!

Oh! Also, Nik and me have our own 'code' language. Some words are specific to the two of us, whilst others are known in our friend group. I forget where most of them came from but for example 'snoof' is how Nik privately tells me he loves me. It's a word for the nose bumps we do when he has stubble and I can't bring myself to deal with the texture for a real kiss. It also means that understanding between us that, when one of us can't do something, the other will accommodate and still carry on loving just the same. It's how we sign off messages and how we keep our mushy feelings time private.

**Sally Cat** I also love making up rhymes and improvising songs. I enjoy finding creative rhyme matches and/or being able to sing an entire, rhymed improvised song without pause. I have made up songs for DD since she was a tiny baby. Some of them she remembers affectionately, such as the nappy changing songs ('Dry Ba Dooboo' and 'Nappy Potato', LOL).

**Alice** I made up songs and word games to play in the car. We had such a laugh in the car! My nephew, on hearing of our word games, once said wistfully 'we have to listen to music in our car'. Some of the songs are instilled into the children, in particular the 'phone number song' (I taught them how to memorise our landline with this) and 'Let's all do the Boo' – a nonsense song with their names in.

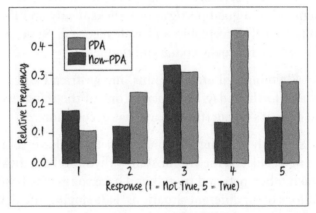

Graph 12: I enjoy wordplay
*From a 'Quick PDA Poll' with 240 PDA and 145 neurotypical respondents*

# WRITING AS A PDAER

From Riko Ryuki's blog

I quite like writing, getting all the thoughts and information from my head to the page feels great. As a PDAer though, this isn't always easy. There's so much preventing me from writing that I'm actually surprised I get as much done as I do, but it's not nearly as much as I would prefer. So what exactly is the problem? And what do I personally do to help?

Perfectionism – the bane of my life. Everything has to be perfect. I'm sure this trait adds to my OCD. Thankfully it hasn't impacted my writing that way; it can for some, but having the need for my writing to be perfect can really impact on what, if anything, I write.

I have always wanted the first draft to be the only draft. I don't like editing as I feel it should be perfect the first time round. This means I may spend ages going over and over what I want to write and how I will write it, so that I end up not writing anything at all. Often, by the time I've perfected it in my head, there's no time or I have no energy left to write it down.

Most of the time I will get stuck at the planning stage and never reach the writing stage because it doesn't sound good enough to me. If it's not right in my head then I won't write it down on paper. If I leave it too long then the original idea starts to sound stupid, so I don't get round to writing, because the enthusiasm for the idea has gone.

The solution – someone once said that it doesn't matter what the first draft is like, it doesn't have to be perfect, it's about getting the overall idea down that's important. Grammar, spelling, correct details, consistency, etc. can all be done in the second, third, and so on drafts. The same person, a published author, showed the difference in their first draft and their seventh (yes) draft. The difference was remarkable. This has helped me loads. I recognise now that my work doesn't have to be perfect the first time round. It's still hard not to make everything right as I write it, but I have learnt to relax a lot. It helps that it was framed as advice as opposed to instruction.

I try not to think when I come up with a new idea. If I think, I'll start to doubt my work. I get everything down as fast as possible then publish it as fast as possible, otherwise I'll second guess the decency and usefulness of the writing. This means posts get published that may have otherwise been binned that are great, but it also means rubbish posts that should have been binned get published too. At least people get to see raw, unsolicited work, kind of like those 'love me or leave me' people who expect others to take them as they are. Sorry, guys, you'll have to accept me as is, crappy posts and all.

Memory – some PDAers have great memory and others have a decent memory. Mine is rubbish. I often struggle to remember what I had for breakfast, so when it comes to remembering ideas I may as well not bother. I often get carried away imagining word for word what I'm going to write, then even an hour later, when it comes to writing it down, I've already forgotten it all. If I'm lucky I can remember the general idea. The details...no chance. I can forget words literally minutes after thinking them. I've had some absolutely brilliant ideas that have been thought up before drifting off to sleep, that have been lost in oblivion by the time I wake. I usually have my best ideas when I am unable to write anything down.

And then there's the stories, blog posts, ideas which I've started and left for a few weeks/months, only to return to with no idea what I was writing. I constantly have to start from the beginning, redoing hours of work, simply because my memory is crap.

The solution – I try my best not to think when I'm not near my laptop. If I get an idea I jot down the basics then hold on to the forming of the details until I am able to write directly from thought to page. I try to finish what I start there and then. I know if I leave something I'll probably never go back to it, so I don't. I've learnt how to, sort of, work around my memory problems.

Handwriting – I love, love, love writing by hand. I don't use cursive or joined-up writing. I use block and I love it. It's taken me ages to find a writing style I'm happy with. Guess what? My writing style satisfies my sensory/autistic needs. It's all sharp edges, smooth rounds and absolutely no dots above the I's. I love the feel of a pen in my hand and I love making marks on crisp white paper.

So why is this a problem? I can barely write a full page before my hand really starts to hurt. My wrist aches, my fingers are sore, and I have to shake my hand to loosen it up. I grip the pen far too hard, but I struggle to write otherwise. I'm pretty sure I either have arthritis or my wrists are generally weak. One time recently I wrote six whole pages by hand. It was a struggle but I hyperfocused through the pain. Even then I had to stop ages before I was finished and needed many, many breaks just to get as far as I did. For nearly a whole week afterwards my hand was useless. I vowed never to make that mistake again.

The solution – sadly I have to severely limit how much handwriting I do. It's easier for me to write a first draft by hand then edit as I transfer it to computer. That option is now out. I write everything on my laptop. I love my laptop but it will never replace the feeling of writing by hand, although writing by type is miles faster and far less painful. It is a better option, it's just not my first preference.

Demand avoidance – did you think I'd forgotten this gem? Demand avoidance is what makes me not write even after I've scheduled time and gotten rid of distractions. It's what causes me to surf Facebook even when nothing interesting is happening and I want to be writing instead. It's what has cost me valuable writing time and many a great idea. My old frenemy, demand avoidance. Need I explain this one?

The solution – I don't schedule time any more, I learnt that lesson the hard way. In fact, I 'decide' to write when something really important needs doing, like filling in a form or cleaning the bathroom. Whenever I get a brilliant idea in my head I look around and find something truly distasteful that needs doing right this second. That prompts me to write for hours. What's that? Just thought up a magical idea for a story? You know, the bin hasn't had a good deep clean in months. Hello, motivation!

I have a rolling 'timetable'. There are three things I spend my time writing on. My blog, fiction stories and Facebook. When I'm doing one thing, such as writing a story, I will start to become demand avoidant. I start to avoid writing fiction by going on Facebook and writing stuff there. After a while I'll start to avoid that so then I'll turn to my blog. Once that becomes too much of a demand I may go back to Facebook or I may start story writing again. It's a never-ending cycle, but I get stuff done. It works for me.

Research – whether it's a story, a blog post or some other form of writing, research can be needed to complete it. What the research is about will impact how long it takes and how hard/easy it is. Some research can take hours because I get distracted with interest, there's so much to learn and some of the things I end up researching are so fascinating I easily get sidetracked. Sometimes research takes ages because I'm avoiding looking, especially if it's something boring or a topic that I've exhausted yet still need more information about. Some things are obscure so take longer simply because it's hard to find. Others mean a long run around trying to find the stuff I need so that it gets too boring. I end up either distracted or giving up.

The solution – I keep a notebook to write down anything interesting that I find. This way, if I start to get distracted by interesting research that isn't relevant to what I need, then I can write down the details and sources to come back to it later, once the writing is finished. If it's boring I will tell myself I will spend 10 minutes looking then have a rewarding break. This sometimes works and often it's the getting started that's the real issue. Knowing there's a small time limit helps get started and I may get distracted and over-run anyway. I will accept that sometimes I don't need all the information to be wholly accurate; I may add in 'facts' whilst making it obvious that it may not be true. It saves on having to do a lot of leg work.

I'm not too hard on myself if I get distracted by research. After all, who knows when that information may come in useful in the future? I've helped a few people out by relating information I've gathered when researching something unrelated. Knowledge is power!

Editing – I've already stated that I don't edit my work. Can you tell? Especially when it comes to blog posts, what you are reading has come straight out of my brain and hasn't much been changed. I know I should edit; my work would probably read better if I did. But then most of the topics I cover wouldn't get published. I'd rather send my work out into the world unedited and have it help someone than have it perfect and sitting in the dark, never to see the light of the internet. Fiction stories are another issue. I sort of have to edit them, even if it's because the only way I will be able to write any more after having some 'time off' is to re-write what I've already written.

The solution – I rarely read my own work. Yup, this helps because then I can't see how bad it is and cringe. If I knew just how bad my unedited work is then it would make it harder for me to write again in the future. I'd become paralysed by perfectionist need to make my writing better. I've also mostly stopped asking people to give me feedback on my writing. They usually only told me my spelling and grammar mistakes anyway.

When it comes to fiction, I tend to leave my writing for a few months/years till I forget most of what was written. I then re-write it all and class that as editing. Apparently this is a really good idea anyway as it gives you a fresh perspective on your own work. Like looking at something with new eyes.

When it comes to writing, as a PDAer I may have it slightly harder than most. Hopefully, I'll be able to keep on writing and one day I'll be a published author, sharing my work with the world in a different way. For now, I'm happy to keep writing on this blog. One step at a time.

# – 13 –

# IMPULSIVENESS

» Impulsiveness as a means to bypass poor
   memory and demand avoidance
» Reining in impulsivity after becoming a parent
» Fear of repeating previous mania patterns
» Executive function issues
» Impulsiveness as a response to self-imposed routines
» Choosing to have a partner handle money to prevent impulse buying
» Being hit by an overwhelming desire to have something
   (applying this awareness to parenting a PDA child)
» Mental health professionals misinterpreting
   reactive behaviour as impulsive
» PDA impulsivity in relation to dieting and budgeting
» Using pre-purchase research to curtail impulse buying

---

Being impulsive is considered a PDA trait. Do you relate to this?
Does this connect to being restrained, e.g. budgeting and dieting?

---

**IMMEDIATE EMAILS**

I tend to answer emails
immediately
I know this can seem impulsive

But I need to do it while I'm 'in
the zone'
And before I get side tracked
And Demand Avoidance sets in

Jenny Penny I'm very impulsive. Often bump myself or drop things as I'm in such a hurry.

Alice I can be impulsive – sometimes it feels as though it's the only way I'll get to do anything!

But on the other hand, if I don't act on the impulsivity quickly, it might just go.

Occasionally I'll be impulsive about a purchase, but as I've got older I've got more canny with spending wisely.

I think I am tempted to speak impulsively, but have learned that it is best to think first, whereas I was less restrained a few years ago.

Riko Ryuki I can be impulsive. I tend to leave plans loose so I'll say I might go shopping on Friday and then I'll decide on the day whether I'm going through with the plans or not. I make impulsive buys. If I get an idea in my head I prefer to act on it straightaway as otherwise I'll forget/lose my nerve/avoid doing it/get distracted. This might look like impulsiveness to others but I see it as playing smart. I know where my weaknesses lie so I work around them.

**Sally Cat** I relate to this. For example, I tend to answer emails immediately while I'm 'in the zone' and before I get side tracked and/or Demand Avoidance sets in.

**Riko Ryuki** Yes, I've had to adopt a 'now or never' mindset because that's how it ends up playing out anyway.

**Sally Cat** I've been accused of being very immediate. I know I can look over-keen (which grates against my masking drive), but I have to do things in a way that works for me. I have so many invisible issues that can prevent me doing things entirely. Also... thinking about it, I do tend to get very enthusiastic and just WANT to do things NOW.

**Pink** I am the one who would have dragged people out of the cave to see what's over the ridge. However I'm pretty sensible most of the time in my impulsive demands, there's usually a good reason for them.

When I compartmentalise then impulsiveness is the only way to get anything done. I know it looks like scatty behaviour but it's often due to worrying about forgetting (again). Though I have learned to add things to a reminder system and then if it's not important by the time it reminds me I'll know.

I wish I could carry that over to conversations sometimes though – I worry too much about saying the wrong thing so then it doesn't get said.

Little Black Duck  My mouth is more impulsive than the rest of me, lol. I certainly have an impulsive streak and for me, it's very much tied to my self-imposed restraints.

Becoming a mother changed quite a bit about me. Becoming a single mother changed even more.

I'm proud of myself for becoming more responsible and considered and considerate...but simultaneously feel a bit stale and stifled.

Laura Mullen  I can be. But I've learned to question it. I spent 5 years suffering from extreme PMDD (I had PMDD since puberty just not nearly as extreme) which included symptoms of psychosis and mania. I was so very impulsive and it got scary. So now any time I feel the 'impulse' I worry. Even though I no longer suffer the PMDD, those feelings scare me. It keeps me from doing many things though. So I've gone from one extreme to the other. I still do impulsive buys based on how I am feeling. If I feel sad, then I want to buy things to make me happy, and no I know that doesn't work. But other than that I fight it all now.

Ruth  Compulsive, not impulsive. I go with gut feeling but still prefer to give thought to decisions.

Stephen Wright  Executive function issues.

Julia Daunt  This made me smile. I'm the most impulsive person I know. I'm terrible. I get an idea and I have to run with it now. Not later but now. I don't think things through very well, if at all, and yes I rush into things when perhaps I shouldn't. I also tend to just open my mouth and say whatever is on my mind – not always a good idea. Unfortunately, due to demand avoidance, most things I start I never finish. I'm useless at budgeting. I know how things cost and how much we need – that bit I get. It's the restraint and not allowing myself to be tempted to buy shiny things. I'm getting better but nowhere near perfect. I've given Paul all control over my money – it's safer that way. I also don't keep up with how much we have or how much bills are because I then have no idea how much 'spare' money we have so therefore, as long as Paul doesn't tell me, I don't recklessly spend it because I'm scared to leave us with nothing.

Tony Enos  It depends on what I am being impulsive about, I suppose. Like Little Black Duck, some of my impulsive is directly tied to my rigid self-imposed routines. Too long following my routines and one day I decide to up and go somewhere random.

I am terrible when it comes to impulse buys. Not big expensive things usually, but small things that add up: food, something that looks fun, and heaven forbid you take me into a dollar-store near Halloween.

My girlfriend handles the money and it is for the best. That way I have to ask her for the money to get something. She is not super controlling. If I really want something she will let me have it; I may just have to wait until it is in the budget. She hates telling me no and feels bad when she has to so I try not to make her feel guilty about it. If she says we can't afford it, she is not being mean or controlling; we can't afford it.

I would have balked at this arrangement at one point in my life and it certainly would not have worked with other people I have dated, but for us, it works really well. I am irresponsible with money and I know it.

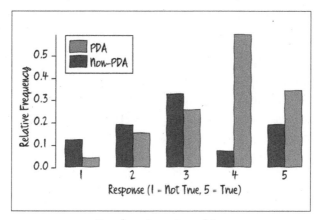

Graph 13: I am impulsive
*From a 'Quick PDA Poll' with 240 PDA and 145 neurotypical respondent*

# IN THE MOMENT

### From Riko Riyuki's blog

Trigger warning.

'Everybody hates me.' 'I'd be better off dead.' 'Everyone would be happier if I didn't exist.' 'I'll just kill myself and then everybody can be happy when I'm gone.' 'Why do you hate me?' 'Everything I do is wrong, why can't I just be right?'

Horrible to hear from someone you love. Horrible to say to people you love.

These are the words family and friends might hear before and/or during a meltdown/shutdown of an autistic/PDA person. There's no doubt that these words hurt; there's no doubt that these words aren't nice. They are worrying words. But are they meant? This is the question someone asked on a Facebook group today. One I quickly responded to.

Sadly, yes. They are meant.

Not as a way of hurting anyone though. Often these words come from a place of deep pain, a lack of self-confidence, a place where the person feels unsure and stressed. Their intention isn't malice, rather they are trying to reach out, attempting to make sense of how they feel and are wanting help. Sometimes they just want to vent, but lack the skills to do so in a socially appropriate way. When a person says these things they are venting their hurt or frustration; maybe they want to be left alone or want to feel better about everything, but they lack the skills to ask properly so they use what skills they do have to get what they need. This means they come across as selfish or mean when they are actually trying to make sense of the situation or wanting help managing themselves.

In the moment, the person does actually believe what they are saying. To them it feels like they are bad or wrong or a waste of space. They actually feel like no one cares about them or that everyone would be better off without them around. They feel like they are simply in the way of everyone else's happiness. It's like a big black cloud of unpleasantness has descended upon them. It's not something they can control and it's incredibly difficult to escape from. In that moment logic has left the building. There's only emotion left and that emotion is one of intense negativity.

In that moment I know realistically that everyone doesn't really hate me, but my brain isn't working properly, the logic side of it has been taken over by an unruly negative emotional side. All I can see and feel is every bad thing that has ever happened to me. It comes crashing down on me and it's really hard to remove myself from this negative thinking. Sometimes my mouth can be saying 'you hate me' and inside my head a little voice will be saying 'why are you saying that, you know it's not true', but my mouth takes no notice, it carries on sprouting non-truths and hurting those I care about. At that point all the positive parts of me have switched off, my mind no longer cares, it just wants whatever caused the situation to stop. At that point I can't connect to other people and how they feel, it hurts too much to try. It's like trying to escape from quicksand. This is when I need to be left alone the most, to ride out this storm until the emotional side has exhausted itself and the rational part of my head can finally take over. For days afterwards I will also be extra sensitive, even the smallest thing can send me back to that quicksand. I need time to recover.

It's times like this that I feel most like my brain is so disconnected from my body. It's like being inside a machine with all these buttons and dials which you use to control the robot. Except the buttons and dials change every few seconds and the window which shows me the outside world is constantly shrinking and enlarging, misting over and clearing, moving around erratically so I can't quite concentrate on one thing for long enough to make sense of my surroundings. And every so often the machine will stop working altogether or will go out of control, going on a rampage which I have little to no control over.

# 14

# ROUTINE

» Love/hate relationship towards routine (liking the certainty, but hating the boredom and craving freedom)
» Routine and time keeping as demands
» Every day as a blank canvas
» Loving routines we are in control of
» Memory issues preventing routine
» Autopilot reducing demand levels
» Is autistic routine-love at war with PDA routine-hate?
» Disliking lists and schedules
» Flexible ordering of mini routines
» Finding lists helpful
» Starting autopiloted routines being the Demand Avoidance hurdle

---

PDA is classed as an Autism Spectrum Condition.
Loving routine is associated with autism. Do you love
routine? Does it comfort? Does it chafe?

---

Joan Watson  Yes, love it. But don't like to be rushed; but if I'm not I'll spend the whole day on it.

Vanessa Haszard  I have a love/hate relationship to structure and routine.

I try to plan things out, literally at length on paper, or digitally, but almost never execute. I consider such to be a huge demand avoidance problem for me.

I feel I need to nail down every last detail for certainty, but then the carrying out becomes a demand. I desperately want that routine in theory, but in practice it becomes traces [an equestrian metaphor meaning to chafe at authority] to kick over.

Sarah Delderfield (mother of PDA son)  Fuck a duck. That's me!

Sharron Madderwords  I need routine because I need to know what I'm doing and when. But I hate routine. It's boring and makes me die inside. There's no helping some people!

Tracy  I would probably benefit from more routine, but I absolutely hate it and always have hated it, ever since I was very very young. I feel confined by it, unbearably restricted. I lose my spark when I feel like my life is inevitably on rails, like a train on the tracks, going from this place to that place with no personal choice or wiggle room. It is the thing that makes me feel like I am going to freak out the most!

I want to just STOP and kick EVERYONE out of my life and only let them back occasionally as I choose, so that I could just do what I want with no one watching and expecting anything – no timetable, no plan, and no reasons. The best day is one where I am alone, with no plans, my family is all elsewhere on vacation, and I can mix everything up and do a lot of things entirely out of order. Cleaning naked in the middle of the night with no one asking questions. Not having dinner. Taking five classes in a row at the gym. Dropping in on friends randomly. Whatever I don't normally do.

Laura Mullen  It chafes. It is a huge demand for me so I'm resistant, hard. In the sense that routine is based on how and when you do things, especially to fit other people in. But because I chafe at routine my life is so chaotic and exhausting.

Sarah S  Nooooooo I HATE routine, and I HATE timekeeping even more!! They are huge issues for me! I'm a fleeter, a fly-by-night, an anti-establishment kinda girl. I subconsciously AND consciously resist all forms of routine!

Silva  When a young woman I loathed routines. They bored me stupid and one reason I chose a nursing career was the variety in working hours – the thought of '9–5' Mon–Fri repelled me.

As I've grown into middle age I find that a certain amount of routine in daily life suits me. I seem to like the structure it affords and it gives me a sense of some security. I still could not stand a routine job though. Having two dogs, there's some need for routine as they need that and that is no problem for me, but how some people do the same thing, day in, day out, for years, I really cannot comprehend. Sally, I just read your comment below and agree – I can find comfort in my own routines, but hate having a routine imposed.

Alice I have mixed feelings about routines. There is a certain amount in the fabric of my life, e.g. hubby and children getting up and going off each day, meds to take, animals need feeding, etc. Then there is the time people return and hope for food! But apart from that there is very little routine. I find that if I decide to do something then I very often can't do it, so mostly I work to deadlines instead of sensible times. Housework has never been routinely done, it might get done as and when. I don't like too much in the diary anyway. I find I am happier with each day as a blank canvas, then I see what happens! There are routines around things like birthdays, I suppose, and Christmas – or are they rituals? I had a lot more routine when the children were younger and when I was working. In my last job I worked term time only, and then I would dread the change of routine at the beginning and end of each term, although once the change had occurred I was fine. So maybe some of that is about change, which I'm not very good at.

Silva Alice, I REALLY get the 'each day a blank canvas' thing x

Sally Cat I like having things to look forward too, like holidays, but I have to have had control in organising them and I like a lot of build-up time. If events are inflicted upon me, especially in close succession, I severely struggle.

Julia Daunt I love routine so long as it's mine and I can change it at any time. I'm routine-like more with things I eat, things I say, things I wear, places I go and TV I watch. I don't really have, or like, a routine with my activities or the times that I do things. My daily routine doesn't exist. Never has and never will. I shower when I'm dirty and I wash up when I can, not when I should, if that makes sense. My way or the highway! Lol

My 'routines' do offer me comfort. Say we go out for a meal it gives me comfort and confidence that it will be in one of a handful of places and when I'm there I will eat one of a handful of dishes. No surprises. No shocks. Very little demand avoidance needed. If it's a routine imposed on me by someone else then all hell breaks loose! Even if I want to follow it I inevitably can't. Strict routines actually make my skin crawl.

**Miguel (9-year-old transcribed by his mum)** M says 'I like routines that are my own routines. They give me comfort and a feeling of security.' 'The ones that others try to put in place are unbearable, like that dust cloud feeling'.

He does like the odd little bit spontaneity too in life if it's something he likes to do.

**Sally Cat** Same for me. I find comfort and the ability to remember stuff through having some self-imposed routines, but I cannot have them imposed on me by other people.

**Becca B** Nik likes knowing that there is a routine – my routine – that it's optional for him to join in with or fit around. I suppose it's the best of both worlds, knowing that plan is there going on whatever happens but with no expectation that he follows a plan himself.

That said, he does tend to fit around it in the same or similar ways.

**Riko Ryuki** I have a bedtime routine, otherwise I forget to do things like take my pill or brush my teeth. I change small bits in it like which pjs I'm wearing or I'll get a new toothbrush. I'm not keen on routine during my day as I can never stick to it and it feels claustrophobic. I can never remember bits of routine so I forget what I'm supposed to be doing. If I'm pushed into a routine by others I'll either go so slow that the routine gets messed up or I'll come up with some reason to not follow it. I prefer deciding what activities to do. I'm more of a 'fly by the seat of my pants' type of person in that I'll only decide what I'm doing as soon as the time arrives to do it.

**Laura Mullen** Sounds like me. I need routine but haven't found a way to establish it so I forget things all the time like self-care and such, but having others' routine imposed on me is a trigger to dig in my heels.

Riko Ryuki  It's taken me years to get a routine down and even now if something interrupts it the whole thing goes to pot. I will also avoid getting started on the routine because I don't feel like I can manage it all.

Sally Cat  Yes, it takes me ages to establish a routine, so it's autopilot. Like getting up, I put the kettle on, arrange the 3 tablets I have to take on the pill box lid, make my tea, use the hot liquid to swallow the pills. Once autopiloted, it ceases to feel like a demand as well, but the trouble is is that I often can't remember if I've actually had my pills! This is why I arrange them on the pill box lid. It gives me a visual memory to refer to. I'm a complex beast!

Sally Cat  Sometimes it feels to me like the autist in me is at war with my inner PDAer. Routines are a great example. Autistic Me likes the comfort and predictability of routines, but PDA Me hates this and finds them suffocating. Autistic Me hates the unknown. PDA Me loves it...

### Routine & PDA

The Autistic part of me craves Routine.

The PDA part of me hates it.

As a result, I only like Routine I have chosen.

It sometimes feels like I'm splitting myself in half.

Pink  This!

Sarah S  Suffocating! Yes!

Vanessa Haszard  Hence me MAKING detailed written plans down to
the last 100g of grain fed to a racehorse, or where every dollar is
going 3 months in advance, but have almost non-existent follow
through...sigh.

Sally Cat  Oh, BUT I can't handle the demand of writing lists and
schedules either!

    I used to be quite good at carrying things in my head, but
this has recently started slipping, so now I keep forgetting
appointments (sigh).

C. Keech  I'm not aware of routine as much as I am being 'set in
my ways'. I have ways I like to do things and efficiency is an
irrelevant factor. So I have routine tendencies but not schedules.
A schedule is a demand, so I will automatically rebel. If I am
told something is happening, even if I'm enthusiastic, I need to
prepare myself mentally so if it then changes last minute I am
left very out of sorts. All built up and nothing to do with it xx

Sally Cat  Yes, I need a lot of preparation time for events, and I need
control of them ideally as well.

    For me, efficiency is a way of carving bulk off demands. If
I action demands efficiently, I am reducing how much energy
and time I give them, so they are partially avoided.

Little Black Duck  For me, it feels very much like a tug of war between
typical ASD (and a helping of OCD) and PDA.

    What this means in reality is that I have no global routine.
But I have lots and lots of mini routines, within my day. Things
like the way I make a coffee. The way I shower myself. The way I
do the dishes. Where I park my car at the mall. Etc., etc.

    So lots of individual tasks follow a set sequence. But the
sequencing of when those sequenced tasks are performed
change. I don't do this, then that, then that. I do what I feel
like doing in that moment...but that moment will be executed
within a mini-routine framework, if that makes sense.

    I love my lists...even if it's just to get it out of my head and
into a concrete form...that I then can choose to ignore or not.

**Sally Cat** I'm with you a lot in this, but I do have my set-to-time routines (like first waking routine and dinnertime, etc.) plus I can't do list writing. I've briefly achieved it and, I must add, benefited from it, but normally it's a demand to me and I avoid.

**Little Black Duck** I'm not dyslexic and that must be a factor for you. For me, it helps my executive function. I need to see it, for it to not be some floating random thought that I'll then keep forgetting. A list 'nails it down', as Vanessa said. So I think it's about how our brains individually process.

**Sally Cat** I am sure my dyslexia and word blindness (plus, likely, my now strongly suspected ADD) all come into play re what is likely to trigger Demand Avoidance in me. I think Demand Avoidance is a very individual thing. What triggers one PDAer may not trigger another at all.

**Little Black Duck** Varies within the one individual too...just to keep things 'interesting', lol!

**Sally Cat** That's true too, if I'm reading you as I think. My own Demand Avoidance varies in intensity. Most thankfully, this week it's at a low ebb.

It's hard to gauge though because when Demand Avoidance is active it's pretty much invisible to me in my low demand-pressure life. I make plausible excuses to myself (and others) about why I don't want to or can't do things and my Demand Avoidance tends to lurk undetected.

Chosen routines also, I think, quash my Demand Avoidance because they become autopilot activities and Demand Avoidance doesn't get triggered.

**Little Black Duck** Yeah that's where the sequenced tasks come in. You just do them, with much less processing demands. It happens, almost like magic, lol.

**Sally Cat** Yup. Individual component 'tasklets', that would otherwise chafe, are blended into a single 'uber task', so less effort is needed to out-think Demand Avoidance.

**Little Black Duck** That's my experience, yes.

For me one of the biggest hurdles is just getting started. Once I start, I fall into the sequence and semi-automatic flow. Like my fridge magnet from many years ago (long before I'd heard of PDA)...'I could be unstoppable...if I could just get started'.

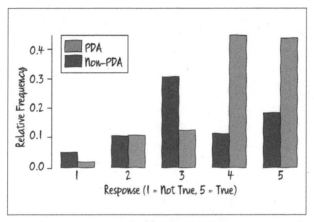

Graph 14: I find routine comforting, as long as it isn't imposed on me
*From a 'Quick PDA Poll' with 240 PDA and 145 neurotypical respondents*

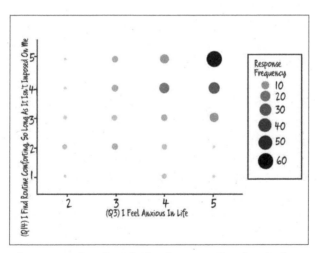

Scattergraph 5: Correlation between Graphs 3 and 14
*There is a moderate positive correlation between 'I feel anxious in life' and 'I find routine comforting, as long as it isn't imposed on me'*

# EXCESSIVE MOOD SWINGS AND IMPULSIVITY

From Riko Ryuki's blog

It's difficult to see how my mood changes are different from typical people's without extensively studying their behaviours. I struggle with understanding how people act/react and the reasons for their actions/behaviour. What I do know is how I act/react and how my mood can change throughout a day.

Most of the time my mood is stable. I don't feel any particular emotion. Often my moods and emotions are triggered by events, mostly external events as opposed to internal, although most of what I feel and do is influenced by my internal feelings and understanding of an external situation. For example: I can become quiet and withdrawn, hardly moving and speaking. This is caused by feeling anxious/threatened/not understanding a situation or how to respond. These feelings are in response to someone speaking to me in a way I'm unsure of the meaning of or about a subject I am unsure how to respond to. Vice versa, if someone were to become angry, raising their voice and being hostile I will feel threatened and scared and will consequently head towards a shutdown, becoming mute and withdrawn.

Sometimes my responses to events and situations can be out of proportion to the thing that caused them. The person that I perceived as angry above might be angry at a situation which has nothing to do with me. Their anger might be slight. They might be joking and I have perceived them as serious. My response therefore will seem excessive and over the top. They may feel my mood has 'come out of nowhere' when in fact it makes sense to me.

It's difficult for people in general to understand how a person thinks. This requires an understanding of their thought processes and how their emotions work. For PDA people, they can have heightened emotions and so have a seemingly higher reaction to events. By typical standards, the PDA person's emotional responses are over-the-top and excessive. It can be hard to control those emotions and act in a way that is deemed 'normal'. Our emotions can come on quickly and sometimes dissipate just as quickly. One minute we can be angry and feeling like the whole world is against us and then feeling happy the next like nothing had been wrong.

Emotionally our responses can seem excessive because of the severity of them. Anger consumes every part of us. Sadness feels like we will never be happy again and the whole world hates us. Happiness can feel like there's never anything wrong, everything is always good and everyone is always nice. Fear is like everything is scary and there's no place to hide. These overwhelming feelings can consume us and not allow anything else to penetrate. Often it's best to let the emotions run their course as they don't last forever.

Because our emotions start quickly and are heightened this can lead to impulsiveness. When we see something we like, we feel like we have to have it there and then. If we don't then it feels like the whole world will fall apart and that we won't survive not having it. A fall-out with a friend can make us feel like everyone hates us and that everyone would be better off without us alive. These feelings can be very difficult for young children to handle. They might not realise that the feelings are out of proportion or that they will soon pass and everything will be all right. Many PDA people don't have the capacity to envision a future where they won't feel those feelings anymore. PDA emotions can often be an 'all or nothing' event.

Explaining what has happened and what might happen can help calm a PDA person as it helps to put the event/situation into perspective. Dealing with the facts and ignoring the emotions can help the PDA person realise that the 'worst case scenario' isn't actually realistic. Feeling like everybody hates you because someone pointed out a mistake you made can feel like that might actually happen. Having it pointed out that the person was only trying to help improve your work and that no one 'hates' you can help you deal with the emotions you're feeling by taking away the power of the feelings. This is a great tool to use for dealing with anxiety. Getting together the facts of what might actually happen, versus what is felt might happen, can help alleviate some of the anxiety.

PDA adults may already have ways of dealing with their emotions and impulsivity. Children will require more help to recognise and deal with their emotions and how they respond to them. Personality also plays a key part in offering help to PDA people as some may be more accepting of help whereas others may respond badly to the offer of help.

# 15

# SCHOOL

» Gifted pupils underachieving because of school structure
» Getting on with fellow pupils, but not the demands
» Being bullied
» Alienation and avoidance
» Difficulties with group projects
» Enjoying school when it is flexible to the PDAer's needs
» Feigning illness to skip school
» Home schooling versus mainstream schooling experiences
» Finding enjoyment through being the class clown
» Adopting a rebellious image to be in control
» Daydreaming to cope

---

How did you get on in school? Did you achieve well academically? Did you get on with your fellow pupils? Did you enjoy it? Hate it? Avoid it?

---

Vanessa Haszard  Shit! I have answered most the other questions, and this is a HUGE one for me. SOOOOOO much to say. Let me take a little time to do it even a semblance of justice.

Ruth  Predicted straight As at GCSE. Did so in the subjects I loved (Art and Science) but not the rest. Aced exams, hated coursework. Teachers held a meeting about me as they were concerned I was on drugs! Ha! No, I just wanted to draw cartoons all day rather than complete their tasks.

Tracy At first I liked school, but although I did very well in some classes, I did very poorly in others. Since it was clear I was verbally quite intelligent and a good reader, it was blamed on my refusal to 'apply myself' or 'achieve my potential'. Even when I was evaluated for learning disabilities (several times) I was deemed to be 'too smart' to have any issues, so it got turfed back to exhortations to 'try harder'. I do believe (now) that I tried as hard as I was able, maybe harder than I should have, because I felt really bad about myself for not being able to do better. I tried to tell them that at the time, but no one really listened. I was very frustrated and sad because I did very much want to learn and do well in school and make people happy and proud of me, but I felt like somehow I didn't have the tools necessary to succeed. Because I didn't know how to predict in which environments I would succeed and in which I would fail, and because I never seemed to be able to explain my failures or get help or turn them around, I found myself very hesitant to commit to anything at all, and my self-esteem suffered.

I had a few friends briefly when I was in early primary school but I quickly lost them as I started to really fall behind socially in about fourth grade. I always felt like I was missing a lot of what was going on and so I didn't give off the right signals and I would confuse people. I didn't dress right and didn't interact right. I was picked on and I hated it and eventually I just withdrew. Later on I found out that people felt I just gave off a vibe of 'leave me alone,' and so mostly the good sort of people did leave me alone, though the difficult ones still picked on me. I felt horrible because it seemed to me that the only people left in my life judged or hated me. I became a very critical person.

Then in late high school, I got contacts and my braces came off and somehow I was now considered 'pretty', and a group of misfit friends decided that their even more oddball friend should ask me out on a date. I spent time with that group of people for the rest of high school, not so much because I liked them as much as because it was something to do and I was lonely. I always felt on the outside and I didn't feel like I understood them or that they understood me. It felt like an uneasy alliance born of necessity – being put into the same unnatural environment and having to deal with it as best we could.

Why I HATED School As A Child
- Social alienation
- Lesson lengths stressed my undiagnosed ADD
- Demand Avoidance against rules, restriction, time tables, the curriculum & authority
- Sensory and emotional overload
- Undiagnosed Dyspraxia made PE humiliating and depressing
- Undiagnosed dyslexia
- Undiagnosed Delayed Sleep Phase left me in pain from sleep deprivation
- Massive Social Anxiety

**Tracy** Oh, and although I have never been able to consistently turn in assignments or study, I am a stellar test-taker, so that was pretty much how I was able to pass.

Also didn't realize it at the time, but I was bullied by my older brother at home starting when I was an infant until I was about 12, and we were both neglected and left alone by daycare providers from age 0–4 years. No place was safe!

**Nicole Dahl** School was awful. Hated class, hated homework. Loved tests. That's how I made it through high school. Failed homework, As on tests. Skipped class most of the time. Best grade I got was in a Geometry class – as long as a student had B+ or better on tests, they were only required to come to class if we had a test. As on all tests – no class – ended up with an A+. I was probably a strange kid – didn't really fit in anywhere too well. Definitely rebellious from an early age. I think I technically failed several grades (2 for sure) but they kept passing me along because I was 'too smart'. Sigh.

**Emily Cool** I managed to make friends but I would always find that I would be friends with someone, introduce them to someone else, then they'd end up being better friends! I was OK with the first bit of getting to know someone, but didn't understand how you get from the 'knowing someone' part to the actual 'proper friends' part. Homework-wise I left everything until the last minute. I would do it in a panic on the bus or in registration. Revision I would always start too late. I would then realise I actually enjoyed it and promised I would start earlier the next time but I never could. Other people would always say they had hardly revised and I believed them but actually it wasn't true. They all revised really hard. I have always been a serial under-achiever. I was lucky that my intelligence got me through to university. I still feel sick at the thought of what I could have achieved. When it came to my music, I found it so hard to practise if anyone else was around as I didn't want to be heard. I also couldn't do it if my mum had told me to. I wanted to play and think I would have done a lot better if left to my own devices. Once I start I find it hard to stop. Starting is so hard though! I remember crying myself to sleep regularly because people were so confusing and I thought I was lazy and useless. I still occasionally have nightmares about realising I'm supposed to be handing in some work that I haven't done, or not being able to find my class!

Tracy Sounds so familiar! Hugs xx

Julia Daunt School was always an issue for me. I've always liked people and enjoyed (mostly) the social aspect of school but I struggled massively with the demands of school life. Although I enjoyed the social side of things I also found it quite difficult to fit in. Children, on the whole, liked me but only at a distance. They tended to keep me at arm's length. They'd play with me at school or sit next to me during coach trips, for example. Not because they were my friends but because I made life more fun for them. I was the class clown and would always do the dare. I wasn't really invited to their houses after school or round for birthday parties. They had other friends for that. I was happy just to be liked and would take whatever level of friendship was offered. Really I was desperate. Things got tougher for me the older I got. I found it harder and harder to mask my behaviours at school and students and teachers were becoming more and more aware that all was not well with me. No one knew what or why but they knew I wasn't typical. I became very disruptive and outbursts happened more and more at school. I was sent home/suspended often. As my behaviour became more and more outrageous children started to distance themselves from me. That left me with no friends apart from others like me – misfits. They accepted me because, like me, they were desperate for acceptance and friendship. When I hit my teens things really fell apart. I was expelled from secondary school after only 5 short months! I returned to education 18 months later, after diagnosis and medication, but to a pupil referral unit. I didn't take any GCSEs but the mocks I took indicated that I would have achieved an A* in English and As in Chemistry, Physics and Biology. I've always known I'm clever so I don't see why I need pieces of paper to tell me what I know already. I'm also a 'Sponge' for pointless facts and my brain stores them up. No idea why as most will never be needed but they do come in handy when taking part in a pub quiz! Lol

Sally Cat I used to love pub quizzes, but my memory is too poor to retain names and dates, etc. I was a self-employed pub quiz writer and reader for a bit. I liked being part of the quiz but being in control and having all the answers! It's how I got together with my partner (he was the champion contestant!).

Julia Daunt Yeah, I never remember the important details either! Lol

Little Black Duck I masked and manoeuvred brilliantly. I think I treated it like an anthropological study (yes, I'm watching 'Bones' this week, lol). Immersed in this culture of people all within 6–7 years of each other (where else does that ever happen in life?) and made observations of everything going on around me.

I've kind of spent my whole life in this kind of observational role, even when I'm an active participant.

Riko Ryuki I didn't mind school. It was boring but I did like being with my friends. I had no clue what I was doing in each of the lessons and I generally daydreamed and doodled the time away. I didn't really care if I did well or not. I didn't really listen to the teachers except enough to stay out of trouble. I rarely did homework and the ones that I did, I did during the actual lesson rather than the work I was supposed to do. I was bullied all throughout my school life only I didn't know I was being bullied until a teacher pointed it out in the last year of primary. Lunch was the best time of school because there was food, but I remember feeling confused and lost many times, especially when my friends were busy or I couldn't find them because we'd been in different classes. There was a bad time when my best friend and I fell out because she wanted to play with other kids which I didn't like, even when she pointed out that I regularly went off with a group of other kids, leaving her behind. I now realise that I wanted her to myself but also wanted to be friends with other people and yet expected her not to play with anyone else. Rather unfair and unrealistic. Despite my oddness, unfairness, sulky, unpopular self, she remained loyal to me. She could easily have been a popular girl with loads of friends yet she stayed hanging around with me and I never realised until now, and I treated her not very well.

Eleanor Smart kid who got bullied a bit (probably more than I realised, actually) for being smart. Always been a bit (quite a lot...) socially awkward and would 'tell on people' a lot, or generally act like I was older and better than other kids. Always did what I was told – which is odd for PDA but I think I liked the routine of it. Scared of getting in trouble. Only really grew into myself aged 14/15 when I lost some of the nerdiness and awkwardness. At uni now.

Sarah Johnson Enjoy, Eleanor! Wonderful time spent with clever people. Absorb the cleverness...

Eleanor Thank you! Am loving it – uni is such a good chance to get involved in lots of things.

Sally Cat I loved uni too.

### University Versus School

I achieved very little at school, beyond learning I was a misfit

And that I wanted to be Free.

I later went to Uni as a mature student

Unlike at school, there was no expectation for me to toe the line and attend every lecture.

I was treated as an adult and given respect and autonomy

And I earned firsts for most modules.

**Becca B**   Nik was badly bullied in secondary school, ended up having suicidal and psychotic episodes and eventually left with no qualifications. He tried again at college and ended up dropping out there. He can't deal with exams or any form of testing, so even though he's really intelligent it doesn't show up that way.

I was a full scholarship kid at a posh, fancy school. I used to play at taking tests, so the entry exam was like a game for me and I flew in – no one told me it was important or what it'd mean if I passed. I daydreamed my way through the social bits as much as possible and was generally considered to be a bit odd, I think, but my scores and work were good enough for them to ignore most of my quirks, low attendance, etc. and the other students were mostly protective rather than difficult. I think school was where I could act out a role like everything was OK while home was falling to bits. Anyway, I stayed on through sixth form then ran hundreds of miles away for university. Hid in the library a lot, did well in all my work and exams, scored myself a first... Then lost out on a grant to do my Masters because I accidentally wound up my personal tutor and he 'forgot' to sign the forms by deadline. In the end, I had to drop out and get a totally unrelated job.

We both have some serious 'what if' moments for totally different reasons. If I'd not avoided all the department get-togethers, optional personal tutor stuff and whatever maybe I'd be doing what I loved. And if they'd just diagnosed him sooner, he might have gotten the support he needed.

Gillian Mead (mother of adult PDA daughter) Never fitted into school, always came out half-dressed, school did nothing to assist her, until the day she came home with her privates torn and bloody, I took her straight to GP who said, 'This warrants further investigation.' Before I knew it, she had a Statement of Special Needs and was moved out!

C. Keech Hated it. I was out before I completed my first year of secondary – on the teacher's suggestion! It was just plain school refusal so being there caused way too much distress. Nothing in particular put me off. I just hated the whole thing, inexplicably but emphatically xx

Jenny Penny Terrible in every possible way. Endless suffering and torment. No friends. Confused, lonely, bullied, lost. Learned NOTHING. I just held myself tense for most of my childhood – it's no wonder my first Alexander technique teacher later commented that I seemed barely alive. Looking back, I fail to understand how I made it to adulthood... If it hadn't been for my beloved friends in Barcelona, and my AT teacher... It's weird now to realise that I am so unusually talented and clever compared to a lot of NTs – if those qualities can be harnessed and helped in our kids, they will be some sort of super race!! And we're so nice too...it's a shame we suffer so. Are we really unteachable? If so, there needs to be such crafty ways to bring out our desire to learn.

Tracy That's right, it's best we teach ourselves and find good role models to study. We are extremely sensitive to hypocrisy. 'Do as I say, not as I do' does NOT work!!

Sarah Johnson Hated it. Worst days of my life. Spent a lifetime trying to work it out. When I realised I had PDA it all fell into place – like a magic formula. All self-initiated based on pain, confusion and an overwhelming desire to fit in and rebel all at the same time. Did I know what I was doing – no. Can I fix it now I know

– yes. So I am onwards and upwards, knowing what failed at school and what I can fix now. Never again...

Oh, and I am lovely and kind and ace. Not things your peer group tell you ever at school. School was cruel, unkind and judgemental. Took me ages to forgive both them and myself. Some I have never forgiven...

Sally Cat I still sometimes have nightmares about school.

Sarah Johnson Me too...nasty bastards...

Sally Cat I remember as a school child yearning to outgrow the 11-year prison sentence that school was for me so I could interact with adults, who I perceived as less vicious and kinder.

Sarah Johnson Yeah – got to college and there were still nasty bastards, but some were just lovely. Still friends with them...

Sally Cat Adults, I think, tend to be less outwardly vile, but society has still been a minefield for me to navigate.

Lauren When I was in high school, if I had to do homework and wash my hair in the same night (which happened frequently as you can imagine), I would get so worked up over it that I wouldn't do either one and I would refuse to go to school the next day (or would go in late). And when I got my first job in high school, working at a restaurant on the weekends, I wouldn't be able to do anything before my 4pm shift. My mom would ask me at 10am if I wanted to go get breakfast and I would freak out and yell, reminding her that I had to work that day...even if it was 6 hours away.

Sally Cat I had a similar experience, except I didn't get on with my secondary school art teacher. I did very badly at school in general (though consistently better in all my final exam results than predicted). I then repeatedly dropped out of college courses, but clicked doing Art GCSE aged 19. I bought a book called something like *How To Succeed in Art GCSE* and mimicked the workbook styles shown in the book. My tutor was excited to tell me that the external examiner had agreed to score me the first ever 100% he'd awarded (I'd achieved the equivalent of 40% in art at school).

I then continued to dip in and out of education sporadically, eventually ending up at uni aged 30 to do a multimedia art degree and earned a fully paid scholarship to Australia to do a graduate diploma in Animation and Interactive Media.

I never wanted a job at the end of it though. I just liked learning and having something to do. I have also trained up to Level 4 as a person-centred counsellor.

Lauren I hated (and still hate) group assignments in school and at work. I always find everyone to be lazy and that they don't keep up their end of the assignment. It bothers me so much and usually I end up doing almost the whole project myself. (I'm a control freak but also most people don't live up to my very high expectations for school or work assignments. And I don't want to look bad/incompetent to a teacher or boss.)

Sally Cat Team projects at uni were soooooo stressful to me. I learned some valuable team skills from the agony, but, like you, Lauren, I used to end up doing a big bulk of the workload to maintain control.

I decided to put myself forward as Director of the class project in the Animation course in Oz. Very stressful! My style was to meticulously brainstorm all the students' ideas, get them to agree on a plan and then police it rigorously.

Lauren I could go on and on for this topic...but I think I'll stop there.

Miguel (9-year-old transcribed by his mum) Loads to say too from M. School was horrendous.

It was a good school and it became eventually supportive but still led to multiple restraints and ended with a two-year period of complete isolation in a room, one to one. M's new school since September has completely acknowledged PDA and has done everything to support him to feel in control. He only likes his school because his school tailors it specifically to him and are flexible with him.

They have even been picking him up every day for the last month to help with flexibility. He has control over his timetable.

Can choose preferred people to work with.

Has farm and forest school there.

They take him scootering and incorporate his interests.

He still has days he can't manage but his school to me is how PDA school should be. His tolerance at home also suffers but he wants to be there.

He could not go without these adjustments x

Sally Cat  Please tell M I think his current school sounds wonderful. I wish I could travel back in time and magic my old school to have been like his x

Silva  As a little girl I loved school and did well there. It was quite a small school and back in the 1960s so didn't have the pressures modern kids get. Secondary school started off okay but I'd been sexually abused as a kid and as hormones kicked in, I just couldn't deal with it all. I would stay home, refuse to attend, etc. When I was bullied/threatened into going back for weeks at a time (before I'd avoid again) I was bullied as I hadn't a clue what was going on in lessons because I'd missed so much. Managed O and A levels somehow (shows my age) and opted to do a degree in psychology because I was desperate to understand what made people tick – myself and my friend's severely psychotic mom included. In third year, as usual, started to avoid and missed lots of time. This is why I now know I work best on my own via online courses. At school, trying to cope, I would disappear into one of my own worlds. Sally, I know you have a wonderful term for this, like a waking daydream where I could cope by altering my reality. It was real to me! I never told anyone about the abuse until I was having counselling, in my forties, as part of my treatment for cancer…wish I'd done it years ago. Oh – and when I first started school I was a wreck – separation anxiety doesn't begin to cover it. We didn't have pre-school/playschool back then so I'd been with Mom 24/7 till suddenly one day – I was handed over to a strange lady in a classroom full of kids, many of whom started earlier (you could then if you had an early-in-the-year birthday). Sorry so long and for rambling. I will shut up now xxx

Sally Cat  The name I came up with for my deep, serial daydreams, was 'Life Dreams' x

Laura Mullen  I was home schooled until fourth grade and my mom was too sick to continue. Then I was in a small public school and my whole life got turned around. I was a good student. I wasn't like the smartest kids, but I tried to be. But I was different from everyone and didn't automatically fold to peer pressure so it made my life in school very hard. I don't have good memories.

The kids teased me, the teachers teased me. I dropped out when I was 16 and went to college.

Elizabeth  I got sent to the headmaster on my first day of primary school for scratching the face of the older girl who was showing me around. I was frustrated because she wouldn't explain to me why I wasn't allowed to use the climbing frame. I couldn't sit still for long or understand rules that weren't explained, which was why they suggested to my parents I be assessed. I briefly had a support worker who the school just used as a general classroom assistant, thinking I shouldn't get too much attention. That led to mum home schooling us. She did try sending us to school again in a different area when I was 10 and it lasted a term. I was good at the work but developed massive anger issues because I didn't get to be in Year 6 owing to a September birthday. I also got a massive crush on a boy who was a bit of an underdog and left a love letter in his bag which got me told off in Assembly. I was going through puberty at the time and had started periods which didn't help. I had an obsession with animal rights. I once got a butter knife confiscated because I was allegedly threatening someone with it. After that term I was home schooled again and never went to big school, which is a relief in hindsight!

Out Of My Element

At school I was like a fish out of water

I was completely out of my element
I was trapped
Floundering
I just wanted to escape and be able to breathe again

Sarah Johnson In juniors I got the 'dap' [was hit with a plimsoll] in assembly for flicking mashed potato in the pudding, a nickname from the teacher, 'jaws', which I hated. But some attention was better than no attention. I worked really, really hard. Then my parents took me away and I moved in the penultimate year to another school. So then I was buggered cos I didn't have any friends and couldn't infiltrate the group – so it went downhill from there...till I was about 35. Then I realised they were all just nasty. Now I choose who I hang around with...

Sally Cat I was 7 or 8 when I stumbled across how to be the class clown. I made all the children laugh by giving a deliberately wrong answer to the teacher and couldn't hold back from then on. I was too scared to talk to the other children one on one, but as you say, Sarah, some attention was better than none.

Sarah Johnson Isn't it sad that we could be so sensitive and no-one notice? Frightened, clever, creative children dumped in a world of competition and clever remarks. We did what we could to survive.

Sally Cat Me too!

Sarah Johnson Bless our cottons – we are the new age. My friends tell me that now. If only someone could have cultivated my wonderfulness then...

Sally Cat I had a strong sense of justice even in infant school. I used to be outraged at Blue Peter for, at this time, having two male and only one female presenter. In the second year of infant school, one hot summer's day, all the boys had taken their shirts and vests off to cool down, so I did too. They were shocked. They told me I couldn't because I was a girl. I told them that this was stupid. If I could they could. I joined the queue, bare chested, to ask the teacher how to spell 'it' or something and was shocked when the teacher on seeing me told me I had to put my vest and shirt back on immediately. It didn't seem fair!

Sarah Johnson I wore a vest and stretchy trousers and wellies well into my eleventh year...got looks, but I didn't care...

Sally Cat I once insisted to my parents on going to school wearing a waistcoat I'd sewn haphazardly together out of material scraps I'd thought pretty. A boy in the playground ripped it and I rushed to the duty teacher irate, telling her that a boy had ripped my jacket. I can remember her saying, 'Oh, you mean the one you made yourself?' Then dismissing me entirely. Again the injustice!!

**Sally Cat** I can remember my first ever day at school, aged 5. I'd been desperate to start school so I could be big like my older brother and not be missing out. I remember first being in that classroom. The teacher seemed kind. She told us all to sit down on mats on the floor. I took a look around at all the other children sitting there, crowding me and I thought, 'I want to be the teacher.'

And I hated school. So. Much.

I couldn't cope with being imprisoned and I didn't get on well with the other children. They used to call me names. Treated me like a dirty outsider. This stung me deeply. I used to cry and beg every morning to my mum or stepdad to let me stay at home. So did my older brother. We traded tips on how to feign illness so as to avoid school. As I grew older, I took to feigning sickness once in school as well or just skiving off and forging sick notes.

## Skipping Shool

I specialised in missing as much school as possible

I used to feign illness.
My older brother gave me the tip of claiming heador stomacheache because there were no outward symptoms for our mother to check.

As I grew older, I avoided school by just wandering the streets for days then handing in forged sick notes when I finally went back

Alice I don't think I ever enjoyed school. I was a good reader before I started primary school (my mother taught me to read at 4), so I was already 'different' and had to go to the class above to get reading books which singled me out and I hated this. I was never very happy. I wanted to stay at home every day and until recently put this down to an insecure maternal attachment. I passed the 11+ which only took note of IQ and went to a 'chalk and talk' Grammar School which I believe didn't suit me and where I was unhappy and had a lot of time off as I feigned illness to avoid school. I didn't achieve my potential as a result, however I later returned to education as a mature student where I was very successful.

It is a sadness of mine that my mother didn't seek help; it surely must have been obvious that something was wrong, although I dare say that in that era it would have been misdiagnosed so goodness knows actually what I would have been diagnosed with and what the consequences would have been. I am so glad that things are slowly improving for today's children.

Eleanor I was off ill A LOT. I missed over half my classes for certain subjects because I had severe emetophobia (fear of vomiting– I'm less severe now) and would bail at the slightest sign of anxiety or nausea. Got pretty housebound – still struggle to do nights away from home/uni. Not really PDA, again, but general anxiety as to life.

Silva Ah, Alice - once more I find myself reading a post I could have written myself. Huge hugs! And I couldn't agree more about today's children.

Sally Cat I don't think there were any aspects of school I liked. I just hated some parts less than others.

I'd always be painfully tired going in (I have had lifelong Delayed Sleep Phase Syndrome and couldn't get to sleep at night early enough to have had enough sleep before getting up for school) I never wanted to go into school and I only did so if I'd resigned myself to not being able to somehow skip it.

My older brother used to verbally bully me walking in.

I felt anxious around my classmates. I did have a best friend in secondary school, I felt safer with her around (although she used to tell me things like 'You've got no common sense!') and she – plus everyone else – refused to call me my preferred name, Sally. Despite this, her friendship made a huge, positive difference. I in fact joined the wrong class because I connected with her in the very first assembly. I was supposed to be in the 'brainier' class, but no one ever commented about my switching. I wonder how I'd have got on if I hadn't switched?

I found lessons interminably dull and excruciatingly restrictive. It was an ordeal for me to sit still for hour-long stretches at a time. I used to daydream a lot as an escape route. I also used to disrupt the class by acting the clown. It boosted my ego when everyone laughed and helped pass the time.

Lunch was an issue because of the social problems I had with the other children (especially in junior school, when I used to have to play on my own, embarrassedly) and I hated school lunches. I now know I have hypersensitivity to taste and food texture. My daughter, in fact, has 'sensory issues' and 'fussy eater' alongside 'concerns of pathological demand avoidance' on her Autistic Spectrum Condition diagnosis.

In secondary school, my best friend organised for us to trade our free school lunches with older girls for cigarettes. This worked better and the rule flouting felt liberating, but my weight probably plummeted even more.

I was called a lot of names at school, like 'Bambi, watch out your legs might snap!', 'Rat!' and 'Sex Symbol!' I wished I could gain weight so I didn't stand out any more. I believed I was so far removed from being attractive that there was no point even pulling a brush through my hair to groom it.

The happiest day of my life was the last day of school, but I pretended to be sad like the other girls so as to mask.

Alice  Those years sound so hard, Sally, I feel for you xxx

Sally Cat  Actually, thinking about it, I did enjoy it when I made the whole class roar with laughter.

I once drew a caricature of Mr Rose, our big-nosed French teacher on the blackboard before class started with this limerick alongside it:

There once was a bloke named Rose,
Who went to bed with a hose,
He said, 'I do beg your pardon, But I can't get a hard on,
Is it alright if I use my nose?'
The class was in hysterics. Mr Rose, when he came in, was NOT amused!!

I was confused when I read up on PDA because all the info was about nightmare children having violent meltdowns I wasn't like this as a child I hid my anxiety

Sarah S  Hated it. Desperately wanted to fit in. Ran out of school constantly because of anxiety from the very first day. Always controlled, forced to be there, despite my feelings. Very shy, and anti-social. On to middle school aged 9 and it was all too much, lots of people, but immersed myself in my work. Did well academically, but was always angry, anxious, bullied horrifically mentally. Expelled for bad behaviour. Forced into a Roman Catholic school, settled a little there, not sure why. A year later into upper school, back together with previous bullies, plus a highly controlling atmosphere. I started to lose the plot a bit. Home life was awful, mother preferring the other two. Made school worse. Ran away a lot. Picked up by police on a few occasions. Nobody cared. The only control I had in my life was school, and I did quite well in exams. Moved on to A levels but didn't like the pressure, so left school and left home. Went to college. Enjoyed the freedom of that much more, but couldn't handle the routines. Left after doing a few courses. Was the start of a self-destructive path.

Vanessa Haszard  I don't remember much about the first primary I attended, from 5 through 7 and a half.

I remember the names of 2 classmates, but no more about them, and a teacher who I really liked, as I went to him for reading first, then was asked if I would like to go up to his class for everything my last partial year there, which I happily accepted. Mum tells me that my teacher expressed concerns at the start of my second year about my lack of social interactions with my peers. In all honesty it is very hard to hold a conversation with a 6-year-old, and adults generally made a little more sense.

Nothing academically particularly excited me, as little was done at school, but at home I had access to a great personal library, and regular trips to the public library with Mum. Mum encouraged reading in the sciences, I spent time doing maths with Dad, and it was probably the time I enjoyed most with him.

As a consequence my level of understanding of a lot of these things FAR exceeded my classmates, and was probably around secondary level by the time we moved in 1982, a few months before my eighth birthday.

Moving to the country from the suburbs should have been awesome. It wasn't.

I remember standing opposite the bus stop watching the kids, and a scrawny, freckly, white blonde boy with the worst teeth I had ever seen started giving me shit. When the 'bus' arrived it was just a van, and we were literally 3 deep in the back seat, and several others.

From the start I was told I was fat, and that this meant I was on the bottom. This was backed up by the bus monitor, and the driver. I HATED them touching me, and was always in trouble for fighting. I got out of the bus a number of times.

I was pretty miserable for about a year, had no friends, and as such was vulnerable to an older boy neighbour over the Xmas break.

When I returned in the new year in 1983 I was befriended by Michelle, who nicknamed me Jumbo, but was fiercely protective of what anyone else might say, and took me along socially in ways that were eye opening to me. She was my first friend. We were just about joined at the hip. School was OK for a bit. Michelle in hindsight ran interference for me, as my partner does now.

She was academically fairly bright, and nothing ever challenged me, so school went quite well. Our teacher in 1984 wrote a very favourable report, but noted that criticism generally resulted in tantrums.

The following year they separated us, nominally because she was so academically ahead that she would go forward a year (she was already a year ahead of me, but they were combined classes), but we weren't stupid and were aware not everyone was so thrilled we were as tight as we were.

My classroom behaviour became more confrontational, and I worked out I was considerably better at most of the things the teacher was trying to teach, than he was. This was slightly disastrous, but out of class I still had my Michelle, and we still spent weekends at each other's places, and secretly planned to run away.

At the end of the first term I went with my brothers to my grandparents for the holidays. When I arrived back I phoned Michelle's place, and her mother told me she was out somewhere.

I put down the phone and panicked!!! I knew she was gone.

They attempted to bring her home several times, but she couldn't stay, and ended up in foster care.

School was hard without her to 'translate' for me, and I frequently fought, and was identified as a bully, because I escalated things to the physical too often.

Mum says she was lucky to get through a week without a phone call or meeting regarding my behaviour.

I had been promised a pony at 13, I got her 2 years early at 11, which I now know was a last-ditch effort to try and turn things around, and find a lever. About the same time another child who often got at me threatened to throw a chair at me. I ended up hiding locked in a toilet cubicle, with a lynch mob of my classmates outside, and she ended up needing stitches in her face, and never coming back to school. She had the lead role in the end-of-year production only days off. Yet another nail in the coffin socially.

In Form 1, 1 had a teacher who actually made an effort with me, and was more perceptive to the class dynamic, and had insight into some of my social issues. He was a good, and competent teacher, whose gentle ribbing was actually very inclusive, and he subtly manipulated things to my advantage for the two years he taught me.

I doubt he has any appreciation of how much I saw, and how much it meant to me.

Unfortunately we had music class with a total twat, and by the end of the first term my music education was over, and I was out gardening in the greenhouse during music for the remainder of the year, as the nasty little man refused to teach me.

On the last day of school I stayed after as many did. Mum worked literally over the road from the school. I walked into the pool compound and was on my way to the changing room when he pushed me in.

Not content with this piece of what might be construed as good-natured fuckery he then picked up my dry towel and threw it in.

I lost it. Chased him round the school grounds throwing water and whatever else I could lay hands on at him and swearing, until someone had the sense to go and get Mum. We were made to apologise to each other some weeks later and he quit teaching.

Form 2 was again eased by the teacher from the previous year, and there ends my primary experience.

Sarah S Well that sounds pretty shit mostly, Vanessa! How did secondary go? Did anyone suggest anything other than 'naughty' then? I think you're maybe 2 or 3 years older than me – and I know autism wasn't heard of then. Special needs was someone with Down's syndrome. That's it. Did you have SS involved?

Vanessa Haszard I was assessed for a couple of 'gifted but fucked up' programs but my parents were resistant. I alternated between genuine masking, and overt hostility.

Sally Cat Vanessa, coincidentally, we moved to rural mid Wales from a city when I was 14. I too thought this was going to majorly improve my life. My school 'bus' was a Land Rover for 3.5 miles followed by a coach. The farm boys used to tease me mercilessly.

I resolutely refused to react at all (in retrospect, I think this was freezing). I made some friends at school, but then lost them. I was desperately depressed and lonely. Developed terrible skin issues (itchy blisters all over me). I travelled back to my home city for every holiday. I realised that the friends I had back there, although they teased me and put me down, at least existed.

### One Teacher...

When I was about 14 or 15, one teacher questioned me about the lack of effort I put into my appearance compared to the other girls.

At this time I couldn't even motivate myself to pull a brush through my hair.

Although his concern meant the world to me,
I felt hugely self-conscious
And was too anxious and shy
to respond at all.

Plus I had one, sole teacher who recognised I had issues. He once asked how come, while all the other girls in my class were dolling themselves up, I made no effort with my appearance. I couldn't tell him – too anxious about exposing my vulnerability – that I felt so far from human that it felt pointless to even pull a brush through my hair, but I deeply appreciated his having compassionately noticed me. I used to secretly long to be rescued during my long, grim school years. But no one ever did.

Vanessa Haszard At the start of secondary school the college I attended streamed initially on information from primary, but then did a comprehensive and broad assessment of language, maths, sciences, logic skills, etc.

I later found out unofficially, as these tests aren't graded and returned, that no one in my year came anywhere near to my almost-perfect score, so they kept me in the top class even in the face of some pretty appalling behaviour and disruption.

Three days into third form 2 classmates decided to call me Jabba, and it was chanted at me as I walked down corridors by entire classes at a time. You can't beat them all, but you can just randomly beat whoever is unlucky that day, and that is pretty much how I operated.

I read on the school bus, as a barrier to interaction, and hated every minute except for when I was handing them their arses academically.

By the last term I was a mess, my allergies were out of control, and fucker classmates had figured some of the spray cleaners triggered my hay fever (and asthma, but nobody had diagnosed that yet), and I don't think I attended after the second week at all.

They put me in the top class again in fourth form, despite my lack of attendance, and a few weeks in Scott (the one fellow student that spoke to me, rather than teased and tortured me) handed me a poem he wrote for me one day.

He didn't want to talk to me at school, but gave me his phone number.

I took the phone into my wardrobe where no one could hear, and poured my heart out to him for a couple of months.

He actually had helpful suggestions regarding my reactivity, and strategies to reduce the harassment I was on the end of at school, but I burnt him out fast, and I was devastated when he cut communication. I became suicidal.

Meanwhile I was top of the form for maths, science, extension maths, and accounting regardless of the ongoing torture and drama.

I sat in class biting myself quietly, trying to curb my anxiety, or was disruptive as hell. I deliberately badly failed the few subjects I couldn't excel at. A classmate in art branded me badly with a heated pallet knife, and I got in as much damn trouble as the arsehole that burned me so badly the skin got stuck to the knife!

Infractions that would normally result in suspensions landed me at the back of the dean's class for a week instead, and when I chose a bitchy girly swot classmate for a beating in late fourth form they decided they had had enough, and the ultimatum was either find another school, or do sixth form the following year, which was only on the table because my science teacher was all kinds of amazing, but the entire school except me, and his wife, seemed to hate him.

I just read in sixth form, didn't even try to really get involved with anyone else.

The Jabba shit continued, but I hid in a book, or my form class, as that same science teacher took on a sixth-form form class for me.

Sadly he left after the first term, and the new form teacher/ physics teacher/science head of department was OK, but he was certainly no replacement, despite it being impressed on him that I needed his office as a bolt hole, and him being OK with that.

Sixth form certificate was internally assessed, and there was substantial assignment work, practicals, and exams, and I didn't want to get found out, so made a bit of effort.

I made the cut of top 4 students that received a cash scholarship award, and got taken out to lunch with the best of all the schools in the greater area. Most schools had flash senior uniforms and blazers; our school was mufti from sixth form. I attended in my Docs, shredded tights, houndstooth skirt, Cure T shirt, and teased hair freshly dyed purple the night before. I remember walking through the packed-out events centre beside the fuckwit ex gang member that was one of the seventh-form deans that accompanied us, and the crowd literally parting before us! Fuck, it was gratifying!

For the first time in my life the staring was in MY CONTROL!

So they assigned me the fuckwit ex gang member as form teacher as well as Dean, and we went to war. He had pissed me off enormously in third form as my science teacher, and I requested a change but was refused, so more or less didn't attend at all after the first term, preferring to get pissed and stoned with a friend I made via my pony.

I had been aiming for a Bachelor of Vetinary Science since about age 8, so asked if I could go back and have a proper crack at seventh form again the following year, especially as on attendance I was ineligible to sit exams, but I was told to sit regardless of attendance eligibility, and managed to scrape a low A bursary, when 8 months earlier I was their best scholarship contender.

I never attended a single social function, was the only senior not to attend the ball in one of my senior years, and one of three in the other.

My horse 'friends' from home avoided me like the plague at school, and of the few from school who talked to me, they would only do so on the phone outside school hours.

I was angry, confused, lonely, suicidal, and anxious from third form on, and at that age it was suddenly occurring to me that I was the common denominator here. Humanity couldn't all be terrible. It must be me!

They were extremely black years, and had I not had my horse I genuinely think there would have been deaths. I am not sure exactly whose, but there would have been a body count.

Alice It's quite amazing that you survived all that, Vanessa – physically and emotionally. You did – you are one incredible person x

Vanessa Haszard Thank you, Alice.
It was a fight. My adulthood has also been a fight. I would love to stop fighting, but if you don't fight you get buried. Sadly if you fight too hard you go to jail. It is a balancing act!

Sally Cat Amazing! Your comment, 'for the first time in my life the staring was in MY CONTROL!' matches my own experience, I think, of 'going punk' and feeling that I was in control finally of people staring at me. What a feeling of freedom and finally grasped power that was! X

Catherine Cross I haven't read the other comments. I daydreamed my way through primary school. Other children weren't too keen on me. Apparently, I was a bit of a bully (when I didn't get my way, I expect). The teachers thought I was 'different'. My reading age was very high.

I don't have fond memories of comprehensive school. For a lot of it, people thought I was stuck up. At about age 14 or 15, I turned into a bit of a tart. Attention from boys was easier to obtain. They made me feel better about myself (I've grown up and learned since).

I never skipped classes, but would try to avoid going to school in the first place. My mum was canny to my tricks though. I started smoking at 15 too. The adrenaline from sneaking out of the grounds to smoke made it a fun thing to do!

I did well enough in school to go to uni. Languages were my strong subjects.

When people used to say, 'Enjoy school, because life gets much harder when you leave', I could have just ended it all. The thought of anything being worse than school? No. Thank. You!

Dee Dee Mmm...school, In my early years I was quiet and shy, a clinger...and a 'looker out the window' dreamer in my last bit of the junior school. I had no interest in the other kids in school. High school I was cheeky, moody, bossy and had lots of interests, collecting, borrowing and stealing...smoking and making a huge profit on selling cigs at school...bunking off quite a lot, hanging round the town. I was overly nice to other kids so I didn't get bullied, I was a bully occasionally myself though...I survived.

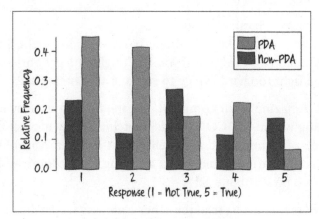

Graph 15: I enjoyed school
*From a 'Quick PDA Poll' with 240 PDA and 145 neurotypical respondents*

# SCHOOL?

School – a place where a bunch of kids are placed into a room and told they have to do certain activities to learn skills that may or may not be needed in their future lives.

For kids, school can be incredibly hard. It's a place full of sensory difficulties, social struggles, loss of control, lots of change and strict routine. Many kids love school and thrive in its environment, but few of these are PDAers. For kids that need adaptability, controlled change, control over activities, lots of space and downtime, school can be full of difficulties which can make it extremely hard and, for some, dangerous.

Some PDA kids mask their difficulties and differences. They appear to be managing okay but they let all their frustrations out once home in their safe place. This makes it hard for schools to see any problems and hard for them to put accommodations in place. Some schools refuse to accept there may be an issue because the child appears 'fine' and they blame the parents for the child's behaviour outside of school. Some kids mask at home and let it all out at school and some kids don't mask at all, meaning schools can see the problems but even with appropriate accommodations school may still be simply too hard for the child to manage. Some kids can end up suspended from school or excluded, some end up in special schools for SEND (special educational needs and disabilities) kids or behaviour problems, sometimes this makes things worse for the child and sometimes it helps.

Many parents home school their children either because they see it as a better option, they think it better suits the child or because the child just can't manage school so it's the only option left. There are a lot of PDA children faring much better home schooled because they have more control, the environment is better for their sensory needs, they socialise on their own terms and in smaller groups if preferable, they learn things they need to know, will use and are interested in and at their own pace or a pace which suits them. There are many positives for home schooling but not every family is able to take this option.

There are many different types of schools too. Some are stricter, some are more flexible, some have knowledge of SEND and readily accommodate, some don't, some have relaxed/reduced timetables where needed, some have smaller class sizes, some have no classes, some have a fixed timetable and curriculum, some are entirely child-led, some are faith schools, some aren't. There's a wide variety out there but not all are available and some are select in who they let apply.

So what is a PDA family to do? Many try mainstream or are mainstreamed before they realise the child has difficulties. This may or may not work for them. Some have tried mainstream and it's failed their child or the child just hasn't been able to cope. Some have always home schooled or gone to a non-mainstream school and it's worked for their child. Whatever the circumstances, the family will know what works and what doesn't for the child/ren.

It's very important that whatever learning environment the child/ren are in that the people working with them fully understand the child's individual needs and are willing to accommodate in every way possible. This is especially essential for PDA kids because of the specific techniques that are required and the difference of environment in which they thrive. There can be no one-size-fits-all thinking when it comes to PDA. PDAers can be vastly different from neurotypical children so they require very different managing.

As parents, especially ones who understand the child's needs, we will advocate for the help our kids need. Sadly, all too often this falls on deaf ears. Either intentionally (what do parents know? they've only got years of experience working with this specific child after all!) or unintentionally (who knows better than a qualified teacher, parents are too soft/anxious/clingy/helicopter). Many teachers/professionals ignore the parents in favour of their own experience/training/opinion, and while it's fine to rely on these things it's also essential that they realise parents do know the child best, they do know what they are talking about and 90% of the time they are right. It would be so much easier if everyone involved with a child collaborated fully and put their egos to one side.

Then of course there are teachers and professionals and parents who do work their best to ensure the child has everything they need, but sometimes it's just not enough. PDA is a disability and as such sometimes no amount of accommodation can over-ride the child's difficulties. There's little people can do at that point except just keep going with what does work, even if that does mean unschooling.

Not everyone learns in the same way either, some PDA children refuse anything that looks like school work; this means the people around them have to teach skills in a way that doesn't look like teaching. Sometimes not teaching the child anything at all frees them up to learn things by themselves. I've heard many instances where a parent or teacher has tried for ages to teach a child to learn something (reading, math, time, toileting) and it's only when they've given up or taken a break from it that the child has suddenly learnt or started learning it by themselves. Learning comes in many forms and not just from school books in a classroom. What we learn isn't all just Maths and English and Science; we learn every day just by being alive and thinking, seeing, hearing, feeling, moving, etc. If a child learns nothing in a school setting, that doesn't mean they know nothing. They may have vast amounts of knowledge in subjects people might not have considered or realised. After all, there was no school when humans learnt to read and write, learnt to grow crops and cook food, learnt to sail and fish and swim and make up sports and discover medicine and build so many wonderful things. For some, school doesn't equal learning, and that's fine – we just need society to accept that.

# – 16 –

# WORK

» Not being able to work because of the demands
» Being unable to comply to unreasonable-seeming directives
» Needing recovery time
» Preferring zero hours contracts and multiple jobs
» Wages being a demand
» Issues with working full time, including
  social, and negative health impact
» Needing friendly treatment and autonomy
» Freelancing
» Demand avoidance against jobs that have become too routine
» Pressure to work despite Demand Avoidance (should
  demand avoidance be accommodated?)

---

Has PDA impacted your ability to work? How are you
with bosses and managers telling you what to do? How
do you get along with colleagues? Deadlines?

---

Julia Daunt  I've never worked so I guess that answers that question.
I would like to say that I've tried getting ready for work by
setting strict routines and by volunteering in a charity shop one
afternoon a week but it all became too much. The demands and
routine needed for employment are just too much. I can't see
that ever changing. This used to upset me but now I think it's

actually not that important. I'm happy and I'm healthy – those are the really important things.

**Fleeing From Jobs**

I've never been able to have a career because I've always felt an overwhelming need to flee from workplaces.

I've just HAD to get away and be Free.

**Vanessa Haszard** I am not sure, given I am probably a complete clusterfuck of comorbidities, however in almost 43 years I think my longest PAID employment was maybe 3 months, maybe twice in that time. I have worked without pay for up to about 18 months.

**Little Black Duck** PDA has impacted my ability to work. And work has impacted my ability to function across the various other aspects of my life. The net result being that I've spent most of my life being qualified, yet under-employed.

I gravitated to a position where I was separated from the gate-keeping onlookers...yet they were still there, in policy and procedure.

I recently left because I felt more policed than I could stomach. I'm pretty good at policing myself, thank you very much, and was drowning in system BS.

**Sally Cat** I think that we PDAers need autonomy in our lives. Being policed by others doesn't work for us.

And being paid a wage doesn't buy out our PDA souls. Being told what to do, how to do it and being constantly monitored remains an issue no matter how much financial recompense is awarded.

Little Black Duck  I understood I was working within a system. All cogs of a bigger machine. That was fine whilst I was in general agreement about the way the machine was operating. But once my values stopped being incorporated into those of the bigger machine, then I had no wish to remain part of it. It was like conscientious objection. I just refused to yield to it any more than I already had been. I'd reached an impasse.

Sally Cat  I think that, as PDAers, we must have a meaningful input into what we plough our energy into.

Little Black Duck  Right. I could adapt (reasonably) to system changes and quality improvement. BUT not when it's not my definition of either quality nor improvement, lol.

Things have to make sense. Can't say that strongly enough. When they stop making sense, I stop participating. The final straw was when we were all told to 'make time to document'. We were all staying back giving unpaid overtime to do this already. So I was like, 'I'm not Mr Time, you deluded, pencil-pushing, bean-counting fuck!', lol!

Sally Cat  For me, I can't act against my heart.

And I certainly cannot act at the behest of a w**ker who's using me like a tool.

Little Black Duck  Documentation is drummed into us from Day 1. It's an essential part of the whole process. The catch-phrase being 'If it's not documented, it didn't happen.' So we all know this. We all do this.

It was the context and tone of this newly appointed uppity bitch that got under my skin. I just knew we were going to have problems.

The business had appointed some master bean-counter. One day, they just escorted the Director of Nursing out of the building, like a criminal, after almost 20 years of loyal service. That was the start of the end, for me.

Perfectionism causes anxiety: hard to keep up

Anxiety over colleagues' opinions

Not motivated by wages, but will work long hours unpaid

Anxiety over wording

Can't cope with deadlines

PDA & Autism issues

Difficulties with multistep processes

**Work issues reported by PDAer & autistic adults**

Can't cope with being told what to do

Demand Avoidance

Extreme issues with paperwork, e.g., tax returns

Can't cope with being confined to workplace

Needs a lot of authority and/or autonomy

**Cara K** Here goes – got a 2:1 degree in accounting, specialised in taxation and went on to get my professional tax exams. work for one of the top accountancy firms in the world at manager level and 1 HAD the potential to progress further. Extreme anxiety which eventually resulted in depression 5 years ago. Have been off on sick leave ever since. Tried to go back to work twice but both attempts failed with disastrous effects for my family. Reason – 1 really struggle to talk to people and meetings are particularly difficult. 1 think 1 coped with work initially as 1 was able to chill and recover when 1 came home from work but when 1 had a family, and especially after my youngest lb was born – he's ASD and PDA – it was impossible to get this recovery time.

**Emily Cool** 1 totally get what you mean about recovery time. 1 think that's why 1 feel like such a failure at the moment. 1 can't cope with much at all because 1 have practically no recovery time, and when 1 do get a bit of time off it's random when it'll happen, like my eldest decided to be asleep all day so 1 have the day free. But because 1 don't know how long it will last and it was unexpected, 1 don't know how to manage my time effectively. Everything feels chaotic. 1 think you did brilliantly before and it's perfectly acceptable to take time from work for child rearing. How old are your children?

Cara K  14, 12 and 8. I have no plans to go back and think I have accepted that I am unable to do so. I can barely cope with family life and all that it brings – I need lots of downtime. I know it's hard but you really should try and get some downtime – take it when you can. I have discovered my dirty bathroom, untidy house, etc. can wait and only do it when I feel well enough. Prioritise what actually needs to be done and remember you are a priority too.

Pink  Yes! I'm much better on a zero hours contract where I (in theory) know I can refuse work, or being a contractor, where I have control over whether I work or not. I'd love to be fully self-employed but I'm not yet knowing what service I'd provide with that aspect. Having multiple jobs with different things to do in each suits my brain.

Sally Cat  I actually do much better working voluntarily than being paid. I can work happily for hours and hours going above and beyond any call of duty unpaid, but wages tend to make jobs into demands for me and then I lose all motivation.

Some Of My Work Issues

I can't cope with being confined in a workplace

I have to have personal autonomy

I need to be spontaneous, not follow directions

I can't cope with bosses telling me what to do

I panic about what bosses and colleagues think about me

Every second I'm at work is Hell

Ruth I have a great full-time job in a position that many are envious of...but, and there's always a but, I have a manager who does not deserve her position and micro-manages to make herself more important. And she loves to take the credit for others' work. She returns from maternity leave in September which I'm dreading.

I also have issues with attendance as I often burn out and migraines, immune disorder and sickness kick in. But I still have my job.

Hate the commute, love the work, but would love to be a full-time author. Working on that.

Sarah Johnson I need smiles, approval, no criticism and lots of love. Then I excel and work my hardest. Bad feeling, bitching and micro-managing. Then I leave. Nice people – I approve and will do my best. Nasty people I will seek and destroy at the first opportunity. Stupid people who are in charge and pretend they are better, I disregard. Grafters who talk sense, I listen. No bullshit and genuine kindness I love. Grumpy resentful workers. I hate. Pay – I don't really care.

Don't do deadlines (too much stress), managers need to leave me to it but keep an eye from a distance. They can't criticise me openly, just make loving suggestions – then I'm like a puppy wanting to please. Colleagues – you better know what you're talking about or I'll write you off. Bullying and snide – I get all agitated and run. Need me? Ask nicely and I'll be there until I fall asleep on the desk. But you have to ask nice...do I make a difference? You bet I do and that's the best bit...

Elizabeth I can work in jobs where I get left alone to do a task without too much disturbance. I've had other kinds of jobs where I started feeling so enthusiastic and as time went on and the pressure built I just lost it. I've been fired twice. Still trying to find my niche.

Riko Ryuki I haven't really worked much. When I did work after a couple of months I wanted to not have to go in anymore. I was relieved when I was let go from one job. I found dealing with a mass of customers during busy hours very difficult; I'd dread the time leading up to it. I really struggled with instruction because I regularly misunderstood what they wanted or forgot what I was supposed to be doing. I also scared the other employees by being weird and deliberately freaking them out (people get squeamish far too easily). I also made silly mistakes and over-stepped boundaries.

Sally Cat  Oh, I'm now dying to know an example of what you did that made your colleagues squeamish!

Riko Ryuki  Lol I used to like telling people facts like 'did you know every night you eat at least 3 spiders' and 'the Egyptians used to pull people's brains out through their noses with a hook after they'd died' and 'you know when a fly lands on you, it pukes on you so it can try to eat your skin'. Some of my facts weren't 100% correct but I don't think they noticed as they were usually too busy trying not to be sick, lol.

Sally Cat  You are a master of conversation!

Riko Ryuki  I've learnt to tone it down now as most people don't like it when you start a conversation with, 'they should always bury people in wooden coffins so that it's easier for the maggots and bugs to get in and eat your remains', haha.

C. Keech  I have only worked as a session singer and a bar person. As a singer, more gigs than not would involve ritualistic meltdown ahead of going on stage (I hate this job, I have nothing to wear, I'm fat, I dunno why I put myself through this) and psychosomatic illness generally of the sore throat variety. As a bar person I loved the social/serving aspect (both customers and colleagues) but hated the clean-down at the end. My manager came up with a system where cleaning jobs were itemised and we signed the ones we completed. My friend Luke used to whip round at twice the speed and then let me sign some of his.

Sally Cat  I've done bar work. I found it less excruciating than other jobs I've done, but still not something I could do much of. I got flustered when it was busy, felt trapped and bored to death when it was quiet and kept getting told off for hanging around chatting with customers instead of working!

C. Keech  I always got in trouble for that but also had the most takings so f*** them.

Sally Cat My first job was in the civil service. I hated every moment of it. I couldn't cope with the shared office environment. The having to stay in one place. The apathy over lost files costing an ex-employee, who had a family, much needed benefit payments. Speaking on the phone (traumatic!) Working within their bureaucratic system that had no room for my personality. I used up all my three weeks of holiday time within the first five weeks then quit!

The paid work I have managed to do beyond bare minimum has been largely freelance art and multimedia jobs, including backdrop painting, leaflet and web design. I have done bar work, but couldn't handle it frequently (too stressful). I very much enjoyed working as a pub Sunday roast cook. I even enjoyed the pressure when it was busy (but was always angry if anyone broke the routine by ordering dessert!). I have enjoyed (and been anxious) DJing and being a caterer. I love to have control and creative input. I was also a self-employed pub quiz writer and reader. My current partner was the champion contestant!

For the majority of my adult life I was technically unemployed. I genuinely couldn't cope with employment. This didn't mean I didn't want to contribute to society. I just couldn't fit the moulds required by the vast majority of job descriptions.

I was so chuffed when at uni to be able to tell people I was a student (and therefore fulfilling a recognised role in society). Beyond this, I've done voluntary work, some of it innovative and commended. Oh, and I also used to organise techno raves, often donating all proceeds (such as they were) to the local drugs education charity. And did I mention managing a cave disco in Turkey? ...

And waitressing there too. That wasn't a labour of love!

Although I did get a buzz out of being useful and wanted, it's always been the humdrum demand of keeping going at a job that has caved me.

Tracy Holding the same job for too long has at times led to me literally wanting to not live anymore. I just can't handle needing to meet the same work expectations day in and day out for more than a few years no matter what I do. I know that's extreme and it's hard to explain to people sometimes, but it's TRUE.

**Sally Cat** For me, the concept of a steady career has always felt like a horrific prison sentence: terrifying to me.

**Tracy** I had the best job. At first I loved it. After I gave it up, people said, 'Why did you give it up? You could have just done anything with the rest of your time.' I didn't even have to BE there most of the time. I could do whatever I wanted and my work took me hardly any time at all. But after a few years, I just couldn't even do the minimum anymore. I couldn't bring myself to meet the job requirements! I couldn't explain it to anyone but I HAD to move on.

I didn't even care what I was going to do next, just so long as it wasn't THAT and THERE. It was driving me CRAZY. Now I'm in the same position, in a job with people I actually love, and I'm scared to let people know I need to leave...

**Wanting To Work?**

To me the Demand of being employed feels like submitting to being shot in the head.

I had an epiphany aged about 30 that some / most people actually want to work as employees

And be told what to do.

This is a totally alien concept to me

But it doesn't mean I don't want to be a productive and helpful member of society)

I just need to do things my own way.

**Sally Cat** I worked for a while as a self-employed pub quiz writer and reader. I had three different quizzes every week. I used to enjoy coming up with new question formats, designing nice answer sheets in Photoshop, but before long, the demand of coming up with new questions several times a week became stifling.

Silva  Tracy, however much I like what I'm doing, I find my tolerance for it has a shelf-life – if that sounds similar to you?

Tracy  Silva, yes, EXACTLY. But I don't know what to do about it because I do need to pay the bills and get health insurance. How do you build a career when you just get sick of what you do so easily?

Silva  I would imagine the stress of knowing that doesn't help at all either xxx

Tracy  No, it makes me much less likely to do what I know is right for me, especially when my partner gets so fearful about it and asks me, almost pleading, not to want to leave my job. I can't help what I WANT.

Sally Cat  The American system is really hard going I think for PDAers with its demands to work and have health insurance.

Tracy  Sally, I hate it, especially now it's going the wrong way.

Silva  Tracy, I get that completely. A previous partner once told me 'I know you're miserable but if you leave we won't cope financially and you know I can't live with debt...' It guilted me for years. Please don't let yourself be miserable, Tracy. There has to be a way through this... Complying to that misery I am sure was a factor in making me ill (physically).

Sally Cat  What your disabled husband could maybe acknowledge is that you are also disabled?

Silva  Sally, yes!

Tracy  My husband is willing to acknowledge my being disabled right up until it threatens his sense of safety. So he can acknowledge demand avoidance and ADHD and their impact on my life in an abstract sense, but if I tell him how much I hate work we usually can't continue the conversation because he can't go on, because he is so absolutely sure he is going to end up a street person dying in a box with no health care. I feel so terrible that I end up promising I will just keep on and pretending I don't hate it anymore even though I do.

I know my hopelessness as far as work is concerned is making me depressed and I just stop wanting to do anything, even things I enjoy.

Sally Cat This is an unfair power balance. Your husband is emotionally blackmailing you.

Silva Tracy, I see where you're coming from but please don't forget that you have a right to feel safe as much as your husband does. It is hard when you're being 'guilt-tripped' and he would probably be horrified if you told him that's how it feels. But your feelings are valid and your needs are equally important to his.

Tracy Sally, I don't know how to handle it. I know I should have the strength to have my own perspective and make my own choices, but then when I actually have to face him I...just can't do it. Yet.

Silva, my husband is visually impaired and he is used to having people accommodate what he can't do. So I think he is unaware that he is unconsciously expecting me to pick up the slack so he gets the environment that makes him feel safe. He absolutely melts down when he thinks I'm not going to, even if I can't. I know we need to talk about it but we've never been very good at having that kind of problem-solving conversation, and of course there's no way to do it if either of us is freaking out at the time. I'm not sure how to handle it and I've been avoiding it for that reason.

Silva I get it. Thank you for sharing that. But it sounds as if you've been accustomed to fixing everything and shouldering more than your share. I am just concerned that it will become too heavy for you. You have coped so far and deserve a break. I feel for your husband, and I understand why it is very hard for you. Is there anything in the past you can draw on to inspire yourself? A time when you've had to face him before with something?

Sally Cat Is your husband able to read with his visual impairment? If so, might it work to write him a letter explaining these things to him?

Tracy Sally Cat, he's actually suggested that, it's a very good idea. I struggle to finish my thoughts when I talk with him about it; writing it down might help. The problem is that I don't know what I WANT to do, I just know I'm tired of doing THIS.

**Sally Cat** And you can take your time composing this letter as and when you have inspiration/overcome Demand Avoidance. Plus, if your husband has even suggested it, it means he's going to be receptive.

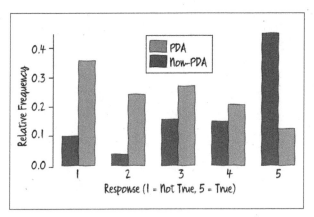

Graph 16: I am able to work to earn a wage
*From a 'Quick PDA Poll' with 240 PDA and 145 neurotypical respondents*

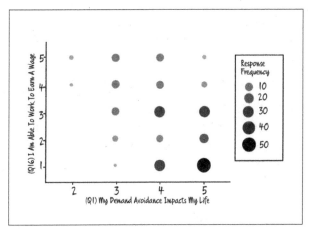

Scattergraph 6: Correlation between Graphs 1 and 16
*There is a moderate negative correlation between 'Demand Avoidance impacts my life' and 'I am able to work to earn a wage'*

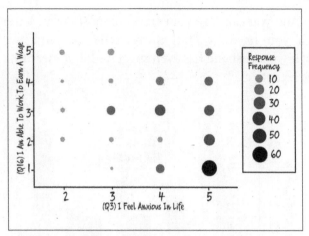

Scattergraph 7: Correlation between Graphs 3 and 16
*There is a moderate negative correlation between 'I feel
anxious in life' and 'I am able to work to earn a wage'*

# WHY ARRANGEMENTS DON'T ALWAYS WORK WITH PDAERS

### From Riko Ryuki's blog

I know most parents at some point will try to agree an arrangement with their kid/s: 'you do this and I'll do that' or 'if you don't do that then I'll do this'. It's a good concept, a little give and take between two people, coming to a compromise between two opposing forces which may want different things. Mutual agreement is a great idea.

So why then does it not work quite as well with PDAers as it does with other kids?

'We agreed that he would take a bath on Tuesdays and Fridays if I didn't nag him to wash the rest of the week, but when Tuesday came around he refused to bathe, even though it was his idea in the first place.'

The thing about Demand Avoidance is that it isn't something the PDAer can control. Agreements, however willing when given, are done by a person who doesn't have full control over their actions. When faced with a demand, the brain causes the body to react however it sees fit, regardless of what the individual wants.

This is one of the biggest frustrations for PDAers, and it feels like a constant fight between what we want and what our brain tells us we must do.

When making an agreement with a PDAer, you're making an agreement with someone who has little control over whether that agreement is carried out.

This can be frustrating for both parties, as one side will feel like the PDAer is deliberately manipulating them to get what they want and the PDAer will feel helpless to carry out the agreement, thus making them feel like they are letting the other person/s down. This is one of the reasons I dislike agreements for behaviour between a school and a student, especially in primary schools, because they under-estimate the control any child has over their own actions, let alone a PDAer. They are just setting up the child for failure.

If PDAers had control over their actions there wouldn't be a need for a PDA diagnosis, and perhaps the condition would never have been discovered. In PDAers there seems to be a large disruption between the brain and the individual's conscience. This is more than likely to be a result of the amygdala being in control over most of the PDAer's actions due to the almost constant alertness from the constant perception of demands. Basically, everything a PDAer does in response to a demand is decided by the amygdala, the part of the body which deals with keeping us safe by using Fight, Flight, Freeze to respond to threats. The amygdala can take over the brain and force us to act without any conscious decision. This is supposed to keep us safe by allowing us to respond immediately to threats. This is helpful when an actual threat appears, but often the amygdala cannot differentiate between actual threats and safe things, hence people having an exaggerated response to tiny spiders or people challenging our morals. With PDAers, we perceive almost everything to be a threat, so our amygdalas tend to be working overtime.

So when a PDAer agrees to an arrangement, we may consciously intend to carry out our part of the agreement, but when it comes time to do so our brain perceives the task as a demand, our amygdala starts up and stops us from complying.

There are ways around this. We can use coping strategies to help us work around our amygdala. These don't always work and for children it is much, much harder to go against Demand

Avoidance. So while it's a good idea to use agreements, even with PDAers, don't expect them to always happen, and be prepared for Demand Avoidance.

# COPING STRATEGIES

» Worry about other people's opinions over-riding Demand Avoidance
» Keeping daily demands and expectations low
   and factoring in recovery time
» Buying clothes that don't need ironing
» Logic puzzles and Facebook games as calming recharge tools
» Making demands into a fun game
» Role playing a character to meet demands
» Distraction
» Meditation and yoga to aid relaxation
» Going with Demand Avoidance (avoiding everything)
» Pressing for people and organisations to
   communicate via email not phone
» Batch cooking
» Disengaging from toxic people
» Self-awareness and acceptance of Demand Avoidance
» 'Bursting' Demand Avoidance by focusing on it
» Compassion Focused Therapy, mindfulness, Alexander technique
   and professional training as a person-centred counsellor

---

Do you have any strategies for coping with PDA issues such as Demand
Avoidance and anxiety? What works for you? What doesn't work?

---

Vanessa Haszard  I will let you know when I find a healthy one!
Most of mine are terrible.

Ruth  I use my worry about what other people will think to force
me into doing things. It's taken years and doesn't always work,
but self-imposed demands are better for me than demands
from other people.

Sally Cat  My weekly counselling course used to be great for
motivating me to bathe and wash my hair the evening before!

Ruth  Now that I can identify with! Plus, someone's coming over?
Take a week to blitz the house...do NOT turn up unannounced!

Sally Cat  Definitely!! Unannounced (or early) guests are an evil!

Pink  There's a couple of friends I've discovered motivate me to
clean before they come over. No one else. And they don't care
what state my house is in, either. They say, 'Don't worry about
it.' I say, 'Don't be daft, I'm taking this motivation and running
with it while it lasts!'

Sally Cat  No demand, maybe?

Pink  Maybe!

Julia Daunt  I've kinda covered this in my other answers but it
doesn't hurt to go over things again. I keep daily demands and
expectations as low as possible so as to keep my anxiety low
enough that I can function and enjoy life. I do this by reducing/
removing unnecessary demands and routines, by changing
tack often, taking naps when I begin to feel overwhelmed and
by planning my weeks carefully so I don't end up with a few
days out of a month crammed full of stuff and the rest of the
month empty. Spreading events/demands out means I'm able
to have prep and downtime too. This is vital. I meltdown if I'm
not able to do this. No surprises. When I'm not coping I hate to
be crowded or babied. Just leave me to it. Don't ask me when I'm
melting down stupid questions like 'are you okay' – of course
I'm not okay! I'm in meltdown! Also, no, you can't help and, no, I
can't just stop. Just leave me to rant and get it out of my system.
Don't baby me after too. I'm not made of glass and I don't need
mothering. I'm often emotionally exhausted and embarrassed

after a meltdown so just having you act normally will make the world of difference.

Alice I'm learning as I go along. Things that I thought were just silly or lazy are possibly DA issues. I can usually shower/wash my hair the day of a doctor's appointment. I can sometimes get something done by starting it with no end expectations. There are lots of things I don't do at all, e.g. ironing, cleaning the car, plus lots of jobs that I'm struggling with even if I could do them because of health conditions, e.g. hoovering.

People turning up unannounced is quite a fear, really, but not enough to make things as nice as they should be. I used to force myself when the children were smaller to do lots of things for the whole family even when every fibre was screaming 'no'; this was when I thought I was lazy.

I seem to have lost that ability to make myself do things if I don't want to.

I'm hopeless at ringing people. I sometimes don't answer the phone even when I know who it is. I could go on for ages about this so will stop! It affects everything in my life.

Providing a family meal each day (even when I don't know who will be in to eat) feels like a daily test. When something is sorted or even in the oven, I feel a palpable relief.

Sally Cat I have reduced my domestic demands down to the occasional load of laundry (if I feel motivated to do it); hoovering the living room quickly (most days); and cooking family dinner in the evening. I sometimes feel guilty that I don't do more, as I perceive other mums to do, but then I remind myself that I have PDA, Chronic Fatigue Syndrome and other impacting invisible health conditions. What I do is perfectly adequate in this light.

Alice I do a load of laundry at least once a day; I find the main problem is putting it all away.

### Housework Thoughts

I do a few simple chores every day, such as making the bed, because I like them to be done,

but even these are a BATTLE
And I feel cheated of my time.

If someone is coming to visit, I feel anxious about extra cleaning, sometimes for months ahead of time.

I rarely actually do any extra chores, I just feel guilty that I haven't.

**Pink** Laundry, I have to peg things out grouped together so they get folded up and put away together. Socks get pegged out in pairs. Putting a fresh load of washing on will motivate me to put the previous lot away, particularly useful if it's been nagging me for days to be taken down. I don't iron anything. Unless I take it out of the cupboard to wear and can see it needs it. There are very few things in my wardrobe that need ironing, and those things that do look amazing so are worthy of the effort.

**Sally Cat** Same!

**Silva** Me too guys x

**Elizabeth** Still learning, but I find things like logic puzzles and tactics-based Facebook games very calming, so if I play a bit before I have to do something it gets me in a much calmer frame of mind. Having a little quiet time before also helps me get my head in gear. When I was working for other people I used to get up much earlier than I needed to in order to have that time.

**Sally Cat** Me too. My customary wake up routine is Facebook Scrabble. I was just playing it now, in fact, I dip into it throughout my day in order to recharge my brain. I have a lifelong sleep disorder that means I need to sleep and wake later than most people, but when I was doing a morning counselling course, I found it easier to get up half an hour earlier so I could play Scrabble, than jumping out of bed without time to ease myself awake (the resulting sleep deprivation unfortunately triggered an autoimmune disease!).

**Dee Dee** Me too...Facebook coffee Facebook coffee Facebook and flick through the news app. A To do list for my day off. Arrrh 10 more minutes and I'll write me a to-do list!

**Becca B** A million and one strategies in our house!

We both find it easier to get things done if we can laugh about it and generally mess about, so if we can make things into a game then we do.

I have my 'demon possessing a fragile meat body' strategy when I can't handle things and need to focus on getting things done without hurting myself or freaking out. I focus on pretending to be the person who can do the things whilst being an entity apart which needs to not draw attention rather than get things done. Also, there's an ongoing thing with our friends that I'm a super smart bear in a great human costume. 'I'm a bear, bears can't do x' is seen as a legitimate excuse or reason for needing help.

We both distract ourselves with debates, music and made-up songs/rhyming games whilst getting things done if we're able to do a job on autopilot.

I do meditations, yoga and relaxation things for my anxiety, but Nik can only do yoga – he can't visualise things when he's told to so most led meditation makes him angry!

Sally Cat  I discussed this in the Fantasy and Role Play section, but guided meditation irritates me as well!

Also, thanks to reading Riko's blog, I've just realised I have used role play to meet demands (e.g., imagining I'm being filmed for TV as I do cleaning).

David Lees  My coping strategy is to avoid everything I don't want to do even if I want to do them. I live in litter and refuse because I refuse.

Once in a long while I might fill a bin bag or three. Not very often.

It gets me down and I don't maintain relationships. I refuse the demand of knocks on the door. And telephones alarm not ring.

Sally Cat  One strategy I've implemented is to press for institutions to communicate with me via email, not phone or even face to face. This works better for me. I am more in control of my own world in that I can choose when to deal with emails and take my time considering my responses (somewhat ironically, these tend to be dealt with immediately, but I still need that space between myself and the other party). I hate phone calls and keep my mobile permanently on silent (another strategy). Very few people even have my number.

Silva  Sally, I love the emails only idea. Thank you so much for sharing xxx

Silva  Too many to list really, Sally. Couple are: I will always text or email rather than having to phone people. I have caller ID on the phone and answer-service so I don't need to 'pick up' if I'm avoiding. I hate it if people drop in uninvited. Or stay too long. I buy clothes I don't need to iron. I work for myself to avoid the demands of 'routine/regular work'. At the extreme end – I never had kids and I am now happy about that as I avoid the demands of being a parent (I do like kids, just not 24/7). I could go on all day...

Pink  I have the same thing for breakfast and lunch every day, so I only need to think about an evening meal. Occasionally I'll shake it up a bit by forgetting to have breakfast, or having double the amount for breakfast and missing lunch. I like to meal plan a couple of weeks ahead and then pick from the list on the other days if I can't bring myself to make what I've allocated. I can't abide food waste so buying food kinda forces me to cook at times. Taking on a plant-based diet has enabled me to have greater control over what I eat. I've also learned to be more tolerant of the wrong food being presented to me, which I found curious when I spotted it.

My food cupboards are generally overflowing, my freezer full of food. Means that whatever I can bring myself to cook on the days I'm unmotivated I can generally find something to make. I batch cook for the days that I can't.

Becca B  Batch cooking is one of those things we never manage to do, so I'm a bit jealous!

Pink  I had chronic fatigue for a few years so it was essential back then, as I needed to have decent food otherwise I'd feel even worse. As a result I've discovered that I can't be arsed to make faffy things like meatballs just for one meal's worth. It seems I'd rather make enough for 18 adult portions, get so utterly fed up with them by the time they are ready to go in the oven to cook, then forget how much of a faff they are over the following 6 months as we work our way through them!

Chuck sauce ingredients in the slow cooker overnight and by the time the sauce is ready that motivates me to be bothered to portion up the meatballs, thank goodness!

Sally Cat I have arranged my life to have minimal demands in it. I only get anxiety, I think, with Demand Avoidance if I am pushed (even by myself) to action the demand. Having fewer demands means I'm avoiding this stress. Also, understanding about my PDA means I don't feel so guilty about not doing stuff. Self-awareness is very important for me.

Silva Brilliantly put! X

Sally Cat Thank you x

I've succeeded in reducing the amount of anxiety I feel through years of counselling and, perhaps most effectively, one-on-one Compassion Focused Therapy and a small group Mindfulness course. These two techniques have both been proven via brain scans to rewire the brain to have fewer 'threat' responses (Fight/Flight/Freeze). I still feel a lot of anxiety, but less so. It's hard to quantify how much anxiety I feel because I've never been without anxiety. This is the least anxious in life I've ever been. I continue to perform Mindful meditation every day (but only very briefly because it feels like a demand!).

Also, in gaining self-awareness, I now notice when I need time out (plus accept that I need it, rather than fighting the urge as a lazy indulgence) and, also, have learned to notice and say if I'm starting to feel angry. This has resulted in my having far fewer meltdowns.

Silva So, so with you here, Sally!

Sally Cat Oh, and I've learned to spot when people are toxic to me and disengage from them. This has helped me A LOT.

And one more coping strategy I realise I have is in having learned to dismiss demands. People may tell me what they think I SHOULD do. This triggers avoidance, but I have learned (connected closely, I think, to my having learned to disengage from toxicity) to not respond. In the past, I'd have argued and become increasingly distressed/felt increasingly out of control and pressured. But nowadays I have an inner strength and if people start telling me what I should do, I can sense myself being triggered and just not respond (TBH not always, but more often than not!).

Being more aware of my 'Avoidance Reaction' has also empowered me. Knowing how I tick/what my triggers are is very helpful. Demand Avoidance still exists, but it's now no longer so likely to escalate into a Bomb.

Also, I can sometimes 'burst' Demand Avoidance by focusing on it. I think it distorts my idea of doing things, or even thinking about them into something completely abhorrent. The more I can coax myself to think about my demand avoidance, the less power it has.

Sometimes I can squeeze past Demand Avoidance by finding something exciting or otherwise appealing about the thing I'm avoiding. It's all about thinking about the avoided thing and the process of avoiding it rather than, umm, avoiding thinking about it.

**Jenny Penny** I started Alexander technique lessons in my teens, for foot and back pain. I've been a teacher myself for over 20 years and I now realise this was the best thing I could have done. It gives me a level of physical control and comfort that mostly can overcome the negative symptoms of PDA.

Defusing My Meltdown Bomb

Being more aware of my "Avoidance Reaction" has empowered me.

Knowing how I tick and what my triggers are is very helpful.

Demand Avoidance still exists,

But it's now less likely to escalate into a Bomb.

Becca B  I've always wanted to try that!

Sally Cat  The person-centred counsellor training I've done (right up to Level 4) has been a coping strategy for me. I was at all points conscious that these courses were honing me with invaluable social interaction skills. I had feedback from experienced tutors and fellow students in how I was coming across; how empathic I was; how much warmth I was expressing; how well I'd understood; what my body language conveyed; how genuine I seemed: all in all perfect mask coaching, but also, I think, an education in how to ditch my mask. This is not something I feel I've been able to achieve fully (ditching my mask). I suspect my mask is actually a hardwired and involuntary part of me, but my counsellor training has empowered me to trust mySELF. To believe that I might be OK as a functioning, interacting member of society.

Also, my training has fed back to me that, despite my autism, I am able to be empathic to a level acceptable by scrutinising counsellor tutors AND that I have exceptionally developed self-awareness. This training also, I feel, has empowered me to express myself to create my graphic memes about my experience of living with PDA and, perhaps most importantly, to feel that I'm OK inside.

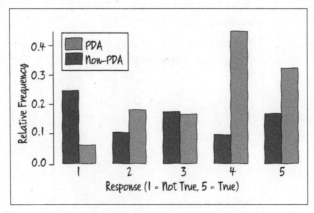

Graph 17: I avoid talking on the phone
*From a 'Quick PDA Poll' with 240 PDA and 145 neurotypical respondents*

# ADULT COPING STRATEGIES

## From Riko Ryuki's blog

As an adult I have developed many different strategies and coping skills to help manage the more difficult elements of my PDA. Some of these strategies I've learnt to adopt and others have come naturally to me, even before I knew what PDA was. Now that I understand my difficulties better I can see what skills I have developed that have helped me growing up, and I can better utilise them now I know why I do them and how they work. What follows is a list of the strategies and skills I've developed. They may help PDA kids and/or adults or they may not. They work for me but every individual is different and so what works for one may very well have the opposite effect for others.

Role play – many PDA people use role play as a way of coping, especially with demands. Parents may find their child is more able to follow instructions and suggestions when they are role playing a character. I myself have found chores easier when pretending I am being filmed for TV. I adopt a character (say, a cleaner) and pretend I am doing a job for TV. I'll imagine cameras following me everywhere, watching what I'm doing and that people are asking me questions or commenting on my actions. I'll run an entire conversation in my head, and get the dishes done at the same time. I also found this useful during uni. I would pretend I was being filmed completing my coursework, this certainly helped me pass many grades.

Doing the opposite – I find if I need to do something, say, have a shower, I will tell myself I don't need to have a shower. My brain will then think, 'No, we are having one' and then I will be able to take a shower. This doesn't work for everything as I also have to consider my energy levels when dealing with demands and this definitely won't work for high-class demands such as making a phone call; however, it can work for smaller demands.

'You don't have to' – I've found that by giving myself an 'out' then it is much easier to meet demands, because I know I can change my mind whenever I want. I'll tell myself, 'You don't have to if you don't want to.' This works quite well.

Avoidance – one way to meet small demands is to order myself to complete a bigger demand instead. This won't work for everyone. I will tell myself to make a dentist appointment if the dishes need washing, then I will find myself avoiding the phone call by doing the dishes. The phone call demand will become harder to meet though and this needs to be taken into consideration when using this tactic. So far I've been trying to make that phone call for the past 2 years, but I've done plenty of dishes.

Not thinking – this is one I discovered as an adult and is fairly difficult to adopt. Our minds are always thinking about stuff so trying not to think about a demand that demands our attention is hard work, however I find that if I am able to distract my thoughts from the task I am better able to actually get the job done. This works best for getting out of bed. It used to take me hours to get up. I would get more and more worked up because I needed to get up but the pressure made it harder and harder. My body would freeze so I couldn't move at all. I found that by not thinking of getting up at all my body would automatically move of its own accord. It's a bit like when you're walking somewhere but are distracted; by the time you stop thinking, you realise you've gotten to where you wanted to go without even realising it – it's a bit like that.

My choice – it's difficult to take demands from other people. I've come to realise that making it my choice to do what others ask of me makes it a lot easier to do what they ask. So when my partner asks me to get something for him, I'll think, 'I'm only doing this because I want to, not because you've asked me to.' It works. It does breed a bit of resentment though.

Having some control – another way to cope with other people's demands is to think, 'Fine, but I'm not going to be happy about it' or 'I'm not doing it your way though, I'll do it how I want to do it.' This helps cope as I have some control over how I do a demand as opposed to whether I do the demand.

Excuses – people would be surprised at the range of excuses I can give for avoiding or putting off a demand. This is very useful for when demands are sprung on me and I don't have the ability to meet them straightaway; by delaying them I can wait until I am better equipped to do the demand, rather than struggling.

Making a list – similar to the avoidance tactic. I will make a list of things I need to do that day and then avoid them all, thus completing a whole different list of demands that also needed doing but were deliberately being ignored. Result!

Taking it easy – I try not to meet too many demands in one day. It really does depend on how I am feeling that day too. In general I will start each day with just one demand in mind (obviously I'm not including eating, dressing, talking, etc., by demand I mean big demands like chores). Some days the demand will be simple because I know I don't have the energy to deal with a big one (taking a shower) and other days I'll have a bigger demand because I feel better (phoning someone, cleaning a room). The aim of this is to not avoid all demands, although I'm not too hard on myself if I can't manage the demand for that day. But I hope by only having one demand in mind I might manage to do more without pressurising myself beforehand. I also take breaks in between each demand and find easy, fun things to do scattered throughout the day; this makes it easier to manage because I know there are times when I don't have to do anything at all. If I manage nothing then I accept that and take it easy on myself. Life is hard; no need to make it harder by beating myself up about it.

Deciding not to – I go to quite a few groups and social events along with needing to do shopping and other outdoor activities. Every time, I feel anxiety beforehand and feel like I want to stay at home and hide. I have had many meltdowns before a big social event, even a meal out with friends causes a meltdown. Sometimes I'll decide not to go. This means I either don't go or the anxiety is immediately removed and minutes before the time for leaving I may change my mind and go anyway. This helps a lot because it removes the anxiety. I know some parents have mentioned how their kids have struggled so much leading up to an event and the relief they feel when the event is cancelled. They say it's like they wanted someone else to decide for them not to go. Yes, we want to go but the anxiety becomes so big that it feels better to be told we can't go, especially since that is often a decision we cannot make ourselves.

Mixing it up a little – regular demands, things like showering, eating, getting dressed, etc. can become so stressful that we avoid the activity completely. I have found that introducing something new or mixing it up a little can actually help. PDA people prefer novelty; there's less anxiety sometimes around something new as we don't know what to expect. It sounds contrary but it's true. New is less anxiety-producing than old. When I feel myself avoiding daily activities I will do something to change the activity, even a little. I may buy new bath products, try new foods or eat out, buy new clothes or try a different fashion style. Anything that changes the demand – even moving the demand to a different time of day can help. Showering before bed, for instance, or having cereal for dinner. For me, change is good.

# – 18 –

# REASONABLE ACCOMMODATIONS

» Time alone and space
» Flexibility
» Acceptance, trust and respect
» Re-wording things and explaining rules
» Don't take things said during meltdowns personally
» Notices to start with 'please'
» Recognise that PDAers are highly sensitive (even if this is masked)
» Don't judge
» Allow email (rather than phone) communication
» Allow the freedom to come and go
» Keep PDAers informed
» Processing time
» Being allocated a quiet place to work
» Fast tracking in queues
» Flexibility in work
» Precision with given times (e.g., 'at 10 o'clock', rather than 'at tennish')

---

What accommodations do you feel would be reasonable
to expect for PDA, bearing in mind how our condition
impacts our ability to function in society?

---

Silva My immediate instinctive reaction is 'anything I need to do to stop myself imploding'. Mainly, my gut is screaming, time alone. Space. I have a need to be alone for at least a part of every day. Unless it's torrential rain, I need to walk. Every. Single. Day. And flexibility, in most, if not all things. Don't ask much, do I? Seriously, flexibility is the key, I think. Not to be forced to fit, as a square peg, into a round hole.

Sally Cat I love that expression: forcing a square peg into a round hole. It's so descriptive for me. I'm a squiggle-shaped peg and I fit NONE of society's bloody holes.

Alice Acceptance. Allowing me to be me. Trust. Understanding. Dare I ask for love?

In a perfect society this would be for everyone, always.

In an imperfect society such as ours is, I'd hope that I could at least be heard.

Riko Ryuki Flexibility in nearly everything. Re-wording things so it feels less demandy. Giving options in how we do things. Explaining rules that are important and why we need to do some things, and doing away with anything that isn't essential. Allowing us space when we are struggling and giving us time to do tasks and time to recover afterwards. Offer to help but don't insist we accept help. Don't take things we say and do personally, especially during meltdowns/panic attacks.

Julia Daunt   Give me a little more time to process things you say and situations, don't nag me, don't demand that I do it your way and that I do it now, listen to what I say and read between the lines, be willing to compromise, don't rush me and don't treat me like a freak. One of my biggest issues with how people treat me is the assumption that because I have PDA they can't talk to me if they have an issue with something I've said or done. A lot of people just assume that I won't listen or that I'll become angry and defensive when actually the opposite is true. I'm normally the first to admit wrongdoing and to apologise for that. Sad but true. I don't want or need to be treated like royalty but just small adjustments can make the world of difference to me. Like when in a restaurant, seat me near a window or by the air con or when at the doctor's let me wait outside rather than the hot and crowded waiting room. Simple.

I'd also like all command signs to start with 'please'. 'Please no diving', 'please no smoking' or 'please keep off the grass'. Those are signs I could happily follow.

Sally Cat   And perhaps also followed by a reason, e.g. 'Please no smoking. We wish to keep this a clean air space.'

Julia Daunt   I'm not fussed about the reason but can see why it could help others. 'Please' is just an under-used word. X

Sally Cat   Interestingly, in Turkey they do put 'please' at the start of some signs, like 'lütfen dikkat' (please attention) – which feels nicer, but perhaps just because it's in another language, so feels exotic! – but they hardly ever use 'please' in conversation and say things like 'give me a cigarette' which always irks me. I have often retorted with, 'only if you say "please"!'

| How different statements trigger my Demand Avoidance | | |
|---|---|---|
| STATEMENT | EXAMPLE | DEMAND AVOIDANCE |
| Command | You must go out | V high |
| Aggressive command | Move it! | V high |
| Pressuring | I'd want you to | High |
| Assumption | You'll love it | High |
| Decisive suggestion | Let's go out! | Medium |
| Polite request | Please come too | Medium |
| Unpressured suggestion | Maybe we could go out? | Low |
| Unpushy opinion | I'd quite like to go out | Low |
| Consultation | What do you think? | Low |
| Unassuming | Come if you like | Low |
| Forbidding | You can't come | Inverted! |

Dee Dee  My bed is my reasonable accommodation!

Little Black Duck  It starts in recognising that this is an exquisitely sensitive individual. Even if that sensitivity is masked or hidden behind a false bravado.

Then you build trust. Enough trust that this exquisitely sensitive individual is willing to risk.

This is done through respect, kindness and gentleness. Respect that a No is just as valid as a Yes. Respect that there are reasons that they don't necessarily need to share but still exist. Allowing them that self-determination. Honouring them as an individual with rights and choices and providing the space where that's known.

Then, you will get some participation, as they can. You will have achieved collaboration.

Sally Cat  Beautiful. PDA 'false bravado' really struck a chord with me because this is DD's way of dealing with the loss of pets. All your words here are perfect x

Sarah Johnson  Be nice, don't judge. And don't give me that look of revulsion because 1 offend your finer sensibilities...your poo poo still smells like mine...and the irony is my observations and critical analysis means I'm always right anyway. My presentation might be a bit ropey though...

Sally Cat Thinking about accommodations I could ask for from institutions, such as the health service and potential courses and work places (plus friends and family), I would say: please think of what you're communicating so it is not telling me SHOULDS (which are demands). These are your opinions. Own them. Leave me free of your implied demands to make my own choices. Please be flexible with me. Please don't insist that I adhere to your arbitrary system.

Allow me, for example, to communicate via email rather than phone (in fact, cease to have phone as a forced automatic communication default).

Please allow me freedom to come and go, thus respecting my hardwired need to be free of constraint.

Please respect me to come to my own decisions and do not, please, tell me what to think.

Please keep me in the loop. I need to know what's going on. Keeping me informed is necessary if I am to avoid intense anxiety.

Please consult me about appointment times and allow me plenty of notice. Further, if I miss an appointment, be lenient with this.

I'm sure there's more I can add here, but for now, finally, I'll say, please also treat me with respect.

Silva Respect really resonates. And communication xxx

Barry Ha! I'll second 'never having to communicate by phone'!!!!
For me, at the moment...maybe...I'm not sure how to say this. A chance to cool down and re-state something. To repent? To be able to correct a first reaction? Also, enough time to process, without listening to more words. The ability to get things in writing, and go through them in relative solitude, before responding.

Elizabeth Being allowed a quiet place to work and focus on one task at a time would help me.

Sally Cat Me too! When I was training to be a professional counsellor and we covered reasonable accommodations for disabilities, I was at the same time having to seek a counselling placement.

I was aware that the counsellors in my training facility had to share noisy offices and I debated whether it would be a reasonable accommodation to ask for a broom cupboard of my own. If denied this, I knew I'd not be able to cope. Similarly, I started adult teacher training and had a placement with students in my former uni course. The department then moved from an old terrace of houses with lots of little rooms to a modern open-plan office. I then quit the course...

**We're going on holiday!**

Both myself & Milly Cat love the novelty of new places
Although I find travel exhausting
And airports are especially stressful:
> My autistic hypersensitivity is stressed by bright lights & crowds
> My PDA, by queues, confinement & enforced demands
We're trying out an airport autism wristband system
Which should bypass some queues
And EasyJet have allocated us free seats near the front of the plane
These accommodations will really help.
See you all soon!

Sally Cat  Another accommodation I feel PDAers should be entitled to is fast tracking in queues, as well as being given priority in choosing seating, appointment times, etc. We recently benefited from this as autistics in flying from Stansted Airport. They have an autistic wristband system that allows the wearer and a small group to join the fast track queue for customs and EasyJet allocated us free reserved seating at the front of the plane. As PDAers, I feel our need for accommodations is arguably even greater. We are highly prone to overloading in crowds; suffer great anxiety and intolerance of uncertainty; and being forced to wait and be penned in triggers Demand Avoidance. I have previously tried to negotiate with hospitals to allocate me a small private room when I've been due to stay in, but they have refused. When forced to stay in a noisy ward bed, I have gone into severe overload then meltdown and discharged myself early.

T.C.  With work, flexitime was really helpful to me and time off in lieu...it allowed me space when I needed it.

I did better the more latitude I had to make decisions about what I did when, and the more it felt like deadlines and expectations were reasonable. In one job I got to arrange my side of the office to suit me and reorientated my desk which helped. I prefer teamwork to hierarchy. The unknown makes me anxious. 'Can you pop in to speak to me at 10ish about x' is better than 'I need you in my office at 10.00 precisely...'

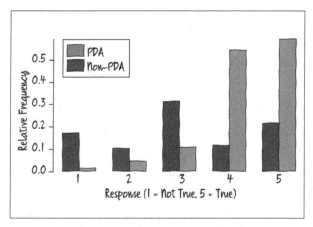

Graph 18: I need access to a quiet place
*From a 'Quick PDA Poll' with 240 PDA and 145 neurotypical respondents*

# DO MY DISABILITIES DEFINE ME?

### From Riko Ryuki's blog

Define: State or describe exactly the nature, scope or meaning of.

Some people say, 'Autism doesn't define you' or, 'Don't let you disabilities define you' or, 'Don't let your past define who you are today', etc.

Other people say, 'How can my past not define who I am when it's impacted upon my personality and character?' or, 'My autism is a part of me so it does define who I am' or, 'Autism is as much a part of me as my hair colour or loyalty.'

If our disabilities incorporate a large part of our lives, so much so that they impact on the way we learn, how our personality develops, the way we form relationships with others, the way we view the world, our limitations, how people perceive and respond to us, etc., then it stands to reason that our disabilities have defined/are defining us.

I have ASD/PDA amongst other disabilities (or differences) such as OCD/OCPD, emotional lability, ADD, SPD, auditory processing disorder. These things affect the way my brain works, how it takes in sensory information, how I process and make sense of the world and information, how I form opinions and rationalise ideas, how I communicate and form relationships, etc. The definition of 'define' states that it describes the nature, scope or meaning of the thing it is defining. If I were to define myself I would say things like: I'm loyal, interested in acquiring knowledge, trustworthy, quiet, boyish, bad at maths, fidgety, etc. I'm not sure how others would describe me but in the past I've been described as quiet, soft and weird. All these things are a part of who I am. Many of them are traits that have been affected by one disability or another. It's difficult to unpick what parts of me are affected by my disabilities as opposed to what isn't. I've never not had these things.

Some people say they don't 'have' autism, they are autistic. Their autism is such a part of them that they don't feel it's right to say it's something they have as opposed to what they are. Well, we don't say we have loyalty as much as we are loyal. It's a part of what makes us who we are. It's what defines us.

Many disabilities are seen as negative. Some think disabilities make a person less than what they were before they became disabled or less than what they could be without them. The same for a bad past. They say things like, 'You'd be a much better person if X hadn't happened to you' or, 'You'd be able to function better now if you hadn't had a bad past.' Not only is this like saying the person they are now isn't worth much because of something they have/are or have had happen to them, it also presumes the person would be better off without disabilities/a bad past. This is rather presumptive. There are plenty of people out there who aren't particularly nice and yet have no disabilities or negative influences on their lives. Similarly, I know many people who have gone through difficult times and/or have disabilities/differences and those people are some of the nicest, kindest most helpful people you'd ever meet.

Our disabilities/differences do define who we are. They play a part in our personalities, the way we behave, the way we view life and the world and how we form relationships. To say they don't is rude at best. Without my disabilities I'd be a completely different person. Who knows whether that person would be good/bad/kind/interesting/loyal/girly/mischievous/mean/honest/a liar/etc., etc. I can't see into parallel worlds.

# — 19 —

# PARENTING

» Defining mutual expectations
» Be respectful, listen to the child and accept them for who they are
» Be mindful of the high impact of negativity on PDA children
» Remember that PDA children are not just being naughty and discipline will only damage them
» Allow PDA children to have safe space
» Allow PDA children to do things their own way, rather than trying to mould them
» Nurture rather than shame PDA children
» Pick your battles and be flexible
» Admit to your child if you have lost your temper and explain that you still love them
» Learn to take time out when you need it also

---

Not all of us have children (PDA or otherwise), but we were all PDA children in our pasts. Most interest in PDA has been focused on the parental perspective of 'managing' PDA children. What do you personally feel would help PDA children to flourish? If you are a parent with PDA, what challenges do you face?

---

**(Not) Tidying My Room**

My Mum used to tell me tidy my room when I was a kid.

I wanted to be good, but the idea filled me with dread.

I'd sit and stare at the pile of mess, but feel unable to lift a finger.

Laura Mullen I'm PDA, and I believe both of my girls are PDA. My husband is likely PDA. It is daunting to parent as PDA to PDA. I'm constantly fighting demands on me from children and others. But trying to be a good role model for them as well. We also home school currently. The demands made by home schooling on all of us are pretty incredible at times and I have to make sure that when it is too demanding we take breaks from it all. I also am in the process of writing up how-tos as well as family expectations/house rules regarding things that need to be done for us all to be happy and healthy. It takes a lot of work but it does seem to be helping a bit. When we all know the actual expectations of each other we have stopped 'biting' each other's heads off as much.

Julia Daunt Parents need to understand that their child probably doesn't see themselves as a child. If that's the case try to see them as the adults that they see themselves as. Listen to them and try to understand. Please don't say that you understand how a meltdown feels if you have no clue. It's patronising and not helpful. Children aren't stupid and will know you don't understand. It also makes light of what is an awful thing to go through. It trivialises it. Not good. Offer small choices. Start commands/requests with 'please'. Remove unnecessary demands where possible. Accept that your child has PDA and stop trying to make them have a typical life. After-school clubs or birthday parties may hold no interest for them so please stop forcing them to 'join in'. So long as they are happy and healthy, what more could you ask for? Accept that they might not follow a typical path or the path that you want them to. Don't pity them. Don't force them. Believe in them. Love them. Understand that their behaviour isn't personal, although it might not seem like it at the time. If praise is an issue try to keep it low-key or indirect. Always be ready to adjust and compromise.

Ruth  My daughter has meltdowns that become violent and when seemingly resolved, waves of anxiety re-start the meltdown sometimes three or four times. As a PDA parent, empathy is one thing, but my DD's demands drain me to the point of exhaustion. As a kid I internalised most of my worries and they came out in different ways, one of which was an immune disorder, psoriasis. I wouldn't have dreamed of attacking my mother. But then, I had two loving parents. My little girl watched her father emotionally and financially bully and belittle me all her life. She has learnt some very negative strategies that we are slowly trying to replace with stronger coping mechanisms.

Silva  Oooooooooooh! I'm a non-parent but recall a turbulent childhood. I think now my mother was PDA too and Dad was narcissistic. He liked to be in control and I resisted. Remember constantly feeling like I never fit in anywhere. I just wanted to be left alone to do my own things. I loved words (taught myself to read before I started school using comics belonging to older siblings). I was the youngest by quite a few years and felt like an only child. So much noise and chaos – older sister (11 years older) was very domineering and we shared a room. Would escape into books and act out characters. I think PDA kids need space and time. To feel safe is paramount. To be shown affection and taught that it's okay to love and be loved. Coldness and lack of communication is very isolating for any child but feels intense to a PDA kid. And please don't ever emotionally blackmail these kids because we never forget it and it scars.

Sally Cat  Hear, hear.

Silva  Sally, hugs! Xxx

Sally Cat  I suspected my mum had narcissistic personality disorder before discovering first my autism, then my PDA. I now think she has PDA too, but her PDA expresses itself as narcissism because she doesn't dare look into herself and blames her issues on those around her instead. I used to be one of her favourite scapegoats.

Silva  Sally, that must be so hard.

Sally Cat  We strive to survive under whatever conditions we are dealt x

Silva  For me, it was the coldness/lack of affection and the guilt-tripping that was most damaging. Hey – thank goodness we've found like-minded souls in this group x

Sally Cat  Definitely! X

Nicola T  I will have a think on this one, but I can tell you that beating, slapping and screaming, to try and make a child conform, doesn't work, just makes them grow up to be glad when you die. I cried with relief when my mother died which in hindsight is so terribly sad, and such a wasted life. So to those who (no one in this group) think that a child is just naughty, and will eventually give in if the discipline is good/harsh enough, I would like it to be known that you are wrong!!!!!

Joan Watson  *hugs* that's rough.

Sally Cat  I made a best friend when I was 7. We used to fantasise for hours about how great it would be if we were orphaned and were sent to live with better families x

Silva  Nicola, that is horrifying. Hugs.

Little Black Duck  Essentially it's about creating a space where you are psychologically safe and 'good enough'.

Joan Watson  My mum never gave me pointless rules to follow; she always let me do me. She took me for long walks or playground sessions to stop me getting restless. Let me stay up drawing if

I needed to in order to get out bursts of creativity. She used distraction methods to give me boundaries without a battle of wills. I still had issues but these things really helped.

> ### Naughty Child
>
> As a child I was often naughty, loud and argumentative.
>
> I often laughed inappropriately.
>
> I didn't realise that this pushed people away.
>
> They saw me as not caring, rude and awkward.
>
> Really I was just anxious,
>
> Had a PDA drive to talk
>
> And hardwired attention issues
>
> I wanted to get on with people, but didn't know how.

Little Black Duck  'She always let me do me' is awesome...and what it's about. My son said, 'Just let me be.' And another PDA child said, 'Allow me to be me.' That's so crucial.

Sally Cat  I think PDA kids cannot be moulded to the shape that parents, schools and larger society deign fit. PDA kids IMO can only flourish if allowed and encouraged to be themselves.

    So many parents of PDA kids have lamented, 'But will my child ever get a job?' And, 'They failed at school, I'm so worried about their future!' I feel their angst, I'm a mum myself, but I believe we PDAers need space without the pressure of parental hopes to begin to flourish and grow as the unique individuals that we are and find our own, amazing potentials x

Little Black Duck  I always think we are outliers or 1-percenters. That doesn't mean it's the bottom 1%.

**Little Black Duck**  And that is good general parenting, across the board. The difference is just how badly it can go wrong with PDA. The child feeling repressed, oppressed, victimised, overpowered and insignificant. It can cause extreme emotional dysregulation and psychological splitting. When your self-concept is already delicate, it can disintegrate with very little 'help'. A PDA child doesn't need any more confusion and fear.

## Unpicking My Past

As a child, I didn't bond with my parents... at all
They never gave me praise
It was all about Them
About how They coped with Me
How I was a Troublemaker
I really didn't flourish

As an adult, I have unpicked the pieces
And learned to seek people who support me
I feel good about myself now
Despite my limits
And am productive

**Sally Cat**  Exactly! Guidelines for parenting PDA kids, I think, work for non-PDA kids, but are especially crucial for PDAers, who are hypersensitive and cannot bend to directive whims.

It is similar to the person-centred counselling ethos, which I trained in (I think it is not a coincidence that, as a PDAer, I was drawn to this model). Person-centred counselling theory places the client (in this context, substitute child) as the expert and the counsellor (here substitute parent) as an unfailingly warm/positive, non-judgemental and empathic facilitator – edited to add: who does not direct the client/child, but encourages them to find their own way.

And, I add, empathy is not just a thing you have. It is an activity that necessitates constant striving and assumption questioning to attain.

My mum used to assume all sorts of things about me: that I was angry (when I was sure I wasn't); that I didn't care about various things (when I thought I did); that I saw her as a failure (when I hadn't, but this feeling mounted as her failure to listen to me continued unabated over the years).

Heidi H  Freedom. Validation. Nurturing. Security in knowing that they are understood. No shaming. No condemnation. Patience. Tolerance. Alternatives. Persistence and most importantly... TONS of communication and the listener with an open mind. My childhood was tough. I developed this inferiority complex and severe low self-esteem. I always doubted myself and was never given tools or alternatives for my emotional responses. I had nothing instilled in me other than everything I do is wrong, everything I feel is wrong, every emotional response is wrong and I was an explosive kid and beaten into submission so fear became my guiding force. I was afraid to speak, afraid to act. I internalized and feared physical reprimand with every situation I encountered that prompted a panic/anxiety/impulsive response in me. So I withdrew. I became that shy wallflower, always afraid of interacting with others because everything I did or said seemed inappropriate or wrong. Any feeling or opinion was wrong. And the sad reality? I'm 46 now and still feel this way. I'm constantly filled with self-doubt and hesitation. I withdraw impulsive comments. I avoid situations where I may actually be spoken to, particularly any situations that may lead to debate on sensitive issues or that have very strong control policies in place. Time limits, restrictions, verbiage restrictions. I cannot, with great confidence, just be myself and feel good about myself on anything. Being mindful constantly when in public and having a moment where I express myself freely in a situation or respond emotionally in a way that is less than 'PC' because I'm feeling like a caged animal with the circumstances, leads me to feeling immense shame and self-loathing. This is NOT something I want for my son. My son is a lot like I was as a child and I see the similarities...so he is given everything that

I wasn't. So far, I see him as a different child than I was. By his age I was meek and timid, afraid to do anything or say anything. My son is not hesitant to speak his mind and make his point and try to explain his feelings. I am his mother and it is my sole responsibility to ensure that he grows up with the tools to be a strong, confident, self-assured individual with the ability to contribute to society in a positive way and if we need to take an alternative approach to parenting and life, we do it. I will never force him into a situation 'because I say so'. He has a voice and I listen to it. He will not be reprimanded for impulse control failures that are beyond his control but rather guided to learn from them so that he is equipped with the skills necessary to mature with confidence. IDK...this may not be what you were asking for but this is the feedback I'm providing based on how I understood the query.

Sally Cat   Heidi, beautiful and so much like my life. My daughter has been showered with compliments and praise since she was born. She KNOWS she is lovely and lovable (unlike myself as a child). She is PDA and autistic like me and shy at school, but loved by her classmates (unlike childhood me) and loves school x

> ## If I could go back in time and speak to my Mum...
>
> I'd ask her to notice my good points
>
> And realise I was trying really hard
>
> But I was just a child, and vulnerable.
>
> I couldn't help my Demand Avoidance, anxiety, oddness, hypersensitivity & awkwardness.
>
> And even though things were tough for her and she said she was at her Wits' End,
>
> I needed her to back me
>
> (Not put me down and moan)
>
> Because I noticed every time she was disappointed
>
> And this stunted my growth.

Silva  Heidi, your son is so lucky to have you to parent him. I could
so relate to this. Thank you so much for sharing. My father used
to say, when I couldn't cope and flipped out, 'You're bl\*\*dy mad
you are! They're coming to take you away in a white van later
on.' I used to sit at the window, shaking, looking out for the van.
I was about 6 and didn't understand his brand of 'humour.'

Heidi H  Oh, that's awful. My feeling is that we, as humans, are
always evolving and it's so important to better ourselves with
each generation. As psychology advances and identifies so much
more, and behavioral/psychological issues are becoming less
stigmatized in the sense that it's no longer something you lock
someone up for and throw away the key as a derelict of society, it
has allowed those of us who suffered emotional brutality by our
caregivers and even our peers, to be able to identify the roots of
our 'misbehaviors' and emotional volatility. This is then giving
us, as parents, the opportunity to make a choice. Either do it
better for our own, next generation or travel the same path and
live in denial that 'that's how I was raised and I turned out okay'
and carry out the same, if not more deplorable child-rearing
philosophies as our own parents did which will either continue
to remain complacent or be worse. To me, the choice is clear.
Do better. So, for me, I'm not perfect.

Some of those knee-jerk responses to certain things will
prompt the instilled response that was projected onto me but
I'm mindful and a work in progress so I am able to backpedal
and learn from each 'slip' to repeating bad habits. It's hard...very
hard, to take a new approach, especially when it's not widely
accepted or tolerated. But my hope is that my son will benefit
and evolve to be a better person than I was able to be, in spite of
my stumbles along the way. Heck, I've never done this before.
But at least I'm doing my best to make sure it's better than
previous generations. Thank you so much for your kind words.

Silva  Heidi, bless you! I am so glad to know there are women like
you out there!

Gillian Mead (mother of adult PDA daughter)  Hardest part... Getting the
professionals to listen and work collaboratively with families,
such arrogance out there!

Jenny Penny  My son goes to a little private school (clever dad fought to the point of tribunal for him, so county pays!) where it works as a democracy. The teachers don't dominate the kids. Very few demands are made. When issues arise, the whole school decides what to do. In practice this means that in his first year my son went to less than 50% of his lessons; swore and yelled at people until they nearly had to ask us to take him away; spent lots of time in town or up trees and moaned constantly about how much he hated it there. Then, he gradually began to get involved; go on outings, make his sensible opinions known and get his aggression a bit under control. They all love him there and when he's ready, the teachers will gladly share knowledge with him if he wants. I think it is the perfect school for someone with PDA. I wish I could have gone there. I hope my son will see it eventually, as it's a bit tough being screamed at for being the cruelest witch, etc. As he's so intelligent, well supported and has improved so much recently, I'm quietly optimistic :)

## PDA Parent to a PDA Kid

I have PDA and autism. So does Milly Cat
I need to be in control. So does she
I need to be heard and so does Milly
I need to do things my way. So does she.
I bend to do things Her Way, because I'm Mummy.
She'd like me there Her Way all the time,
We have lots of cuddles.
I love her so much and Milly loves me.
But I quickly overload and need quiet time.
My partner, Daddy, is great at enabling this.
I feel guilty not to Be There for her more,
But she knows 'Mummy gets tired'
and that I love her.
With Daddy's support, our relationship works
xxx

Sally Cat  I'd say, remember that your PDA child can't help having Demand Avoidance and being anxious. Remember that they are very sensitive and will bruise easily emotionally. Forcing them causes lasting damage, even if they mask this from you. Meltdowns are not a choice and are distressing for your child to experience. Pick your battles. Be flexible. Explain why you have rules. Discuss things with your child and negotiate. Ask them how THEY feel. Let them know you love them, respect them and care. If you lose it at your child, own this. Rather than denying it, or blaming it on external factors/them, admit that you lost it; that sometimes you crack and let them know you still love them. This will give your child a model on which to base their own emotional expression.

Be conscious of how you phrase things. Telling a PDA child that they have to do something (even if YOU think they do) is going to trigger demand avoidance. Even enthusiastically urging them is likely to trigger them. It works with my daughter (and me!) if people say what they themselves are going to do; she then often wants to do it as well. Also, telling her she doesn't have to do something tends to 'de-claw' any implicit demand. Offering choice is important too, I think. And keeping things light-hearted, even making a game of things (again to 'de-claw' implicit demands).

As a PDA parent of a PDA 6-year-old daughter, I find I get overloaded very quickly. DD likes to be in control. So do I. Her attention span flits around. So does mine. Trying to stay focused on what SHE wants me to focus on is draining. Very draining. I need a lot of quiet time. Now I understand why I need this, I feel less guilty about it.

Sally Cat In retrospect, I can see my mum had similar issues with us 3 kids. We're all definitely on the spectrum and likely PDA, definitely our mum. She'd sit on the stairs weeping, but claiming she'd wanted no one to see her. I intuitively knew she'd chosen that spot to maximise likelihood that she WOULD be seen. She'd never admit to being stressed, but it was blatantly obvious. I was left assuming it was my fault. That I was intrinsically such a terrible person that I caused suffering and pain without even trying or realising. I think this is why it's important to admit to our children when we're upset. They're going to sense it anyway and likely blame themselves if you don't explain the reasons.

Silva  Sally, I wish I could offer 'child-Sally' a hug xxx

Riko Ryuki  I find it hard as a PDAer to parent PDA kids. I have 3 boys and at least 2 of them I know have PDA. It's very difficult relinquishing control of tasks and activities in order to make it easier for the kids to handle. Even before I knew about PDA I was using the correct strategies instinctively and I didn't really give my kids as many demands as other families do because trying to get my kids to do all those inconsequential things like use the correct cutlery or wear the 'right' clothes was just another demand for me too. There were times though when I fought against my kids, trying to force them to do something without complaint and I found myself unable to handle their avoidance. Managing my kids' demand avoidance alongside managing my own is an exhausting, never-ending task. I get a little jealous of non-PDA parents because at least they get a break when the kids aren't around; there's no escape for me. In some ways I understand my kids on a level most probably don't. I can know exactly how they feel when faced with a demand that seems simple to others but feels like an impossible mountain to them. There are times though when I just can't fathom my kids or times when I don't have the strength to consider the feelings behind their behaviours, I just need them to get on with things instead of constantly fighting. We have a lot of ups and downs but I think overall we get each other and are working on getting on with each other. It's a work in progress and in some ways it will always be an exhausting uphill battle, but we are all trying our hardest to overcome our demand avoidance. One day at a time.

Cara  Likewise. I need a lot of quiet time and as horrible as it sounds, there are days when I find it immensely difficult to listen and/or talk with my kids. I have 3 kids, youngest (age 8) being PDA. Endless chatter and questions physically make my head spin.

Sally Cat  Christ, yes, can my daughter talk! Non-stop! (Apart from at school, where she's quiet as a mouse.)

Cara  Apparently my three are all really quiet at school too. Save it all for me.

Sally Cat  Sigh.

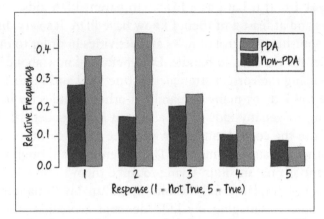

Graph 19: I felt my parents understood me as a child
*From a 'Quick PDA Poll' with 240 PDA and 145 neurotypical respondents*

# TIPS FOR PARENTING YOUR PDA CHILD

## From Riko Ryuki's blog

Parenting a PDA child can be quite difficult as they require a parenting technique which is rather different from typical parenting and even autistic parenting. Due to the high levels of anxiety and the constant need for control, PDA children find it intolerable to follow commands, whether these come from an outside source or themselves. Parenting PDA children involves a lot of hard work, flexible thinking, the ability to stay calm even under great stress and a high level of understanding and compassion.

It's important to remember that many PDA children have lagging skills, skills which aren't developed enough to deal with circumstances that are expected of their age group. An excellent explanation of lagging skills comes from Ross. W. Greene's *The Explosive Child*, a book which can be bought from many online bookstores and is also explained on his website: *www.livesinthebalance.org*.

PDA children also have difficulty understanding and feeling their emotions, which can become a problem when dealing with sudden, extreme bouts of emotion. They often live in the moment and so, when feeling heightened emotions that they don't quite understand and/or know how to deal with, they can over-dramatise events. Coupled with a sometimes literal thinking and black-and-white way of viewing the world, they might often see things as 'always' being 'bad'. One such example is when a child may be told off for breaking something (whether intentional or not) they may angrily state that, 'I'm always breaking things, I can't do anything right.' Problems socially may cause PDA children to react, stating, 'Everyone hates me. No one likes me. I don't fit in anywhere.' These reactions may appear to others as attention seeking and over the top, but to the child they do actually feel this way. They might know logically that these feelings aren't correct but they are unable to stop feeling them. Knowing that their feelings aren't right but not being able to control their outbursts can make the PDA child feel even worse as they wish they could stop, they just don't have the ability to separate their logical mind from their emotional body. Most children will feel terrible afterwards and may apologise. They may also try to avoid situations that caused the outburst in order to avoid the same thing happening again.

PDA children feel a need for control in order to reduce their anxiety. They think that if they can control everything and everyone in their environment then they won't feel anxiety from unexpected events. However, this level of control, whilst appearing to reduce anxiety, can actually increase anxiety felt when something unexpected does occur. Parenting techniques include framing demands so as to give the child the appearance of control while the parent actually maintains control and the demand is met.

Due to the way their brains are wired, PDA children may not understand what people say. Things like sarcasm, play on words, tone of voice and body language can all be misunderstood. Some PDA children believe that if someone's tone of voice is anything other than neutral then that person is angry at them. This can be confusing and frustrating for both parties involved. PDA children usually understand written instruction better than verbal instruction and many families use visual guides to help their children understand what is required of them. When giving verbal instructions it helps to keep to simple sentences and only give one prompt at a time.

# MORE TIPS FOR PARENTING YOUR PDA CHILD

From Riko Ryuki's blog

Due to demands being so hard for PDA people to take, the way you verbalise demands is very important. Since every child is different, even within PDA, what might work for one may not work for another. PDA children also have a tendency to prefer novelty, which is why new tactics may work for a short while but will soon stop working as the child becomes accustomed to it and/or works out that it's a veiled demand. Some PDA children may be okay with having demands presented to them as a choice while some tactics might never work for others.

*Here are some tactics which I've come across which seem to work:*

*Asking nicely. Who doesn't want to be asked nicely? After all, if someone said to you, 'Pick that up right now' you'd probably look at them like their head had suddenly turned to mush (I know I would). So why should our children be any different? Asking, 'Please could you pick that up for me?' sounds much better and is more likely to be favoured.*

Respect their no. If someone asks you to do something and you say no and then they get mad at you, wouldn't you be a bit annoyed? It's important to teach all children that's it's okay to say no. If we don't, then how can they refuse to give in to peer pressure when they've been taught that their opinion doesn't matter? If it's important that they do it and no isn't an answer that's available then don't ask them to choose. One of my pet hates is when people frame a demand as a choice and then get annoyed when the answer is no as they were expecting a yes. This is different from giving PDA children the illusion of control over a demand in the form of a choice because the child still gets to choose, the options just aren't a yes or no choice.

Give them a choice. Open-ended choices and questions are difficult for PDA people. When giving options it is usually best to stick to a choice of 2 options. Unlike yes/no, this tactic doesn't allow the child to choose whether they do the demand or not but rather allows them some control over how the demand is done. 'Would you like to use the green toothbrush or the red toothbrush?' The child is being 'told' they have to brush their teeth but they get to choose which brush they use.

The non-offered choice. Whenever my partner asks me if I would like a tea or a coffee, quite often my reply is a hot chocolate. This is for one of 2 reasons, the first is that I actually wanted a hot chocolate and the second is that sometimes my demand avoidance won't let me choose even one of the options given. Parents of PDA children have also commented on this. One example is where a mother asked if she could have a sweet from her child, the child seemed to think for a moment before saying, 'No, but you can have two sweets.' This isn't because the child is being manipulative or defiant, but rather that the need to avoid the demand (giving of a sweet) is so great but the child's desire to follow the demand clashes and the only way out is to work around the demand (by offering 2 sweets instead). It might sound strange to those who aren't used to PDA. So if you give a choice of 2 options and the child picks a third option, unless it goes against the demand, then it's usually best to let it go. The child is showing that they want to work with you, but they really struggle to do so in the way a typical child would.

Countdowns. Giving a countdown in the run-up to a transition and/or demand can help prepare the child and give them time to get used to the change and/or implementation of the demand. Imagine being told you have to give a speech to a hundred people right now. You'd probably panic. You won't have time to prepare. One second you're doing nothing and the next you're thrust on stage and expected to talk. Well, transitions and demands are like that for PDA people. Because of our heightened anxiety and emotions, even small things like getting dressed and eating lunch feel like being told to get on stage and make a speech. Overwhelming, right?

'The wait was worse than the actual event.' Sometimes, the lead-up to something is worse than the actual thing. Our minds go over what's going to happen and what could go wrong. The longer we have to dwell, the worse the event appears. It's only afterwards that we realise the wait was worse. I've found it's sometimes easier to tell a child about a demand shortly before it's due to happen, rather than days/weeks in advance. This is especially helpful for things like dentist appointments, hospital visits/operations, holidays, meetings, and other unpleasant and unpredictable events. It's important to give enough of a warning (i.e. not seconds before leaving the house) but not so much warning that the child starts to worry about all the things that could go wrong.

Race to the finish. Some kids find making a demand into a race to be a good motivator. Saying, 'I bet you can't get dressed before me' can get them up and moving in their need to beat you.

Pretend play. PDA kids often use role play or pretend play to cope with everyday demands. Some talk through their toys saying, 'Charlie Bear doesn't want to eat his food.' Often the parent/s can cajole the child to do something by talking back through the toy, saying, 'Can Charlie Bear get dressed?' This means the child can accept the demand because it's not aimed directly at them. They may blame a character or toy for any mistakes they make; it might be easier for parents to go with this and discipline the toy instead of challenging the child. The child probably already knows that what they did was wrong and are anxious about being told off, so blaming something else is often easier. This can make it easier for the parent to explain why what the child did was wrong, what they should have done instead and how to make things right, because without the medium of the toy, the child may become overwhelmed by their emotions and may not hear what's being said.

Asking the room. Direct demands can create an immediate refusal to comply in many PDA people; sometimes it's best to use an indirect way to communicate demands. One way to do this is to ask the room, 'I wonder if Annabella could get dressed now?' Similarly, asking, 'Is there anyone who can help me tidy this up?' This might not always work and may be ignored, since this isn't a direct demand; any refusal to comply shouldn't be challenged.

Reducing and increasing demands. Anxiety and the ability to cope with demands changes every day, sometimes even from hour to hour. This means the parent has to become tuned in to when their child is struggling and when they are able. When anxiety and demand avoidance is high, it is best to reduce demands, as they will struggle to cope otherwise and this can lead to meltdowns/shutdowns/panic attacks. When the child is managing fine and their anxiety and demand avoidance is low, then you can increase demands as now is the time when they are most likely to be able to comply. It's important to be careful when increasing demands though, as anxiety can quickly escalate, making it difficult for them to cope. With practice it will become easier to judge how and when to increase and decrease to make the most of what the child can do when they are able.

Give them breathing space. Everyone needs breaks from time to time; this is more so for PDA children. They need room to relax and get their emotions under control. It might be helpful to give breaks in between demands so they have time to recharge. When anxiety is high, it helps to give them more rest than usual, as this is when they'll need it most.

Don't rush them. Everyone works best when left to their own pace. Some people work best when given lots of time, others work better under stress. Some PDA kids leave everything till the last minute then jump into action in a panic. While this may seem unhealthy, it's one of the ways some PDAers manage demands best, as the panic over-rides the anxiety, making it possible for them to act. Other PDAers need lots of time with no deadlines to be able to act, as deadlines and panic make them unable to do anything at all. You will know best what works for your child.

Let them stim. Stimming is a form of self-soothing. It can be flapping hands, spinning in circles, touching everything, clicking pens, watching lights, rolling objects like balls, jumping up and down, etc. There are many different stims. Stimming is very helpful, especially for concentration and as a coping mechanism. As long as the stims aren't harmful (some stim by banging their head on walls) then it's fine to allow, and even encourage, stimming.

Remember...Demand Avoidance is not a choice. Every child wants to do well; they struggle because they 'can't help won't'.

# OUR ACHIEVEMENTS

» Training champion racehorses
» Graduating from college and university
» Working full time
» Marriage
» Surviving abusive relationships
» Running own business
» Remaining stable
» Concert performances
» Winning scholarships
» Long-term sobriety after addiction
» Doing everything well
» Roller derby
» Teaching in a hospital
» Living abroad
» Happy long-term relationships
» Speaking at conferences, writing a book and
  raising money for PDA Society
» Helping people and being kind
» Purple belt in karate
» Creative achievements
» Successfully achieving after geographically relocating
» Overcoming own toxic childhood and raising confident PDA children
» Winning back own life
» Opening own home for battered wives

» Being a facilitator to help others
» Planning a business to give grants to support PDAers creatively

---

What things have you achieved? Sharing our triumphs can show others that PDA doesn't have to be the killer of potential. Have you, for example, landed a great job? Done well academically? Oraganised a group? Sold artwork? Won an award? Anything really.

---

Vanessa Haszard I have trained a winning racehorse, and produced a pony that has multiple national level showing titles. All on an almost non-existent budget, from raw material horses that were given to me, often as 'no good'.

I made a 50,000% profit on the show pony!!!

And I am bloody exceptional academically, and one day will finish my degree. What is the point in having A and A+ tertiary grades if you don't finish the damn degree!? Lol

Joan Watson That's so cool and glamorous.

Tracy I just graduated from college this past May! I was incredibly close to getting honors (didn't get them just because of a technicality). I am 34 and have been working on it on and off since I was 18. I've been working full-time that whole time except the first few years. It's not much but it's a big accomplishment for me!

Dee Dee I'm still thinking. Two marriages, two kids...a few near misses, hopefully settling down for the last 30+ years of life...so tiring. Working to survive and pay for my house. I should really be getting myself ready for work...

Silva Attained a degree in psychology back in the 1980s and an MA this year at 55. Survived child sexual abuse, a toxic relationship and low self-esteem and met and married my lovely husband in my forties. We're getting back on our feet after near bankruptcy. Fought cancer twice, once at 22 and again early forties. Am a qualified (retired) psychiatric nurse, holistic therapist and counsellor. Had my own small business and was co-director of my husband's, when he had it. Now working on becoming a writer, artist and photographer. I'm still standing! All of us need to be proud of just that!

Editing just to add – I think one of my achievements is to have survived a lot of cr*p! I think so many of us can relate to that. They can knock us down, but we always get the hell back up! X

Riko Ryuki  I have a HNC in Business and my blog seems to be doing well!

Sarah S  Errrr, getting out of bed is an achievement for me right now!

Astrid van Woerkom  I graduated a high-level high school (I think in the UK it's called grammar school) with pretty good grades in 2005. In 2007, I met my now husband and we've been married for nearly six years now. Shortly after first meeting my husband, I fell apart mentally and had to be admitted into a psychiatric institution. I left this institution last May to live with my husband. I do not work but consider it a major achievement that I manage to go to day activities each morning and am able to stay relatively stable (so far) whilst my husband works long hours.

Sally Cat  Your stories made me smile.

Emily Cool  The only thing I feel I've done well is my children, but even that has been a disaster recently. My eldest has mental health problems and I don't know how to help him. My youngest wants to be home educated but everything is a shambles due to me not being able to have a proper routine or any time to myself to organize anything, so I don't feel I could cope with that at the moment. I feel like I need everything else to stop so I can catch up! I have done the odd concert or show here and there that I feel has been a success, but overall I could have achieved so much more with my music. I have a lot of personal music goals that I need time and space to achieve. I also want to be more knowledgeable, so will only really feel success when I have the time and space to reach my personal goals. It's the personal goals that are most important to me even though they won't get me money or anything.

Sally Cat Successful concert performances sounds like quite a big success to me. You're a pianist, as I recall?

Silva Sally, Amen to that!

Emily Cool Yes, a pianist. I usually accompany other people. I haven't done much solo stuff and I generally scrape through! I'm never properly ready due to procrastination so a successful concert for me means getting through it without any disasters! I really am capable of so much more.

But thanks y'all.

Elizabeth It sounds to me like you're being too hard on yourself, to be honest. Is this a PDA thing, I wonder? My mum thinks I am. Anyway nobody can be everywhere all the time and you're helping your kids with their problems as well as dealing with your own stuff.

Emily Cool I probably am too hard on myself! I did do practically nothing though before having children. I was naturally good at music so probably picked it because it was the least stressful thing to do. I still always crammed before exams, etc. though rather than consistently practising! My parents had high expectations and I know my dad especially is disappointed as none of us (I have 2 brothers) have achieved highly despite being very intelligent. I think he expected at least a doctor out of us! I think from an early age I was the one expected to become the doctor as I seemed more capable of talking to people than my brothers. They were more outwardly defiant. My mum went through a stage of taking us all to church and they would sit there discussing very loudly how it was impossible for God to exist! I was more outwardly compliant though inwardly it was a nightmare. I would always act as if I was toeing the line but not really do anything properly, or I would make excuses rather than defiantly say 'no'.

Donna Spurdens (mother of PDA girl) My daughter achieved a full scholarship at Northern Ballet School. Always a very proud mum.

Nicole Dahl Maintained 26 years of sobriety after recovery from alcohol and drug addiction, survived cancer, currently raising

2 perfectly wonderful kids. Daily survivor of depression and anxiety as well as PDA.

Sarah Johnson Done everything I chose to do well. Been married to a majorly NT guy for 17 years, raised 4 rather charming kids (his genes not mine) and won a medal at a national roller skating dance competition (yes I can skate like a good un). I can also draw, ride a horse, sing, run a business, train dogs and drive rather well. Just wish I could fit in and be perceived as normal too. Now that would be a major accomplishment...

Joan Watson Have you ever considered roller derby? I'm still learning the basics of skating but it's so cool.

Sarah Johnson There's nowhere local. If there was...I'd kill 'em. As happy on my feet as skates and I'm almost 14 stone. I've also played rugby. Knocked a girl over holding a tackle barrier when I was on skates and she was on her feet. Used to take the big boys on (I'm talking the 6 foot boys) in roller hockey and broke my arm in a tackle. I'd kill myself if I played roller derby – I'm so competitive...might just travel though. Discussed it before... hm...

Joan Watson I would love to see you play.

Sarah Johnson I just looked it up – I'd be lethal...honest, I'd get sinned [taken out of the game for a penalty period] all the time...

Joan Watson I'm doing a stint as a timer in the penalty box this weekend. It's my first time NSOing [non skating official-ing], and even in the practice game today it was the same skater I was timing three times.

Vanessa Haszard I seriously think I am slightly in awe of you, Sarah Johnson! You are seriously COMPETENT! And I know this might sound silly, but in my opinion that is one of the highest compliments I can pay a person.

Multiply competent in fact, and I am seriously impressed. And fuck! Apparently I was serious...lmao

Sarah Johnson Why, Vanessa, I take that as a compliment coming from you. We are kindred spirits, honeybun. You with those horses... you've got the whisperer in you somewhere. So thank you. X

Ruth  I teach at Great Ormond Street Hospital School. It's my dream job and I see many children who have issues with anxiety. I feel PDA gives me the empathy required to work with these children and their families. Without it I wouldn't be half the practitioner I am.

Elizabeth  Lived abroad for three months, got a BTEC [Business and Technology Education Council Diploma, a further education and vocational qualification taken in England, Wales and Northern Ireland] and a degree, maintained a relationship for nearly 10 years... I never thought any of this meant anything until I realised I react and deal with things differently. I feel I've done the best I can with most things I've tried, including jobs and so on that didn't work out. I'm just learning to move past it all and move onwards and upwards rather than feeling like a failure.

C. Keech  Oh, God. I'm still hoping for me.

Vanessa Haszard  I feel sure if you think about it you will find plenty, maybe not conventional, but they will be there.

Lucy Tor  Your kids seem pretty damn healthy and happy!

C. Keech  I'm quite a crappy mum haha sounds really unnecessarily self-deprecating but it's true. I have all the will and the ideas but none of the patience or drive x

Lucy Tor  Don't believe that for a second (the crappy bit not the patience/drive!).

Julia Daunt  I've achieved a 13-year loving relationship with Paul. That's pretty impressive, I think. I'm also a proud trustee of the North Devon Forum for ASC and ADHD. I run (or help to run) 7 Facebook PDA support groups, my 'IF' poem is on a wall in a country pub in Devon, I've spoken at national conferences, I'm writing a book with Ruth Fidler, I've supported countless families as they've navigated the whole PDA thing and helped them with things like education and diagnosis. I achieved a bronze Duke of Edinburgh award at school and a few years ago I stood in the local town council elections and even though I was unsuccessful I'm proud. I've also raised around £2000 for the PDA Society through my Facebook craft auctions. I might not work but my life has a purpose and direction. That's what is important.

Lucy Tor  Helped numerous people, am kind to everyone even when I'm struggling. Keep my mum going when she's struggling. Running miles now when I never thought I would. Still surviving clinical depression. Got two pain in the ass rescue rabbits, one of whom should have been dead around 6 times but instead he's healthy (because I have nursed him through the night when he's poorly). I'm also proud that I always do things that scare me/I find hard. Learned to be proud of the small steps as they all count towards the bigger.

I know none of the above seem that amazing but I'm proud nonetheless!

Lucy Tor  Actually totally misread context of your post, Sally, so not applicable for what you want/asked for! Sorry!

Sally Cat  I think this is entirely applicable.

Lucy Tor  Ah bless you x

Silva  Lucy, my hat is off to you! X

Sally Cat  Achievements are personal to us and our own journeys IMO, not what society might count or discount x And huge kudos to you for saving that rabbit 6 times!

Lucy Tor  Oh, how kind you are, ladies.

Joan Watson  2:1 [Second-class honours, upper division] in computing, work as a senior programmer. Passed my roller derby fresh meat [beginner basics] but had to retake due to injury absence. Kept a baby fed for 1+ years.

In the past: purple belt in karate. Nearly sold a sculpture from an art course but decided to keep it. Grade 5 cello, 7 singing. I wish I could maintain special interests beyond role playing for longer than a few months.

Finishing things is really hard. I usually cope by doing bare minimum on the things I don't love – some of my uni project documentation was handed in on napkins. And some of my art coursework just totally sucked largely because of terrible executive function.

Sally Cat I have studied both art and computing also.

Silva Sally and Joan, I did Art at A level and desperately want to get back into it because I love the outlet. When I left school we hadn't had computers but as soon as I could I got my first and learned how to use it. I used to sing. Love to write. We are creative, aren't we?

Becca B I've rehabilitated a few 'damaged' cats, have a loving relationship with a lovely partner and have successfully moved hundreds of miles away from home and made a new life for myself. I picked up a first class degree and I've also been published as a poet, fiction and non-fiction writer, photographer, artist and model.

Plus earlier today I managed to make a complaint over the phone and get both an apology and some apology money without having a panic attack – this is currently what I'm most proud of!

Nicola T Oh my, I am indeed impressed at that as I loathe the phone and I hate confrontation/complaining, so for me that would be terrifying.

Rachel R I feel I've managed to achieve a decent amount thus far. I made a solid group of (male) friends at school and they've remained friends since (despite the physical distance), I've overcome decades of self-harm, passed my driving test, moved away from home to get my 2:1 BSc degree in psychology, met my husband (been together 11 years), moved a substantial distance away from our families and did my MSc degree in social work; I then got a couple of jobs in this field. I went on to have children and raised them (thus far) with no support network (it has been challenging especially as eldest is highly likely PDA). Yes, I am still struggling but now I know why and I should learn to pat myself on the back a little bit!

## My Wasted Education?

I studied multimedia art at university I was expected to get a job at the end, but didn't.

I then got a scholarship to study post grad in Australia

I was expected to get a job at the end, but didn't.

I then trained to be a professional counsellor

I was expected to get a job at the end, but didn't.

I've poured what I've learned into my memes

People have freely told me these PDA memes have helped them.

I consider this more valuable than any paid job x

Sally Cat  Despite having grown up believing I was useless, worthless, bottom of the social pile, ugly, unwantable, irredeemably stupid and a heartless trouble maker, predicted to by my school to be a low achiever, I:

- beat all the school-predicted exam results by 2 grades

- was the first student in my local Further Education college to be awarded 100% for Art GCSE, produced an A-Level Psychology essay that the tutor suggested I enter into a national competition

- became Artist for my local Animal Rights group

- during the height of rave culture, organised my city's harm reduction rave stall that gave out drug information, free condoms and free water

- organised a benefit rave for the local drugs agency with one of the nation's top DJs playing for a fraction of his normal fee

- appeared as an extra in a major theatre production of Roald Dahl's The Witches

- co-managed a cave bar disco and guest house in central Turkey

- worked freelance writing and designing drugs information leaflets for the local drugs agency

- danced on stage at a major, commercial outdoor rave event

- was awarded a Merit in Foundation Art despite failing to finish my major project on time

- discovered I was actually a celebrity in the Turkish village I'd managed the disco in

- visited that village over 30 times, despite living in poverty and it taking at least 36 hours to reach from my home city

- learned to speak moderate Turkish despite having (then undiagnosed) dyslexia

- worked as an usherette in a concert hall and saw loads of big bands for free

- achieved firsts for every semester at university (apart from the crucial final semester when I had issues with my tutor, freelance work and health and only – never going to be happy about this scored 69.25% for my final degree, giving me a 2:1: big, massive boo!)

- was awarded a fully paid scholarship to Australia to do a Graduate Diploma

- received a High Distinction and industry-sponsored award for Best Interactive Project in this course

- back in England, designed the new logo for a pub

- had a regular DJ night in a pub and become quiz writer and reader

- played on the darts team despite having dyspraxia

- went on to be self-employed as a pub quiz master with three weekly quizzes on the go

- formed and captained my own darts team

- studied up to Level 4 as a professional person-centred counsellor

- detoxified my relationship with my mum

- am raising a PDA daughter who is confident, achieving, popular and happy

- have a wonderful partner who supports me (and the negative, toxic pattern of my childhood is not being repeated)

- found out I had autism and then PDA

- have had phenomenal success with my Facebook-published Sally Cat memes

- rallied the wonderful members of the adult PDA Facebook group to collaborate in writing this book!

Silva Wonderful! And with you on the detoxifying mom relationship too!!

Emily Cool Wow!

Little Black Duck I'm the heroine in my own life story. I've stood up when it mattered. I've made a difference in the lives of others. And I'm still here, for the next chapter.

Zoe Davies OK, I'm going to contribute to this even though I'm massively cringing about saying positive things about myself! (It also helps me avoid finishing my work prep and getting kids uniforms ready!)

I have a psychology degree. I had a great career, ending as the head of client services for a homeless charity. I also worked at a think tank and edited a book on reforming the youth justice service. It was covered in the news and I got a response direct from the Home Office. I re-trained after having my daughter and qualified as a Hypnotherapist and Life Coach and set up my practice when my son was 3 months old.

I became a single mum 2 years ago and this year set up a training company teaching organisations mindfulness. I won a large contract almost immediately and have become more financially stable. I'm running my first luxury mindfulness and yoga retreat in September.

But the thing I think I'm most proud of is doing everything I possibly can to improve my wellbeing and mental health, to grow and develop, to be my best self for myself and my children. Little support from family, 3 nervous breakdowns, a marriage break-up and CFS but I'm still here. My kids are happy and loved and I am able to be a positive role model to them.

Hope I don't sound like a complete wanker!! (I'm still cringing)!! X

C. Keech Aww, I'd love to be a positive role model to my children! Your life is one I wish I'd had.

Zoe Davies I bet you are but just can't see it yet. It may be useful for you to ask your friends and family in what ways you are a positive role model. I bet they will come up with many things you didn't realise. I was on a group therapy course once for PND. One of the activities we had to do was go round the room and tell each of the other mums why we thought they were a good parent. It was so powerful. The facilitator wrote everything up so we got to take it away and read it over and over. Once you start seeing it, you notice it more and then can build on it.

Also, half the battle is actually knowing what you want out of life. Sooo many people don't. But you do. So hold on to that vision, picture it full of life and colour, and know that you will get there. Tiny steps. Each in the right direction. You can do it!

C. Keech Yeah, maybe you're right. I know I want them to look up to me but I'm very unsure on how to achieve that. I want to be a beacon of positivity that goes after what I want but I dunno what I want, feel too old to start anything and am pretty joyless and cynical!

Zoe Davies Too old? Are you crazy?! I'm 38, so was 35 when I began re-training (and looking at your picture you are WAY younger than me). Besides, I just don't see age as a barrier. We're going to be working till we are in our seventies, so even if it takes until aged 50 to qualify or set up a business doing what you want to do, you still have 20 years of doing it left!! Plus, you won't get to 70 and look back with regret about what you could have done!

Also, your kids will look up to you when they are young just for the fact of you being their mum. The important thing is that YOU feel proud of yourself. So think about the qualities you would like to possess as a mum and start cultivating them in yourself. If you want to teach them positivity, learn about it, read, watch TED talks and practise, practise, practise. They will learn through watching you. A tool to start you off is to keep a gratitude journal.

Gifts

I know we PDAers can be f**king difficult & unpredictable.
But those of us I know have hearts of gold.
We are proactively compassionate
As well as mind glowingly creative, clever and funny.
I see us PDAers as gifts society hasn't yet learned to unwrap

Every night write about 3 things you were grateful for that day. They can be tiny things (the sun was shining, etc.). This practice starts requiring your brain to notice the positives and has been shown to be more effective than anti-depressants at reducing depression! There's a great app called gratitude 365 you can use to take photos too. You can start getting the kids involved too – asking them at dinner what they are grateful for. I ask my 3-year-old, 'What made you laugh today?' when I pick him up from nursery. Whilst we can re-wire our brains at any age, it's much easier when they are little.

Just a note – we can't always be a beacon of positivity, and in fact that's not a healthy image for kids to see. They need to understand that life is all ups and downs and that parents get upset or cross at times just like they do. The important thing is that we show them how to handle big emotions: acknowledge them, let them out and move on. This develops their emotional intelligence and doesn't present a false image of some happy clappy Instagram world. Hope there is something here that's useful!

Sally Cat I agree wholeheartedly there, Zoe. I firmly believe that in having been stroppy in front of DD and then having 'put on big girl's pants' and apologised to her and admitted my stroppiness plus what triggered it, then being OK (yippee!) has given her a vital model for dealing with her own intense emotions x

Zoe Davies Sally, absolutely spot on! What a great example xx And I love the phrase 'putting on your big girl's pants'!

C. Keech I will get that app now!!

Zoe Davies Yay!!

Alice I am finding this question extremely difficult to answer; I have done lots of things in life that I know others have regarded as successful but I struggle to agree and can always find an opposing view.

Two achievements that I don't do that with, however, are my two children.

Sally Cat Are there any additional things you've done, Alice, that have been personal achievements for you (even if no one else valued them)? For example, overcoming major demand avoidance to do something you'd felt prevented from doing? X

Alice I seem to have a block when thinking about achievements. I don't understand where it is coming from at the moment.

Sally Cat Maybe you're just (unjustly IMO) feeling shit about yourself? X

Alice I've considered this further. I saw my GP this morning and asked about my assessment for ASD/PDA and despite two referrals and the surgery chasing it via phone they are not replying. The lack of a diagnosis except depression, I realise, is the root of my inability to recognise achievements. Unless I can see that the failures that I can talk about with every perceived achievement are not attributable to my own laziness or incompetence, but due to a hardwired condition, I don't think this will change.

Does that make any sense?

Sally Cat  It sounds like you need official recognition of your PDA in order to process it? x

Alice  Yes, I think so.

Laura Mullen  I fought for my life and I won. After the birth of my second daughter I suffered with postpartum psychosis. As time progressed and it didn't go away I was diagnosed bipolar 2, treatment resistant, ultra rapid cycling [bipolar disorder type 2 is when you cycle between depression and hypomania. Hypomania is not to the extreme of true mania, but often in bipolar type 2 you cycle more often]. My doctors prescribed over 50 different psych meds within five years. I was on up to 15 medications a day. I was suicidal and in and out of hospitals. I swore it was cyclical, the mania and psychosis, and no one listened to me. Last year I pushed to get away from those horrible doctors after they said my last chance was trying LSD, yes, the hallucinogenic drug. I swore my problems were hormonal because it all eased up after my period started. I had tried all kinds of things. I had already made two attempts on my life and I couldn't keep doing this to my family. I took a chance, found a doctor willing to go for a drastic treatment of PMDD (premenstrual dysphoric disorder). I had surgery to remove my lady parts. I am no longer on any psych meds. Very rarely have panic attacks and no more psychosis or mania!!! I won my life back!! I saved myself and my family by not completely giving up and ignoring my instincts.

Nicola T  Opened my home to battered wives and their children. The first family was a friend who had to post her children out the window, then climb out after them. She phoned me and I went and got her and they lived with us for 2 months until she was back on her feet. I then applied to do this through social services and the fight I had was monumental and soooooooooooo long. I gave up fighting as women were literally dying while the social services ummmed and ahhhed... We just made it known through lots of different social media dealing with these families, and have since given sanctuary to 4 more families. At least one I am convinced we saved her life. Since then we have had to give our large house up because of hubby being made redundant, and we are in a too small flat, but if ever we climb back up, I fully intend to do it again.

Pink OK, here goes. Although I've never managed to do anything with it particularly, I have a degree in Applied Physics, which is how I met my husband. I've volunteered at various festivals over the years, running some great venues and been a part of some fab teams. I've held down several jobs, even when I felt they weren't the right jobs to have at the time.

I've survived the loss of a child and have gone on to inspire others to find their inner strength as a result. People come into my life for a reason, and they learn to see the world differently because of it.

I've had voluntary positions at times when I've been unable to work, such as helping women with breastfeeding. I've had CFS while bringing up a small child. I continually show my girl how to live and survive in this world, and make it work for us rather than against us.

I am a great facilitator; I bring people together.

Sam I graduated uni as a theatre director with a 2.1 and a first for my dissertation. I trained as a secondary drama teacher. I now run my own drama business and teach primary children. I write plays and have written a PDA play. Struggling to do application for funding but will see...my own PDA is making this hard as the sense I might fail makes applications hugely difficult to do. I have a play currently touring schools. I really want to write a PDA play for children.

I have two PDA children who are helping me learn about PDA and my own journey. We all use PDA strategies on each other, particularly in meltdowns. It is lovely to see.

Our PDA journey only started officially 18 months ago... however I have journeyed with it for 40 years now. I should add that the level of anxiety suffered to achieve all of this is beyond my comprehension. However, I also have this huge fear of failing and the pain that causes me to feel so had to push myself through. I only work very part time. It is all I can manage now as I become exhausted very easily.

Compassionate PDA

Although we PDAers resist commands and requests,

The many PDAers I've got to know in the Adult support network share my trait of strongly wanting to help people.

If you give us space and respect,

You may well find we are helpful and proactive without your asking.

Stephen Wright My company will use grants to get houses around the country to house people with PDA that have a lot of talent... we feed them and will open an online marketplace where anyone in the world can see their profiles and hire them to do websites or logos or anything creative. The houses will have computers and 3D printers and everything for them to just be creative. They will have complete control over their lives. If we meet people with a great idea...we do all the website and funding and develop the brand free and we take a small equity... but its non-profit so it goes into expanding our network. We will have access to 3000 offices around the country...each one staffed with a sales team and fundraiser...if we sell a site for 2500...which is less than half what we charge (we charge 4000–5000 for a site that complicated)...and raise 5000...that's a quarter billion a year going back into the non-profit which funds projects for people on the spectrum...especially people with PDA. We will be sponsoring kids with 10% of the money we get from our contracts getting them things to pursue their talents. And no one will know I did it...we could bring in the people who are so creative they can't live on their own...and one could cure the common cold...I am finally happy. And I'm just taking a small salary and living a normal life and stepping down as CEO once the system is in place...then I will do one of my business ideas with spectrym [his design business] and find someone to mentor. We are also doing an autism walk for PDA in the United States. Soon everyone will know that Asperger's and PDA don't have to be disabilities...and they will think not everyone gets to have autism. Having high functioning autism is a disability because you think different... I want people to stop thinking it is a disability and focus on the strengths and talents that come with it. Eventually I think autism will be something that people can be proud of. Autism makes you special... And if we can give employment and help people on the spectrum learn to live with the autism and be proud then people might someday think that autism is a gift instead of a curse...

Silva  I'm intrigued and proud to observe that so many members of this group have helped others as part of their own path, either in professions or as volunteers or in everyday life, while dealing with our own (pardon the French) cr*p! Fantastic, guys!

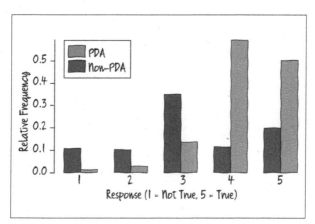

Graph 20: I can achieve a lot, but need space and
autonomy to do it my own way
*From a 'Quick PDA Poll' with 240 PDA and 145 neurotypical respondents*

# Appendix: Statistical Analyses

| Question | PDA | | non-PDA | | |
|---|---|---|---|---|---|
| | Mean | 95% CI | Mean | 95% CI | p-value |
| Q1) My Demand Avoidance impacts my life | 4.24 | (4.14–4.34) | 2.22 | (2.04–2.41) | <0.0000001 |
| Q2) Demand Avoidance stops me doing things I enjoy | 3.99 | (3.87–4.11) | 1.92 | (1.75–2.09) | <0.0000001 |
| Q3) I feel anxious in life | 4.42 | (4.31–4.52) | 3.22 | (3.00–3.43) | <0.0000001 |
| Q4) I mask | 4.09 | (3.96–4.21) | 2.88 | (2.66–3.10) | <0.0000001 |
| Q5) I need to know what's happening (I can't tolerate uncertainty) | 4.42 | (4.31–4.52) | 2.99 | (2.78–3.21) | <0.0000001 |
| Q6) I need control of my own life | 4.58 | (4.50–4.67) | 3.67 | (3.48–3.86) | <0.0000001 |
| Q7) My meltdowns are always obvious | 3.39 | (3.23–3.54) | 2.35 | (2.15–2.56) | <0.0000001 |
| Q8) I overload easily | 4.28 | (4.17–4.38) | 2.80 | (2.59–3.02) | <0.0000001 |
| Q9) I have had obsessions about people | 3.73 | (3.57–3.88) | 2.23 | (2.00–2.46) | <0.0000001 |
| Q10) I respect competency rather than rank | 4.30 | (4.19–4.41) | 3.76 | (3.57–3.95) | 0.000002248 |
| Q11) I have (now or in the past) daydreamed a lot | 4.08 | (3.95–4.21) | 3.20 | (2.97–3.43) | <0.0000001 |
| Q12) I enjoy wordplay | 3.41 | (3.25–3.57) | 2.98 | (2.77–3.19) | 0.001360 |
| Q13) I am impulsive | 3.80 | (3.66–3.94) | 2.94 | (2.74–3.15) | <0.0000001 |
| Q14) I find routine comforting, as long as it isn't imposed on me | 4.14 | (4.01–4.27) | 3.31 | (3.12–3.50) | <0.0000001 |
| Q15) I enjoyed school | 2.19 | (2.03–2.35) | 2.88 | (2.66–3.11) | 0.000001486 |

| | | | | | |
|---|---|---|---|---|---|
| Q16) I am able to work to earn a wage | 2.53 | (2.35–2.70) | 3.87 | (3.65–4.08) | <0.0000001 |
| Q17) I avoid talking on the phone | 3.73 | (3.58–3.89) | 2.82 | (2.58–3.06) | <0.0000001 |
| Q18) I need access to a quiet place | 4.37 | (4.26–4.48) | 3.10 | (2.89–3.32) | <0.0000001 |
| Q19) I felt my parents understood me as a child | 2.22 | (2.07–2.37) | 2.54 | (2.32–2.75) | 0.018607628 |
| Q20) I can achieve a lot, but I need space and autonomy to do it my own way | 4.29 | (4.18–4.40) | 3.20 | (3.00–3.41) | <0.0000001 |

## Q1) My Demand Avoidance impacts my life

| PDA | | non-PDA | | |
|---|---|---|---|---|
| Mean | 95% CI | Mean | 95% CI | p-value |
| 4.24 | (4.14–4.34) | 2.22 | (2.04–2.41) | <0.0000001 |

## Q2) Demand Avoidance stops me doing things I enjoy

| PDA | | non-PDA | | |
|---|---|---|---|---|
| Mean | 95% CI | Mean | 95% CI | p-value |
| 3.99 | (3.87–4.11) | 1.92 | (1.75–2.09) | <0.0000001 |

## Q3) I feel anxious in life

| PDA | | non-PDA | | |
|---|---|---|---|---|
| Mean | 95% CI | Mean | 95% CI | p-value |
| 4.42 | (4.31–4.52) | 3.22 | (3.00–3.43) | <0.0000001 |

## Q4) I mask

| PDA | | non-PDA | | |
|---|---|---|---|---|
| Mean | 95% CI | Mean | 95% CI | p-value |
| 4.09 | (3.96–4.21) | 2.88 | (2.66–3.10) | <0.0000001 |

## Q5) I need to know what's happening (I can't tolerate uncertainty)

| PDA | | non-PDA | | |
|---|---|---|---|---|
| Mean | 95% CI | Mean | 95% CI | p-value |
| 4.42 | (4.31–4.52) | 2.99 | (2.78–3.21) | <0.0000001 |

### Q6) I need control of my own life

| PDA | | non-PDA | | |
|---|---|---|---|---|
| Mean | 95% CI | Mean | 95% CI | p-value |
| 4.58 | (4.50–4.67) | 3.67 | (3.48–3.86) | <0.0000001 |

### Q7) My meltdowns are always obvious

| PDA | | non-PDA | | |
|---|---|---|---|---|
| Mean | 95% CI | Mean | 95% CI | p-value |
| 3.39 | (3.23–3.54) | 2.35 | (2.15–2.56) | <0.0000001 |

### Q8) I overload easily

| PDA | | non-PDA | | |
|---|---|---|---|---|
| Mean | 95% CI | Mean | 95% CI | p-value |
| 4.28 | (4.17–4.38) | 2.80 | (2.59–3.02) | <0.0000001 |

### Q9) I have had obsessions about people

| PDA | | non-PDA | | |
|---|---|---|---|---|
| Mean | 95% CI | Mean | 95% CI | p-value |
| 3.73 | (3.57–3.88) | 2.23 | (2.00–2.46) | <0.0000001 |

### Q10) I respect competency rather than rank

| PDA | | non-PDA | | |
|---|---|---|---|---|
| Mean | 95% CI | Mean | 95% CI | p-value |
| 4.30 | (4.19–4.41) | 3.76 | (3.57–3.95) | 0.000002248 |

### Q11) I have (now or in the past) daydreamed a lot

| PDA | | non-PDA | | |
|---|---|---|---|---|
| Mean | 95% CI | Mean | 95% CI | p-value |
| 4.08 | (3.95–4.21) | 2.20 | (2.97–3.43) | <0.0000001 |

### Q12) I enjoy wordplay

| PDA | | non-PDA | | |
|---|---|---|---|---|
| Mean | 95% CI | Mean | 95% CI | p-value |
| 3.41 | (3.25–3.57) | 2.98 | (2.77–3.19) | 0.001360 |

### Q13) I am impulsive

| PDA | | non-PDA | | |
|---|---|---|---|---|
| Mean | 95% CI | Mean | 95% CI | p-value |
| 3.80 | (3.66–3.94) | 2.94 | (2.74–3.15) | <0.0000001 |

### Q14) I find routine comforting, as long as it isn't imposed on me

| PDA | | non-PDA | | |
|---|---|---|---|---|
| Mean | 95% CI | Mean | 95% CI | p-value |
| 4.14 | (4.01–4.27) | 3.31 | (3.12–3.50) | <0.0000001 |

### Q15) I enjoyed school

| PDA | | non-PDA | | |
|---|---|---|---|---|
| Mean | 95% CI | Mean | 95% CI | p-value |
| 2.19 | (2.03–2.35) | 2.88 | (2.66–3.11) | 0.000001486 |

### Q16) I am able to work to earn a wage

| PDA | | non-PDA | | |
|---|---|---|---|---|
| Mean | 95% CI | Mean | 95% CI | p-value |
| 2.53 | (2.35–2.70) | 3.87 | (3.65–4.08) | <0.0000001 |

### Q17) I avoid talking on the phone

| PDA | | non-PDA | | |
|---|---|---|---|---|
| Mean | 95% CI | Mean | 95% CI | p-value |
| 3.73 | (3.58–3.89) | 2.82 | (2.58–3.06) | <0.0000001 |

### Q18) I need access to a quiet place

| PDA | | non-PDA | | |
|---|---|---|---|---|
| Mean | 95% CI | Mean | 95% CI | p-value |
| 4.37 | (4.26–4.48) | 3.10 | (2.89–3.32) | <0.0000001 |

### Q19) I felt my parents understood me as a child

| PDA | | non-PDA | | |
|---|---|---|---|---|
| Mean | 95% CI | Mean | 95% CI | p-value |
| 2.22 | (2.07–2.37) | 2.54 | (2.32–2.75) | 0.018607628 |

**Q20) I can achieve a lot, but I need space and autonomy to do it my own way**

| PDA | | non-PDA | | |
|---|---|---|---|---|
| Mean | 95% CI | Mean | 95% CI | p-value |
| 4.29 | (4.18–4.40) | 3.20 | (3.00–3.41) | <0.0000001 |

### Frequency of Response to Q1

| Response | non-PDA | PDA |
|---|---|---|
| 1 | 46 | 0 |
| 2 | 45 | 5 |
| 3 | 32 | 41 |
| 4 | 14 | 85 |
| 5 | 6 | 109 |

### Frequency of Response to Q2

| Response | non-PDA | PDA |
|---|---|---|
| 1 | 67 | 3 |
| 2 | 34 | 15 |
| 3 | 31 | 50 |
| 4 | 8 | 85 |
| 5 | 3 | 87 |

### Frequency of Response to Q3

| Response | non-PDA | PDA |
|---|---|---|
| 1 | 14 | 0 |
| 2 | 38 | 8 |
| 3 | 25 | 26 |
| 4 | 35 | 64 |
| 5 | 31 | 142 |

### Frequency of Response to Q4

| Response | non-PDA | PDA |
|---|---|---|
| 1 | 28 | 9 |
| 2 | 32 | 8 |
| 3 | 33 | 33 |
| 4 | 29 | 93 |
| 5 | 21 | 97 |

## Frequency of Response to Q5

| Response | non-PDA | PDA |
|---|---|---|
| 1 | 21 | 2 |
| 2 | 36 | 9 |
| 3 | 30 | 18 |
| 4 | 35 | 69 |
| 5 | 21 | 142 |

## Frequency of Response to Q6

| Response | non-PDA | PDA |
|---|---|---|
| 1 | 4 | 0 |
| 2 | 22 | 1 |
| 3 | 35 | 24 |
| 4 | 37 | 49 |
| 5 | 44 | 166 |

## Frequency of Response to Q7

| Response | non-PDA | PDA |
|---|---|---|
| 1 | 42 | 9 |
| 2 | 44 | 63 |
| 3 | 31 | 59 |
| 4 | 11 | 44 |
| 5 | 13 | 65 |

## Frequency of Response to Q8

| Response | non-PDA | PDA |
|---|---|---|
| 1 | 25 | 0 |
| 2 | 42 | 7 |
| 3 | 31 | 40 |
| 4 | 26 | 73 |
| 5 | 19 | 120 |

### Frequency of Response to Q9

| Response | non-PDA | PDA |
|---|---|---|
| 1 | 63 | 13 |
| 2 | 28 | 32 |
| 3 | 25 | 47 |
| 4 | 10 | 63 |
| 5 | 17 | 85 |

### Frequency of Response to Q10

| Response | non-PDA | PDA |
|---|---|---|
| 1 | 9 | 2 |
| 2 | 10 | 3 |
| 3 | 32 | 44 |
| 4 | 46 | 62 |
| 5 | 45 | 129 |

### Frequency of Response to Q11

| Response | non-PDA | PDA |
|---|---|---|
| 1 | 20 | 5 |
| 2 | 32 | 15 |
| 3 | 27 | 43 |
| 4 | 26 | 68 |
| 5 | 37 | 107 |

### Frequency of Response to Q12

| Response | non-PDA | PDA |
|---|---|---|
| 1 | 23 | 24 |
| 2 | 27 | 31 |
| 3 | 43 | 67 |
| 4 | 30 | 58 |
| 5 | 20 | 60 |

## Frequency of Response to Q13

| Response | non-PDA | PDA |
|---|---|---|
| 1 | 16 | 9 |
| 2 | 42 | 20 |
| 3 | 43 | 57 |
| 4 | 16 | 78 |
| 5 | 25 | 76 |

## Frequency of Response to Q14

| Response | non-PDA | PDA |
|---|---|---|
| 1 | 8 | 5 |
| 2 | 28 | 17 |
| 3 | 48 | 33 |
| 4 | 30 | 70 |
| 5 | 29 | 115 |

## Frequency of Response to Q15

| Response | non-PDA | PDA |
|---|---|---|
| 1 | 31 | 100 |
| 2 | 27 | 55 |
| 3 | 36 | 40 |
| 4 | 26 | 30 |
| 5 | 23 | 15 |

## Frequency of Response to Q16

| Response | non-PDA | PDA |
|---|---|---|
| 1 | 14 | 83 |
| 2 | 9 | 34 |
| 3 | 22 | 63 |
| 4 | 35 | 29 |
| 5 | 63 | 29 |

**Frequency of Response to Q17**

| Response | non-PDA | PDA |
|---|---|---|
| 1 | 38 | 16 |
| 2 | 27 | 28 |
| 3 | 27 | 43 |
| 4 | 25 | 69 |
| 5 | 26 | 83 |

**Frequency of Response to Q18**

| Response | non-PDA | PDA |
|---|---|---|
| 1 | 23 | 3 |
| 2 | 23 | 6 |
| 3 | 42 | 24 |
| 4 | 26 | 73 |
| 5 | 29 | 133 |

**Frequency of Response to Q19**

| Response | non-PDA | PDA |
|---|---|---|
| 1 | 38 | 87 |
| 2 | 39 | 62 |
| 3 | 28 | 57 |
| 4 | 25 | 19 |
| 5 | 12 | 15 |

**Frequency of Response to Q20**

| Response | non-PDA | PDA |
|---|---|---|
| 1 | 15 | 3 |
| 2 | 24 | 4 |
| 3 | 49 | 32 |
| 4 | 27 | 83 |
| 5 | 28 | 118 |

# Glossary

| | |
|---|---|
| **ADD** | Attention Deficit Disorder |
| **ADHD** | Attention Deficit Hyperactivity Disorder |
| **ASC** | Autism Spectrum Condition (an umbrella term) |
| **ASD** | Autism Spectrum Disorder |
| **BPD** | Borderline Personality Disorder |
| **CBT** | cognitive behavioural therapy |
| **CFS** | Chronic Fatigue Syndrome |
| **cos/coz** | because |
| **DA** | Demand Avoidance |
| **DD** | darling daughter |
| **def** | definitely |
| **dgaf** | don't give a f**k |
| **D&D** | Dungeons and Dragons |
| **esp** | especially |
| **FB** | Facebook |
| **ffs** | for f**k's sake |
| **IDK** | I don't know |
| **iykwim** | if you know what I mean? |
| **iyswim** | if you see what I mean? |
| **imao** | in my arrogant opinion |
| **IMO** | in my opinion |

| | |
|---|---|
| **IRL** | in real life |
| **LARP** | live action role play |
| **lb** | little boy |
| **LMAO** | laughing my ass off |
| **LOL/lol** | laugh out loud |
| **MMORPG** | massively multiplayer online role-playing games |
| **NT** | neurotypical |
| **OC** | obsessive compulsive |
| **OCD** | Obsessive Compulsive Disorder |
| **OCPD** | Obsessive Compulsive Personality Disorder |
| **ODD** | Oppositional Defiant Disorder |
| **OMG** | oh my God |
| **PND** | postnatal depression |
| **PMDD** | Premenstrual Dysphoric Disorder |
| **RPG** | role playing games |
| **SEND** | special education needs and disabilities |
| **SPD** | Sensory Processing Disorder |
| **SS** | social services |
| **Stimming/stim** | Self-stimulatory behaviour (the repetition of physical movements, sounds, or repetitive movement of objects) common in autistic people |
| **TBH** | to be honest |
| **trich** | Trichomoniasis (a common sexually transmitted disease) |
| **Trigger warning** | the following content may be upsetting |
| **WTF** | what the f**k |